The Rise and Decline of Faculty Governance

The Rise and Decline
of Faculty Governance

Professionalization and the Modern American University

LARRY G. GERBER

Johns Hopkins University Press
Baltimore

2 4 6 8 9 7 5 3 1

Johns Hopkins University Press
2715 North Charles Street
Baltimore, Maryland 21218-4363
www.press.jhu.edu

Library of Congress Cataloging-in-Publication Data
Gerber, Larry G.
The rise and decline of faculty governance : professionalization and the modern
American university / Larry G. Gerber.
pages cm
Includes bibliographical references and index.
ISBN 978-1-4214-1462-1 (hardcover : alk. paper) — ISBN 978-1-4214-1463-8
(pbk. : alk. paper) — ISBN 978-1-4214-1464-5 (electronic) — ISBN 1-4214-1462-7
(hardcover : alk. paper) — ISBN 1-4214-1463-5 (pbk. : alk. paper) —
ISBN 1-4214-1464-3 (electronic)   1. Universities and colleges—
United States—Administration.   2. Teacher participation in
administration—United States.   I. Title.
LB2341.G47 2014
378.1'01—dc23   2013048635

A catalog record for this book is available from the British Library.

Special discounts are available for bulk purchases of this book. For more information,
please contact Special Sales at 410-516-6936 or specialsales@press.jhu.edu.

Johns Hopkins University Press uses environmentally friendly book materials,
including recycled text paper that is composed of at least 30 percent post-consumer
waste, whenever possible.

*To the memories of Glenn Howze and John Hopper,
two inspirational activists who worked tirelessly on behalf of
faculty rights, literally to the end of their lives*

CONTENTS

This book was inspired by my own participation in university governance, both at Auburn University, where I served as chair of the University Senate in the early 1990s and later as chair of the History Department, and with the American Association of University Professors, for which I served two different terms as chair of the Committee on College and University Governance and three terms as national vice president between 2002 and 2008. As a historian of twentieth-century America, I decided that writing a history of faculty governance in the United States would provide a unique opportunity for me to bring together my scholarly interest in modern American history with my long involvement in college and university governance.

While participating in governance activities over the course of more than two decades, I met and worked with many individuals who exhibited a deep sense of professionalism and dedication to a broad vision of the purposes of higher education. This book is dedicated to the memory of two of those individuals. Studying the history of the role of faculty members in college and university governance has reinforced my belief in the necessity of a major role for the faculty in institutional decision making if American higher education is to maintain high academic standards and continue to enjoy a position of global preeminence.

I want to thank my Auburn colleague Bill Trimble and Johns Hopkins University Press reviewer John Thelin for their helpful comments on the original proposal I developed for this book as well as Ashleigh McKown, formerly at Johns Hopkins University Press, for expressing initial interest in my project and encouraging me to proceed. I am also grateful to Cary Nelson, who several years ago invited me to write an essay for the *Journal of Academic Freedom*, in which I first laid out some of the themes developed in this book.

In the later stages of this project, Greg Britton of Johns Hopkins University Press has been all that one could have hoped for in an editor. His remarkably swift responses to every e-mail I sent him and his strong support at the press for my work undoubtedly helped me complete this book much sooner than would otherwise have been possible. Sara Cleary has also been very helpful in answering all my questions concerning the various technical issues that have arisen. Thanks also to George Roupe for his careful copyediting of the final manuscript. I am especially grateful to the Press's anonymous reviewer of my manuscript, not only for his sympathetic reading of my work, but also for the numerous constructive suggestions he made for improving the final draft.

I also want to thank Gabriel Kaplan for providing me with the raw data from his 2001 governance survey. It was very generous of him to take the time to retrieve these files and send them to me, considering that his professional career has now taken him away from the study of college and university governance.

AAUP colleague Bob Kreiser, copyeditor extraordinaire, deserves particular thanks. As a longtime staff member to AAUP's Committee on College and University Governance, Bob is one of the most knowledgeable people I know concerning governance, and his willingness on short notice to read and comment on a late-stage draft of my manuscript greatly improved the book. I also want to thank AAUP staff member Nanette Crisologo for her technical assistance in making it possible for Bob to get his edited copy back to me so quickly.

I owe a special debt of appreciation to my sister, Mary Gerber, who carefully read drafts of chapters as I completed them. Mary's experience as a professional editor and keen eye for the structure and logic of an argument, and her prodding me to be less equivocal in making my points, helped make this book much better.

Finally, I want to thank my wife, Louise Katainen, whose encouragement and support (both moral and practical) were instrumental in my completing this book in a timely manner.

The Rise and Decline of Faculty Governance

Faculty Professionalization and the Rise of Shared Governance

In recent years numerous books and articles have proclaimed that America's colleges and universities now confront a crisis of historic proportions.[1] Of course, as John Thelin points out, such jeremiads are nothing new in the history of American higher education.[2] Nevertheless, the combination of substantial cuts in funding for public colleges and universities, growing complaints about the increasing cost of tuition at both public and private institutions, greatly intensified demands from governing boards and politicians for new efficiencies and greater accountability, together with unprecedented competition from for-profit institutions of higher learning and the apparent potential of new technologies to transform traditional methods of teaching and research, have created what William Tierney refers to as a "perfect storm."[3] The current situation may well mark a watershed in the history of American higher education.

Directly related to the developments noted above has been the rise in recent years of a concerted movement to recast the system of institutional governance that gradually gained acceptance in American colleges and universities during the century following the end of the Civil War. During that time, a system of "shared governance" that gave an increasingly professionalized faculty a significant role in academic decision making arose as a crucial element in the development of the modern American university. By the middle of the twentieth century, functioning largely within a context of a growing consensus over the value of shared governance, American higher education gained a position of preeminence in the world. That preeminence was made possible not only by the unparalleled resources that postwar America was able to devote to higher education but also by the development of the system of shared governance and academic freedom that prevailed at America's leading institutions of higher learning. The twin pillars of shared governance and academic freedom helped to support an environment that was both hospitable to scholars seeking to create new knowledge and intellectually challenging for the unprecedented numbers of students who began entering college after World War Two.

Today, however, the system of shared governance in which faculty have played a significant role in academic decision making is being challenged by critics who argue that more businesslike methods are necessary so that American colleges and universities can be more "flexible" and "nimble" in responding to changing market demands and new technologies. These critics consider the system of significant faculty autonomy and substantial responsibility for educational matters a form of governance that prevents necessary changes and frustrates efforts to bring greater accountability to American higher education. They call, in other words, for the institution of a more corporate, rather than collegial, approach to governance.[4]

Arguments in favor of the application of business methods of management to higher education have been voiced since at least as far back as the late nineteenth century, when faculty were just beginning to make more assertive claims to a significant role in academic decision making. At that time, defenders of a traditional hierarchical approach to governance were resisting efforts by what was then a newly professionalizing faculty to claim a greater role in academic decision making as a necessary complement to their new professional status. Today, advocates of a more businesslike approach to college and university governance are attempting to roll back the influence that faculty in the United States gradually gained over the course of more than a century.

The narrative to follow traces the evolution of the faculty role in college and university governance since the founding of the first college in British North America. It shows how faculty members in the United States by the 1960s had gained a significant role in academic decision making and how and why, since that time, that role has come under increasing attack. The extent of the control achieved by faculty members in American colleges and universities, even at the peak of their influence, has often been exaggerated by those who are critical of the professoriate. On the other hand, those whose ideal institution of higher learning is a completely self-governing "community of scholars" have in recent years often tended to understate the influence that faculty actually achieved in the century after the Civil War.

Throughout much of the history of American colleges and universities, dating back to the founding of Harvard College in 1636, faculty exercised little influence over the formulation of educational policies or other aspects of institutional decision making. Instead, American institutions of higher learning very early on came to be distinguished from European universities by the development of strong external governing boards and powerful presidents. It was not until well into the twentieth century that the notion that faculty should have primary responsibility for academic decision making gained substantial acceptance. In matters of academic decision making relating to the curriculum, methods of instruction, research, and the determination of faculty status—in other words, those matters most directly related to carrying out the educational mission of a college or university—faculty ultimately gained considerable influence. However, in other areas of the broader realm of institutional decision making, especially those involving budgeting and long-range planning, or nonacademic issues more tangentially related to educational policy, the role of faculty remained much more circumscribed, even by the mid-twentieth century.

American colleges in the colonial era began as poor distant cousins of the British and northern European universities that had served as models for their founding. On the whole, before the twentieth century, American colleges remained relatively undeveloped and undersized institutions. Their primary function was instilling character in their students and passing along to their charges well-established moral truths. As late as the mid-nineteenth century, the typical American institution of higher learning enrolled fewer than one hundred students, a significant number of whom were engaged in a precollegiate course of study. The typical college lacked a strong core of faculty members who considered themselves professional scholars and teachers making a long-term commitment to a career in academia. College teachers rarely had advanced training in a specialized discipline and generally did not see research as part of their responsibilities. Institutional governance, including the determination of educational policies, was largely in the hands of presidents, who more often than not came from the ministry, and of lay governing boards whose members typically had little knowledge of the teaching and research practices that had first come to define the modern university as it developed in Germany in the early nineteenth century. American colleges before the end of the nineteenth century generally demanded little in the way of analytical thinking from their students and generated little new knowledge through original research. In comparison to institutions of higher learning in Europe, especially those in Germany, American colleges through most of the nineteenth century were generally second rate in quality and afforded their faculties little role in institutional governance.

In the last quarter of the nineteenth century, however, American higher education began to come of age. Although the nation's colleges and universities were still characterized by tremendous diversity in terms of mission, scope, and size, many institutions of higher learning in the United States grew to be large enough to make possible greater specialization among their faculties. At the same time, the mission of American colleges and universities expanded well beyond the cultivation of Christian character in their students to include the creation of new knowledge and the provision of advanced training for students entering the professions.

Newly emerging American research universities such as Cornell, Johns Hopkins, Michigan, and Chicago, which took much of their inspiration from the example of the modern universities that had developed earlier in the nineteenth century in Germany, took the lead in changing the character and organization of American institutions of higher education. With their new focus on academic specialization, graduate education, and research, these schools paved the way for the establishment of a new role for faculty and for more demanding standards for their students. Many of America's traditional four-year liberal arts colleges, however, also began to experience substantial changes in the last decades of the nineteenth century, at least in part because of the influence of developments at the new research universities. While retaining their focus on undergraduate education, many liberal arts colleges began to reconceive their mission to focus on preparing their students to go on to more advanced training in the professions or graduate study in the new, more specialized academic disciplines. By 1900, the quality of American higher education had improved dramatically.

An essential element in the improving academic quality of American colleges and universities in the late nineteenth century was the development of a more professional faculty. A growing number of faculty members experienced a process of professionalization that included going through an extended period of advanced training in a specific academic discipline that often led to a PhD, identifying with peers across the country involved in the same discipline rather than only with one's own local college community, coming to see college teaching as a lifetime career, and beginning to consider research as part of one's academic responsibilities. In order to carry out a broadened conception of their role as professors, increasingly professionalized faculty members demanded not only academic freedom in their research and teaching but also a larger degree of control over academic decision making as a matter of professional right and responsibility. Just as practitioners of the traditional professions of law and medicine in the United States had begun in the nineteenth century more effectively to assert claims to greater autonomy and self-government on the basis of their expertise, so, too, did professors begin to lay claim to a larger role in institutional governance. Many faculty members contended that improving the academic quality of American colleges and universities depended on institutions' making fuller use of their professional expertise in reaching decisions about academic matters.

Such claims for a greater role in academic decision making had their first major impact on the ability of faculty members to assert control over what went on in their own classrooms. This was followed by a general recognition throughout American higher education of the faculty's claim to primary responsibility for determining the curriculum and graduation requirements. The rise of the discipline-based academic department became an important locus of such faculty members' claims for greater influence in decision making based on the argument that their extensive training in what had become progressively more specialized academic disciplines made them uniquely competent to render informed decisions about matters involving teaching and research. By the turn of the twentieth century the important role played by discipline-based academic departments in college and university governance came to distinguish the structure of American institutions of higher learning from their European counterparts.[5] Over time, faculty at most well-regarded colleges and universities were able to cite their professional expertise as a compelling reason for the importance of peer review by colleagues in decisions about appointments, promotions, and dismissals. Although the role of faculty in the selection and evaluation of administrators was slower to develop, in this area, too, the idea that faculty should at least have input into the selection of administrators gained traction by the middle of the twentieth century.

To a large extent, the most highly qualified and most prominent faculty members at America's emerging research universities led the way in the late nineteenth century in calling for a greater faculty role in institutional governance. However, the process of faculty professionalization and consequent calls for a larger role for professors in academic decision making were not limited to those teaching at the new research universities. Even before the end of the nineteenth century, growing numbers of faculty members at many four-year liberal arts institutions that retained their collegiate character and focus on undergraduate education also began to earn advanced degrees and develop an identification with a particular academic discipline and to insist on a recognition of the rights and responsibilities that went along with their new professional status.

The development of a significant faculty role in governance was a slow and uneven process. At no time did American faculty members come to enjoy anything close to full control of the institutions in which they taught and did research. External governing boards and presidents at American colleges and universities continued to exercise powers that had no real parallel in institutions of higher learning in Europe—at least not until very recently, when European institutions began to adopt some American practices. Especially in the area of budgeting and long-range planning, faculty influence in the United States always remained quite limited. Nevertheless, over the first half of the twentieth century, as American institutions of higher education matured and came to play a central role in the life of the nation, faculty gained greater influence over academic decision making. By the 1960s, the general principle of shared governance had become a widely accepted norm in American higher education.

At the same time that the principle of shared governance was gaining traction, American colleges and universities rose to a position of international preeminence. After World War Two, scholars and students from around the world flocked to American institutions of higher learning, and American research universities came to dominate global rankings. The rise of American higher education to a position of global preeminence after 1945 was certainly a result in good part of the nation's postwar prosperity, which allowed the United States to invest immense resources in its colleges and universities. However, the preeminence achieved by American colleges and universities was also tied to the substantial professional autonomy, significant role in institutional governance, and academic freedom enjoyed by faculty members. The widespread recognition of these faculty rights and responsibilities helped create an environment that fostered the pursuit of new knowledge and helped keep academic priorities at the forefront in the operation of American colleges and universities. There was thus a direct correlation between the development of a professionalized faculty, an increasing faculty role in institutional governance, and the unparalleled quality achieved by American higher education in the second half of the twentieth century.

Although faculty authority in institutional governance did, on the whole, gradually increase in the century after the Civil War, serious questions about *which* faculty members should be entitled to participate in the formulation of educational policies always accompanied the expansion of faculty influence. Some of these issues continue today to be matters of contention and to create divisions within the ranks of the faculty. From the outset of the movement in support of a larger role for faculty in governance, highly regarded senior professors at the nation's most prestigious institutions most frequently took the lead. In emphasizing the link between professional status and the right and responsibility to participate in institutional governance, the most prominent advocates of what came to be known as shared governance did not initially support an all-inclusive approach to faculty involvement in decision making. Full professors often ignored the claims of their junior colleagues to a place at the table, regarding them as not yet full-fledged members of the profession with sufficient expertise to deserve a role in governance. This attitude was evident in the formation of the American Association of University Professors

(AAUP), which quickly became the most influential voice in higher education calling for a significant and meaningful role for faculty in institutional governance. When it was first organized in 1915, the AAUP was open only to professors with at least ten years of service who had a reputation for scholarship and who received a nomination from another recognized scholar. Excluding from the AAUP those just starting careers in academia and those who lacked a national reputation for scholarship also had the effect of denying AAUP membership to virtually all women and people of color.[6] In the early twentieth century, the most vocal advocates of shared governance thus generally envisioned extending authority in institutional governance to only a quite narrow segment of those involved in teaching.

In subsequent years, however, the idea that junior professors should be excluded from most aspects of institutional decision making would give way to a more inclusive conception of governance. Not long after its founding, the AAUP itself would greatly expand its membership eligibility requirements. While faculty involvement in governance was largely restricted to full professors in the late nineteenth and early twentieth centuries, by the middle of the twentieth century, opportunities for involvement had generally been extended to assistant and associate professors who were tenured or on the tenure track.

More recently, as the number of those holding part-time and contingent faculty appointments off the tenure track—many of whom are women—greatly increased in academe, questions have arisen anew about just which members of the faculty should be entitled to a role in governance and whether those holding contingent appointments, especially those employed only part time, have the independence and institutional loyalty necessary to participate equally with those on the tenure track. Following its earlier moves toward a more inclusive approach to faculty involvement in governance, the AAUP has only recently issued a policy statement strongly favoring the extension of the right to participate in governance to those holding contingent appointments.[7]

Another question related to the faculty's role in governance concerns the role of research as a determinant of the professional qualifications that justify a college teacher's playing a significant role in academic decision making. Research and the creation of new knowledge have become important elements in the development of the professional identity of faculty members. Involvement in research is thus often cited as creating the expertise that is required for informed participation in many aspects of academic decision making. Consequently, some have raised doubts as to whether faculty members whose academic responsibilities do not include research ought to be given a substantial role in the shaping of their institution's educational policies. In particular, this has been an issue in the community college sector, which has experienced rapid expansion over the last half century. These two-year institutions, which generally developed as extensions of the K–12 system of public education, have been staffed largely by faculty who are not expected to engage in research and who often do not have the same academic credentials as their colleagues in four-year colleges and universities. As a result, faculty in two-year colleges have often been excluded from meaningful participation in institutional decision making. However, as community colleges increasingly evolved away from their early association with K–12 education, and as the credentials of two-year college faculty members improved, the debate over the role of community college faculties in institutional governance has taken on new significance.

Yet another issue regarding the extent of faculty participation in governance revolves around the degree to which all faculty members have shared in the desire to devote significant time and energy to governance activities—whether, in fact, a belief in, and commitment to, shared governance is really widely held among faculty members. The rapid expansion of college administration that has occurred over the last century and more was not only a result of the increasing size and complexity of American institutions of higher education; it was also at least in part a product of the desire of many faculty members to avoid administrative responsibilities for both the formulation and implementation of policies. As demands on faculty to demonstrate research productivity and keep up with the latest instructional technologies have increased, many faculty members have come to regard involvement in governance activities as an unwelcome burden. Challenges to the practice of shared governance have thus come not only from administrators and external governing bodies; they have also come from within the ranks of the faculty.

Nevertheless, while these problematic issues about governance have continuing relevance, in recent years the greatest threat to the practice of shared governance has come from those administrators, governing board members, and public officials who seek to corporatize American higher education. A key element of their program of "reform" involves measures that would, in effect, deprofessionalize the professoriate. Many advocates of a more businesslike approach to managing American colleges and universities contend that the need to achieve greater "flexibility" in order to respond to new twenty-first-century "realities" requires the "unbundling" of the tasks performed by professors, so that each faculty member is no longer expected to fulfill all three of the traditional triad of faculty responsibilities of teaching, research, and service (including governance work). Even such tasks as course-content development and actual instruction, they claim, may be more efficiently carried out if performed by different individuals, especially in the ever-growing area of online education.

Similarly, supporters of a more businesslike approach to higher education see the greater use of contingent, often part-time, non-tenure-track faculty as an effective means of reducing costs and maintaining greater flexibility to respond to changes in student demand. In 1975, those working full time made up 70 percent of all faculty, and of those, 57 percent were tenured or tenure track. In recent decades, the casualization of labor that has come to characterize much of the American labor market with the end of the great post–World War Two economic boom has clearly affected the professoriate. Currently, less than one-third of all faculty work full time in a tenured or tenure-track position. In the corporate model, faculty members are treated as "employees" to be assigned to duties defined by management, rather than as largely autonomous professionals working in a collegial setting.

These challenges to the professional status of faculty members are thus closely linked to the effort to restructure the system of academic governance. The deprofessionalization of the professoriate undermines the principal justification for faculty members' claiming a significant role in academic decision making: namely, that such a role is a necessary product of a faculty member's professional status and academic expertise.

Other "reform" proposals that have received considerable attention in recent years also represent serious threats to the system of governance that developed in American colleges and universities over the course of the twentieth century. Some reformers, who would undoubtedly deny the charge that they favor an effort to deprofessionalize the professoriate, nevertheless have called for measures, including ending tenure and limiting the authority of discipline-based departments, that could significantly undermine the ability of faculty to exercise significant influence on institutional decision making.[8] The establishment of the system of academic tenure in the twentieth century was important in protecting academic freedom, not only as it applied to teaching and research, but also as it related to intramural speech that concerned institutional governance issues. Without such protections, intimidation or self-censorship can be serious obstacles to faculty participation in governance. Although it is possible to develop new interdisciplinary structures in which faculty authority is maintained, current attacks on the institution of the academic department threaten to weaken the one administrative unit in which faculty over the last century have come to exercise the greatest degree of control.

The narrative that follows presents a chronological history of faculty involvement in governance. Chapter 1 provides a general overview of the history of college governance before the 1870s, when the modern American university began to take shape. It focuses on the origins of the American system of strong presidents and often intrusive external governing boards, while arguing that the role of American faculty in institutional governance was greatly limited by their lack of professional status and by the small size and restricted institutional mission of American colleges.

Chapter 2 examines the years from 1876 to 1920, that is, from the founding of Johns Hopkins University, the nation's first research-focused institution, to the establishment and early years of the AAUP, the professional association that became the principal voice for the professional aspirations of the professoriate. Although powerful college presidents became highly visible public figures in this period and played a dominant role in institutional governance, the decades before World War One also witnessed the formulation of two key principles that became essential for the growth of American higher education: academic freedom and shared governance. These two principles were closely linked to the professionalization of the faculty—a process that was furthered by the formation of the AAUP in 1915.

Chapter 3 considers the period from the end of World War One to the beginning of World War Two. Both the expansion of American higher education and the professionalization of American faculty continued apace in these years. This chapter pays particular attention to the results of a major survey of governance practices at colleges and universities across the country conducted by the AAUP in 1939. An analysis of these results sheds light on the ways in which the faculty role in institutional governance grew during these years.

Chapter 4 examines the period from the beginning of World War Two to the mid-1970s. These years were marked by unprecedented growth in the resources devoted to American higher education and saw American universities achieve a position of global preeminence. During this period, the idea that faculty should exercise primary responsibility over academic matters also gained widespread acceptance. This acceptance is best symbolized by the 1966 publication of the *Statement on Government of Colleges and Universities*, which was jointly formulated by the AAUP, the Association of Governing Boards of Universities and Colleges, and the American Council on Education. The chapter also considers survey data gathered by the AAUP in 1970 that provide additional evidence concerning the expansion of the faculty role in institutional governance in the quarter century after the end of World War Two.

Chapter 5 traces several developments since the mid-1970s that have undermined the basis of faculty governance, especially the deteriorating economic environment for higher education and the rapidly accelerating deprofessionalization of the faculty that is part of a larger effort to apply the logic of the market and the principles of business management to higher education. Although survey results from the early twenty-first century show the complexity of recent developments in the trajectory of faculty self-government, the implications for both faculty governance and academic freedom of recent trends in academic employment are deeply troubling. The Association of Governing Boards' backtracking in the mid-1990s from its earlier commitment to the 1966 *Statement on Government* is an indication of the breakdown of the consensus that had earlier developed about the proper role for faculty in institutional governance.

The conclusion briefly considers the likely future for the faculty's role in governance and the potential consequences for American higher education if the role of faculty in academic decision making declines further. Key questions for the future are whether current challenges to the practices of shared governance will only intensify and whether such challenges will affect the quality and purpose of American higher education. It remains to be seen whether American colleges and universities will be able to continue to pursue a broad approach to the purposes of higher education in an increasingly market-driven environment or to retain their position of global preeminence if the system of governance that helped make that broadly conceived mission and preeminence possible is fundamentally altered.

CHAPTER ONE

College Governance before 1876

The founding of Harvard College in 1636 marked the beginning of higher education in what would later become the United States. In a number of respects, American colleges and universities would develop in ways that would eventually distinguish them with regard to organization and governance from colleges and universities elsewhere in the world. In their origins, however, Harvard and the eight other colleges that were founded in Britain's North American colonies before 1776 were directly influenced by the examples of universities that existed in England, Scotland, and northern Europe in the seventeenth and eighteenth centuries.[1]

The early British colonists who came to America were most familiar with the English universities of Oxford and Cambridge, which had become major centers of learning centuries before the first British settlements of North America. These institutions had separate faculties of theology, law, medicine, and liberal arts and were largely controlled by the senior members of their faculties, who elected those holding positions of authority. The colonists who established the first colleges in British North America were also influenced by the examples of several Calvinist institutions of higher learning that were a product of the Reformation. These included universities established in Geneva (1559), Leyden (1575), and Edinburgh (1583). Although each of these sixteenth-century Calvinist institutions had its own particular governance structure, in contrast to Oxford and Cambridge they all operated under the authority of local civic and religious officials and were subject to some form of external board of trustees that, at a minimum, oversaw financial matters. Faculty members, however, largely controlled the internal affairs of these institutions and were generally responsible for choosing the rector, who coordinated the faculty's handling of the internal administration of the university. As scholars with influence in both church and state, senior faculty at these institutions enjoyed substantial social status.[2]

Although the American colleges that were founded before the Revolution were all heavily influenced by the precedents established by English and northern European universities, they also quickly developed certain distinctive features. In comparison to European institutions of higher learning, America's colonial colleges, which were created in a sparsely populated and relatively underdeveloped environment, had a more limited mission and were much smaller. European universities provided both undergraduate and postgraduate instruction and were, in many ways, defined by the advanced professional training they offered to those preparing for careers in the ministry, law, and medicine. Universities such as Oxford, Cambridge, and Edinburgh may have relied on young graduates to serve as tutors for students working on baccalaureate degrees, but these tutors taught under the authority and supervision of more established masters, who were responsible for postgraduate instruction, and who, as a body, were largely in charge of internal governance. In contrast to European universities, colleges in colonial America offered no advanced instruction, had minimal resources, enrolled few students, and had very small teaching staffs. Whereas European universities clustered together multiple colleges into a single degree-granting institution and typically had separate faculties for law, medicine, theology, and philosophy, colonial colleges were small unitary institutions. Probably no colonial college had more than one hundred students in any given year, whereas many universities in Europe from early in their histories enrolled more than one thousand students. The University of Paris may have had as many as ten thousand students in the mid-sixteenth century.[3]

America before the Revolution was home to few recognized scholars who could provide colonial colleges with a core of continuing senior faculty capable of commanding substantial respect from society at large. As late as 1755, Harvard had only two professors, while Yale, the College of New Jersey (Princeton), and King's College (Columbia) had no regularly appointed professors.[4] All told, in 1750 only ten individuals served as professors in the thirteen colonies.[5] No colonial-era institution offered advanced degrees or professional training. Although many students attended American colonial colleges with the intention of later entering the ministry, the colleges did not offer any advanced instruction in theology, nor did they offer such instruction in law or medicine. Most instruction for the youthful students attending colonial colleges was provided by young men who were themselves recent graduates and who often did not see college teaching as a career but rather as a form of temporary employment before finding a pulpit or embarking on some other occupation.[6] The absence of a body of senior scholars at any of the still immature colleges in colonial America had significant implications for institutional governance.[7]

Colonial colleges, like Reformation universities in seventeenth-century northern Europe, were organized under the auspices of civic and religious authorities who set up nonresident boards of governors to ensure that the colleges fulfilled their public purpose. The first two American colleges, Harvard and William and Mary, also had resident corporations that included teaching fellows, so that their governance structure was bicameral, but these resident corporations by the eighteenth century had come to exercise much less authority than the external governing bodies.[8] All other colonial colleges, with the exception of Brown, adopted a unicameral structure of governance, in which the only legally recognized governing authority was a nonresident board of trustees.

In contrast to the external boards that were responsible for the overall supervision of universities in Britain and northern Europe but allowed faculty to enjoy substantial autonomy in most matters of internal governance, external governing boards in colonial American colleges, whether under a bicameral or a unicameral governance structure, exercised significantly greater control over a wide range of issues. Colonial governing boards were not willing to allow typically youthful, inexperienced, and transient teaching faculty to govern themselves or determine institutional policies. Only at the College of Philadelphia (later the University of Pennsylvania), where the masters were drawn from the ranks of more mature and socially prominent members of the community, did the faculty exist as "a separate and duly constituted body with clearly governmental functions."[9] Even at the College of Philadelphia, however, such powers were more circumscribed than those exercised by the higher-status faculty in European universities. Rather than delegate to the teaching staff as a body control over academic decision making and student discipline, governing boards in British North America devised a new administrative innovation: the strong college president, who was appointed by and reported to the external board, not to the faculty, and who often acted in an autocratic manner toward his generally youthful and poorly trained teaching staff. Historian John Thelin thus concludes that a "legacy of the colonial colleges that has defined and shaped higher education in the United States to this day" is "the external board combined with a strong president."[10]

The Growth of American Colleges, 1776–1820

In the decades following independence, the most dramatic development in American higher education was the rapid increase in the number of colleges. In addition to the nine colleges in existence at the time of the Revolution, forty-three more were chartered between 1782 and 1820.[11] These new institutions fell into two major groups: state institutions and denominational colleges. Georgia, North Carolina, Vermont, Tennessee, South Carolina, Ohio, Maryland, and Virginia all chartered state-supported institutions of higher learning in this period. A variety of religious denominations, including several evangelical churches, most notably the Baptists and Methodists, which had previously eschewed the need for an educated ministry, also sponsored the establishment of colleges during these years.

During the colonial period, no distinction had existed between private and public colleges, and this remained the case well into the nineteenth century. As late as 1820, many institutions that would later be considered "private," such as Harvard, Columbia, and Yale, received funding from state and local governments.[12] On the other hand, some institutions that received no state support had government officials serving on their governing boards and were considered to be carrying out a public purpose. The celebrated *Dartmouth College* case of 1819, in which Supreme Court Chief Justice John Marshall ruled that the state of New Hampshire did not have the right unilaterally to change the terms of the charter under which the college had been established, did not, as is sometimes claimed, create an iron wall of separation between "private" and "public" colleges, but it did lay the foundation for the subsequent development of such a distinction that became a defining characteristic of American higher education.[13]

In the first decades of the nineteenth century, however, religiously affiliated colleges and so-called state universities had much in common. The diffusion of resources among a large number of institutions of higher learning meant that no American college was well funded. None came close to the size and stature of contemporary universities in Europe, where some institutions enrolled over two thousand students, and many others more than one thousand, a substantial proportion of whom were preparing for careers in law and medicine.[14] In 1817, Yale, then the largest college in the United States, had roughly 275 students.[15]

American colleges, whether state sponsored or religiously affiliated, were essentially preparatory or undergraduate institutions, focusing on the development of character and moral discipline rather than on intellectual inquiry and discovery. Very few offered any form of advanced training in theology, medicine, or law (let alone other specialized academic subjects), since the practice of these professions did not at the time require a college degree.[16] As late as 1800, fewer than one hundred college teachers in the United States held professorial rank, and even among this small group very few could claim significant expertise or a recognized academic reputation in a specialized field of study. Although college teaching was beginning to become more of a long-term commitment, it was still not seen as exclusive of other career options. At Harvard, which pioneered in the creation of professorships and whose faculty was beginning to become more academically specialized than those at other colleges in America, only one of the ten members of the teaching staff holding professorial rank in 1821 viewed his position as representing a long-term commitment to an academic career.[17]

The profile of American college teachers was changing by the first decades of the nineteenth century, but the development of the modern conception of the academic profession based on advanced training in a specialized field of knowledge and reliance on peer evaluation of one's qualifications by fellow experts was still well in the future. As a ministerial career became less attractive in the early nineteenth century because of a relative decline in salaries and greater job insecurity, college teaching began to become a more appealing long-term career option.[18] This increasingly became the case as leading institutions such as Harvard and Yale raised the number of permanent professorships, so that less instruction would be carried out by young tutors who would soon turn to other pursuits.[19] Even the decreasing proportion of teaching staff who served as tutors began to stay in that position for longer periods of time and had more training than tutors half a century earlier.

Nevertheless, as of 1820 very few college teachers had developed a sense of professional identity. Rather than seeing themselves as experts in a particular academic field devoted to the discovery and transmission of new or specialized knowledge, most college teachers continued to view their role as cultivating character in their students, "oftentimes as an extension of an earlier or concurrent ministerial role (the college as parish)."[20] As a consequence of the limited size and narrow mission of American colleges and the relatively homogeneous nature of college communities, typically only the president, who often came out of the ministry, not from the ranks of the faculty, exercised administrative responsibilities and commanded significant respect from the community.[21] College presidents did devote a substantial amount of time to teaching and were thus not yet full-time administrators, but in most cases, together with their governing boards, they ran their institutions with very little or no input from faculty. Faculty played no role in the selection of the college president, who was accountable only to the external governing board. Just like their predecessors in the colonial period, presidents and governing boards in the early republic continued to exercise primary responsibility for almost all areas of academic decision making. Historian Walter Metzger, in fact, observes that "in the early nineteenth century a nadir seems to have been reached" in faculty relations with trustees, as "the system of control by a nonresident board . . . evolved into an instrument of academic government that was officious, meddlesome, and often tyrannical."[22]

Although Harvard was one of the few institutions to have a bicameral governance structure (with both a nonresident board of overseers and a resident Harvard Corporation) that provided for the possibility of faculty serving on the resident governing body, no member of the teaching staff was elected to the corporation after 1800.[23] In contrast to Harvard, which in the early nineteenth century took steps that, in effect, limited the possible role of faculty in institutional governance, Yale was one of the few colleges in this period to take steps in the opposite direction. When Jeremiah Day, himself a longtime faculty member, became president of Yale in 1817, he introduced an important, though not then widely copied, reform by granting his faculty a role in institutional governance. This included allowing faculty substantial authority in the selection and appointment of new colleagues.[24] Yale historian Brooks Mather Kelley refers to this policy as one of Day's "most significant contributions to American higher education."[25] Far more common in the early years of the republic was the approach to governance adopted by the trustees of Princeton, who, according to historian Thomas Jefferson Wertenbaker, gave the faculty, and even the president they had chosen, "no more authority than was absolutely necessary, and that grudgingly."[26]

Antebellum Colleges and Precursors of Change, 1820–1860

American higher education continued to grow at an accelerating pace in the four decades before the Civil War. The number of students rose substantially both in absolute numbers and as a percentage of the population, but as a result of the fourfold increase in the number of state-sponsored and church-affiliated institutions between 1820 and 1860, the average enrollment for American colleges at the end of this period was still only seventy-nine students—a figure that had changed little since 1820.[27] Even the largest colleges had relatively small student bodies. Harvard at this time enrolled between four and five hundred students. Princeton, which was one of the few institutions to draw students from well beyond its own region of the country, had just 314 students in 1860.[28] The typical college on the eve of the Civil War had between four and six faculty members. Although at a limited number of prestigious institutions a gradual process of professionalization among some faculty members—including more specialized training, scholarly publication, and participation in learned societies—was beginning to take root by the 1850s, such professionalization was the exception, not the rule, for most college teachers in America.[29] While a few institutions—primarily those with the largest and most specialized teaching staffs—began to assign to faculty greater responsibility for some academic matters, the basic pattern established in the colonial period of small institutions being run by autocratic presidents and actively engaged governing boards continued to be the norm.[30]

Symptomatic of the limited role for faculty in institutional governance in this period—even at the institution that probably had the most prestigious faculty in the country—was the failed effort by the Harvard faculty in the 1820s to regain representation on the resident Harvard Corporation, which during Harvard's first century had included members of the teaching staff. The non-resident Harvard Board of Overseers' final rejection of faculty representation on the corporation did not altogether preclude faculty influence on academic decisions, especially as the faculty grew in size and prestige. However, the Harvard Corporation, which was increasingly coming under the control of the Boston business elite, closely guarded its authority over the appointment of new faculty. Much to the dismay of the instructional staff, the corporation and overseers also imposed on the faculty a number of important curricular and other reforms in this period, though passive resistance by the faculty did result in some modifications to the original proposals.[31]

Early Efforts to Expand the Role of Faculty in Governance

Although faculties played only a minimal role in institutional governance in most antebellum colleges, several noteworthy efforts to give faculties a greater role in academic decision making did occur in this period. These attempts proved to be precursors of later developments. In most cases, such efforts took place at the nation's largest institutions and were associated with plans to expand the mission and scope of these colleges and to introduce a greater sense of professionalism, including at least a limited responsibility for research, among the faculty. No American institution in the antebellum years was comparable in quality or reputation to the modern universities that were being created in Germany in the late eighteenth and early nineteenth centuries. The modern German university, with its new emphasis on academic specialization, original research, the seminar method of instruction, and freedom of inquiry for professors enjoying high status as professionals would eventually become a model for institutions of higher learning in the United States and elsewhere in the world.[32] In the antebellum period, however, no American institution of higher learning could be considered a "university" in the modern sense. Nevertheless, the roots of the later transformation of some of America's old-time colleges into universities with more comprehensive curricula, professional schools, and a greater commitment to original research, as well as more highly regarded faculties, could be found in this period with the rise of what Roger Geiger calls "multipurpose colleges."[33]

The first significant attempt at governance reform that called for a new role for faculty was Thomas Jefferson's plan for the establishment of the University of Virginia. After earlier failing to remake the College of William and Mary into an institution more akin to a European university, Jefferson became the guiding force in the founding of a new state university that opened its doors to students in 1825. In staffing the newly created University of Virginia, Jefferson sought to recruit faculty who were already established scholars involved in the pursuit of new knowledge rather than young men for whom teaching would be a way station on the road to a career in the ministry or some other occupation. He looked to European-trained scholars to provide the core of such a teaching staff. He also envisioned the University of Virginia to be more like a European university by focusing on advanced training rather than preparatory and undergraduate education. In its early years, the fledgling institution did not even offer bachelor's degrees. In contemplating the hiring of a more professional faculty composed of mature scholars who were themselves engaged in discovering new truths, Jefferson reasoned that such faculty members ought to be entrusted with much greater responsibility for institutional governance than was the case at the typical American college. Instead of creating a strong president chosen by the external governing board, Jefferson's constitution for the University of Virginia provided for copying the European practice of allowing the faculty to elect its own chair on a rotating basis. Faculty members were also given more authority over their own classes, including the selection of texts, than at most other American colleges of the time. Some of these innovations remained in place even after Jefferson died one year after the opening of the university, but the difficulty of recruiting mature students who sought a European-style university experience—rather than boys who were still basically adolescents—and the growing conservatism of antebellum Virginian society, prevented the University of Virginia from fulfilling Jefferson's dreams and thus serving as a model for other institutions in this period.[34]

Although the small liberal arts college with a traditional classical curriculum and little role for faculty in institutional governance remained the typical American institution of higher learning in the antebellum years, this period did witness the development of some new curricular programs in which faculty exercised greater decision-making authority. Some of the country's most prestigious schools, such as Yale and Harvard, established new programs in science and engineering. In addition, many colleges established or expanded legal and medical schools. Although such professional schools did not require a college degree for admission and were typically regarded as inferior in status to the undergraduate college that was the core of the institution, the development of science and engineering programs ultimately contributed to the spread of new thinking about the appropriate role of faculty in college governance. Yale, for instance, furthered its reputation as a pioneer in faculty governance when in the 1840s it established a new department that later became known as the Sheffield Scientific School. Faculty in the new department had even more control over academic matters than did their colleagues in the traditional college, in part because Yale's governing board initially paid less attention to the new program than it did to the undergraduate college it considered to be the core of the institution, but also because the school became home to a number of leading scientists who looked to German universities as a source of inspiration. In 1860, the Scientific School became the first institution in the United States to offer an earned PhD degree. The faculty members at the Lawrence Scientific School of Harvard, which was founded at almost the same time as Yale's Sheffield School, also exercised an unusual degree of autonomy, electing their own dean and being largely responsible for determining the shape of the school's organization.[35]

Another institution whose practices presaged a greater role for faculty in institutional governance was the University of Michigan, which rose quickly to a position of preeminence among state universities in the decade before the Civil War. Chartered by the new state of Michigan in 1837, the university enrolled its first students in 1841. Michigan's board of regents adopted a plan that, in some ways, paralleled Jefferson's constitution for the University of Virginia by initially establishing a rotating presidency among the small body of newly appointed professors and delegating to the faculty primary responsibility for the curriculum. In contrast to Jefferson's vision for the University of Virginia, however, the initial faculty for the University of Michigan was composed primarily of ministers who lacked any academic specialization and who remained committed to a traditional course of study for their students. In fact, only clerical faculty members were eligible to serve as president.[36]

In 1852, however, the Michigan governing board ended the rotating presidency when it selected educational reformer Henry Philip Tappan to become president of the growing university. By 1860, the University of Michigan was probably the largest state university in the country, with more than five hundred students and a faculty of seventeen.[37] Tappan's vision was to build an institution that would be similar but not identical to a German university.[38] Like Jefferson, he wanted to develop a faculty of mature scholars who would pursue original research and to have the university offer instruction in professional and scientific fields, as well as in the traditional liberal arts. Tappan succeeded in transforming the faculty, so that a substantial majority by 1860 had either earned a PhD in study abroad or would eventually earn a doctorate. Moreover, at least in the sciences, two-thirds of the faculty appointed under Tappan would be publishing scholars.[39]

In his initial efforts to reshape the curriculum, Tappan acted more or less unilaterally, but he relied heavily on the advice of the faculty in making new appointments. Moreover, meetings of the entire faculty (which came to be known as the "University Senate") became an important vehicle through which faculty members could express their collective views. Before he was forced out of office in 1863 as a result of a conflict with the board of regents that was personal rather than philosophical, Tappan joined a handful of other antebellum educational reformers in setting forth a strong argument in favor of a significant role for faculty in institutional governance. Speaking to the university senate in 1861 about pending state legislation concerning the governance of the university, Tappan, according to his biographer, outlined "several principles . . . essential to the well-being of the University: for instance, no laws or regulations should be made without the concurrence of the faculties; and the appointive power should rest with the University Senate." Tappan went on to assert with great passion that the regents "should not look upon the professors as 'employees.' The Senate is and should be *The University*."[40]

Frederick A. P. Barnard was another university president in this period who made a similar argument for faculty expertise justifying a greater role for professors in institutional governance. Using such an argument while serving as president of the University of Mississippi in the 1850s, he helped convince the governing board of the school to grant the faculty greater control over educational policy. Barnard would later go on to help transform Columbia into a modern university after the Civil War.[41]

While very few colleges in the antebellum period were organized on the basis of Tappan's conception of university governance, one significant example of an institution in which faculty gained formal recognition of their right to self-government was Oberlin College. Primarily noted for its progressive policies regarding the admission of women and African Americans, Oberlin was also a pioneer in faculty governance. Founded in 1833, the new college immediately became embroiled in a dispute over the admission of African Americans that led the governing board to approve a resolution stating that "the question in respect to the admission of students into this Seminary be in all cases left to the decision of the Faculty & to them be committed also the internal management of its concerns, provided always that they be holden amenable to the Board & not liable to censure or interruption from the Board so long as their measures shall not infringe upon the laws or general principles of the Institution."[42] This approach to institutional governance was exceptional for a small fledgling college that began with only four faculty members. Moreover, faculty self-government was further strengthened by the board's adoption of the college's first bylaws, which gave to the faculty (chaired by the president, and including professors, tutors, and "general agents") control over the internal administration of the college, including the disciplining of students, a responsibility often exercised by governing boards at other small colleges. The bylaws also required the faculty to "hold stated meetings once in two weeks to promote the general interest of the Institute." In 1834, prominent evangelist Charles Grandison Finney made the trustees promise never to interfere in the "internal control" of the college as a condition of his acceptance of the presidency of the college—a commitment the governing board was willing to make and keep.[43]

In 1837, Jasper Adams, who had recently left the presidency of the College of Charleston, set down a remarkably prescient set of principles for the proper relation between college trustees and faculty.[44] His views, though not yet widely accepted in American higher education, reflected the aspirations of an educator who envisioned an increasingly professionalized faculty playing a dominant role in academic decision making. Before developing his mature reflections on college governance, Adams had engaged in an ultimately successful struggle with the trustees of the College of Charleston to gain formal recognition of the faculty's role in institutional governance. As "principal" and "president of the faculty" of the that college during the 1820s and 1830s, Adams insisted on the right of the faculty to be consulted in the appointment of tutors and also attempted to obtain the trustees' agreement on a clear definition of the proper spheres of responsibility for the faculty and governing board. Adams failed to achieve this latter goal during his time as president, but soon after he left in 1836 to become a professor at West Point, the College of Charleston reorganized to become the nation's first municipally sponsored college, at which time the trustees allowed the faculty to draw up a set of regulations for the government of the college that gave the faculty primary responsibility for internal administration.[45]

One year after leaving the College of Charleston, Adams delivered an address to the American Institute of Instruction (the first significant interstate association of teachers and others interested in education in United States history)[46] in which he claimed to be the first American to present a systematic discussion of the relation between trustees and faculty. He premised his analysis on a recognition of the "peculiar skill, knowledge, and experience" that were required to be successful as a professor, and he drew direct parallels between the service performed by faculty and the services performed by the traditional professions of law, medicine, and the ministry. Adams argued that in each of these professions, the typical relationship between an employer and a subordinate employee, who labored under the immediate direction of his superior, was transformed into one in which the "employer" had to defer to the professional's best judgment in accomplishing the task at hand. He observed that college trustees most often were clergymen, lawyers, or successful men of affairs, who had no experience as college teachers. He concluded, therefore, that "however worthy and excellent they may be, in their personal characters, and however distinguished in the line of their several pursuits and professions, [trustees] are no more qualified and entitled to advise and direct a college faculty within their peculiar department, than the client is to advise and direct his lawyer, or the patient his physician." On the basis of his own experience and observations, Adams contended that no college had "permanently flourished, in which the trustees have not been willing to concede to the faculty, the rank, dignity, honor, and influence, which belong essentially to their station." Conversely, "those colleges have been most flourishing, in which the instruction and the discipline have been most exclusively committed to their faculties."[47]

Adams then proceeded to describe in more specific terms what he understood to be "the respective duties of a board of trustees and a faculty." In language that, in many respects, foreshadowed what would become conventional wisdom a century later, Adams recognized that trustees by "right and necessity" were responsible for "the original organization of the college" and, in most cases, the appointment of the initial body of faculty members. Thereafter, according to Adams, the trustees retained the right of assigning salaries and managing the college's funds, a job for which Adams thought the trustees much better suited than the faculty. He also accepted the need for the trustees to have the final authority in "calling instructors to account" if they were "unfaithful" in the performance of their duties and in "removing them for just and adequate cause" if that became necessary. On the other hand, Adams also thought trustees had a duty "to sustain the faculty by their countenance and encouragement, to conciliate public confidence and favor towards their institutions," and, in general, to serve as the "patrons" of their colleges.[48]

Adams argued that the faculty ought to exercise control over the "regulation of the course of study, including the choice of text-books" and that "the mode of instruction, the discipline of the college, and the internal administration of its affairs" ought to be "exclusively committed to them." He also asserted that even though the trustees had the power of appointment of new faculty, they ought "to be governed chiefly by the advice and wishes of the faculty," because nothing tended "more to disturb" the harmony among the members of the faculty, which was "indispensable to the usefulness" of a college, "than the introduction of a member into the faculty, to whose admission the other members are opposed." Adams claimed that his proposed division of responsibility between a faculty and governing board was necessary for the effective functioning of a college: "Without a sphere of duty, in which freedom and independence of action are secured to them, no faculty, whatever may be their talents and virtues, can be useful or successful."[49]

While Adams's views in many ways anticipated a consensus of opinion that would develop in the next century, he did not foresee the growth of administration as a category separate from both trustees and faculty. Rather than regard the president of a college as a "chief executive officer" whose role and responsibilities were distinct from those of the teaching staff, Adams implicitly assumed that the president ought to be considered primarily as leader of the faculty. College presidents at this time did carry significant teaching loads. However, it would have been an unusual college president in this period who would have considered himself simply a first among equals on the faculty. Most college presidents in the antebellum period would probably have claimed that when they acted on their own initiative, they were acting in behalf of the faculty, but in so acting they were not likely to have consulted with their teaching colleagues. Unlike the rectors of European universities who were elected by their professorial colleagues and were thus beholden to them, the typical American college president was selected by, and was responsible to, an external governing board that paid little if any attention to the institution's faculty in making its choice. Moreover, so long as most college instructors themselves lacked advanced training and specialized expertise, it was difficult for them to assert their right to a role in institutional governance that compared to the role played by the college president.

American Higher Education in the Immediate Aftermath of the Civil War

Historians often cite the Civil War as a watershed in the development of the United States in general and of higher education in particular. However, it would be more accurate to view the period of the Civil War and Reconstruction as an extension of the gradual transition that was already beginning to occur in American colleges over the previous several decades.[50] Although many colleges in the South experienced severe disruptions as a result of the Civil War, for the nation as a whole, the 1860s saw more new colleges established than had been founded in the 1850s.

Congressional passage of the Morrill Act in 1862 was an important landmark in the development of higher education in America, even though its impact was not fully felt until the last years of the nineteenth century. In paving the way for the creation of state land-grant universities, the act not only reinforced the slowly developing antebellum trend in both public and private schools toward integrating practical and scientific research and education with offerings in the traditional liberal arts; it also helped build the foundation for the later development of mass higher education. The law, in other words, ultimately had the effect of greatly enhancing the importance Americans attached to institutions of higher learning and to the research they would conduct, and thereby eventually helped to create a greater demand for a professional faculty engaged in the pursuit of new knowledge.[51]

By the 1870s, especially at the larger and more prestigious institutions of higher learning such as Harvard, which by this time probably became the first American institution to have more than one thousand students, an increasingly better qualified faculty began to exercise more control over the curriculum, though not necessarily over appointment and promotion decisions.[52] While the number of institutions of higher learning in the United States continued to grow rapidly, and more educational reformers were starting to call for American colleges to emulate some of the practices of German universities, substantial change in the organization of American institutions, including an expanded and more formal role for faculty in institutional governance, was still decades in the future.

By European standards, the typical American college remained both rudimentary in its offerings and small in size. In 1871, the total number of students enrolled in all graduate programs in the country was 198, and as late as 1880, the average enrollment for American colleges was only eighty-eight students.[53] Changes in the training and career patterns of college teachers in the United States were beginning to occur.[54] However, the typical American faculty member continued to be a generalist who was not a full-fledged professional academician. One study of faculty members at seven leading colleges between 1800 and 1860 found that more than one-third were clergymen.[55] Faculty members were still primarily responsible for maintaining discipline, building character, and passing on received wisdom to their students, but they were not expected to engage in original research and played little role in institutional governance.

College teachers may have thought of themselves as "gentlemen," but professors were only just beginning to enjoy a high degree of social status, and most did not meet what are now thought to be the basic criteria for "professional" status.[56] No form of specialized postgraduate training was required to become a college teacher. The doctoral degree had not yet become a necessary qualification. There were no professional associations or specialized journals for college professors, organized either by discipline or as a whole. Faculty did not enjoy autonomy in the performance of their work or control over the selection of their colleagues. As historian Laurence Veysey observes, even "the idea of a formal academic career was still in its infancy" in the 1870s.[57]

As late as 1874, European-trained Harvard scientist Louis Agassiz complained that

the very fact that there is no university in the United States the intellectual interests of which are managed by professors, but always by a corporation outside, shows that we do not understand what a university is. The men who are in it must know better what are the wants of an institution of learning than outsiders. I believe there is no scientific man who will concede that there can be a university managed to the best advantage by anybody but those interested in its pursuits, and no body of trustees can be so interested.[58]

The last quarter of the nineteenth century, however, would see the emergence of the modern American university. This development would be predicated on the increasing professionalization of American faculty, who would use their new status to lay claim to a substantially greater role in institutional governance.

CHAPTER TWO

The Emergence of a Professional Faculty, 1870–1920

Before 1870, stirrings of change in American higher education pointed toward the emergence of institutions with more expansive missions and more highly qualified faculty assuming a larger role in institutional governance. Only after 1870, however, could any American institution of higher learning lay claim to being considered a modern "university" committed to establishing and maintaining more rigorous standards of instruction and comprehensive course offerings for both undergraduate and graduate students and to assembling a corps of faculty professionals with advanced training and with the academic freedom to engage in research that would allow them to generate new knowledge as well as to pass on already established truths.

A number of factors contributed to the emergence of the modern American university and to the concomitant professionalization of American faculty. The United States experienced rapid industrialization and urbanization that created a demand for new types of knowledge and the training of experts in new specialized fields. Some American colleges responded to this demand by offering more practical subjects to go along with the traditional liberal arts curriculum and by adding research and graduate education to their institutional missions, ultimately evolving into modern universities. The Darwinian revolution undermined static conceptions of the "truth" that could be passed on to students by rote methods of instruction and led to an enhanced regard for the scientific testing of new theories and the use of new approaches to teaching by individuals with more specialized training.[1] Even many of the more numerous schools that retained their collegiate character as primarily undergraduate institutions underwent a significant change as they became more clearly distinguished from high schools and established more rigorous academic standards for both their faculties and students.

Whereas before the Civil War few people saw a college education as having much practical benefit, after 1870, a college degree began to make its recipient a more attractive candidate for many of the jobs being created in America's expanding and modernizing economy as well as for admission to the professional schools that were becoming a gateway to careers in law and medicine. Scientific research increasingly came to be regarded as necessary to the country's industrial and technological progress.[2] In addition, college professors in the newly emerging social-science disciplines began to be seen as possessing expertise that could help the country deal successfully with the rapid social and economic changes of the late nineteenth century.[3]

The increasing importance Americans attached to higher education was reflected in a substantial increase in philanthropic support for colleges and universities. Prominent businessmen Mark Hopkins, Leland Stanford, and John D. Rockefeller funded the establishment of influential new research universities, while other business leaders began to make much more substantial donations to existing institutions of higher learning. A growing trend of businessmen replacing clergy on college and university governing boards had both positive and negative consequences for faculty governance.[4] On the one hand, the increasing secularization of better-funded American colleges and universities contributed to the professionalization of a significant segment of the professoriate. Professionalization, in turn, led many faculty members to demand greater autonomy and academic freedom in order to carry out their expanded responsibilities as teachers and researchers. On the other hand, the trend toward greater representation of business interests on governing boards not only posed threats to the academic freedom of professors who challenged economic and political orthodoxy but also caused tensions over the application of business models of management to higher education. Such tensions would become an ongoing feature of discussions about college and university governance down to the present day.

An 1881 editorial in the *Nation* on problems besetting American higher education used language that bears a striking resemblance to that still being used in the twenty-first century by critics of college and university governing boards. The editors argued that by "more than anything else, except their poverty," American colleges were being held back from advancing because of "the comparatively small value placed on the professors" by the institutions' governing bodies.

> [College trustees] cannot see why a professor's salary should be any higher than is necessary to get you a professor, and having got a professor at their own figure, they despise him for taking so little. Having got him for less than they have paid their bookkeepers, they credit him with a bookkeeper's capacity—that is, with ability to perform faithfully a certain round of rather humble duties, which will fulfil [sic] the object for which the buildings were erected and keep the machinery in motion. In fact, the professor, in their eyes, is rather a man who "tends" college, as a hand "tends" a loom in a mill, than a person fit to govern, or direct, or manage an institution of any kind.
>
> . . . [The businessman trustee] wishes very much, indeed, that a college could be carried on without professors, and has a vague notion that by some sort of improvement in organization this result may some day be attained.

In attacking such thinking, the *Nation* editorial concluded that the "next great step to be taken in the improvement of the higher education in this country is the committal of university management in a greater degree, if not wholly, to the teaching body."[5]

During the last decades of the nineteenth century, the combination of increased funding for colleges and universities, rising demand for a college education, and a slowing rate of expansion in the establishment of new colleges produced a substantial growth in the average size of American institutions of higher learning. Compared to other nations, the United States was still unique with regard to the number of institutions it supported in its highly decentralized system of higher education, but the average number of both students and faculty for the nearly one thousand institutions that existed in 1900 had more than doubled since 1870.[6] By 1909, six universities enrolled more than five thousand students, and three of these employed more than five hundred instructional staff.[7] Even schools that remained more traditional undergraduate-oriented liberal arts colleges, such as Williams and Amherst, enrolled approximately five hundred students each at this time.[8]

The significant increase in the size of many American institutions of higher education made possible the greater specialization of faculty and also created a new organizational context in which issues of institutional governance were addressed. The growing separation of functions within a more complex university structure led to the establishment of new layers of academic administration, with policy implementation in an increasingly bureaucratized setting becoming more distinct from the task of policy formulation. The use of faculty committees and the proliferation of deanships and other administrative positions were both products of these developments.[9] Accelerating academic specialization also led to the rise of the academic department as a key unit of administration. The department would quickly become a focus of faculty concerns about and involvement in governance. As the evaluation of faculty credentials increasingly came to require expert judgment, college presidents eventually came to rely more heavily on the advice of departmental faculty in making decisions about appointment and promotion.[10]

The growing size of many American universities raised issues of governance in a way that had not arisen in the smaller, nonbureaucratized colleges of the pre–Civil War era. Curricular changes, including the creation of new programs, became much more frequent, and as academic departments and colleges became important administrative units within rapidly growing institutions, the method of selecting department heads and deans became an important issue.

The development in the United States of more mature institutions of higher learning in the last decades of the nineteenth century was directly influenced by the model of the modern research university that had first taken shape in Germany earlier in the century. Increasing numbers of American college graduates in fields ranging from history to physics began to seek postgraduate training in Germany. Between 1870 and 1900, well over five thousand Americans studied at German universities. Many German-trained scholars, including prominent future college presidents Andrew Dickson White, Charles W. Eliot, and Daniel Coit Gilman, returned to the United States to foster the development of institutions that would be comparable to German universities and, in the process, adapted German ideas about institutional governance and academic freedom to American conditions.

Ministers of state played a central role in bringing about the transformation of the traditional German institution of higher learning into the modern discipline-based university committed to original research.[11] German professors, all of whom were state appointees under the authority of a minister of education, did not enjoy an absolute form of self-government. However, compared to their American colleagues in the late nineteenth century, German professors—at least those holding chairs—exercised a good deal more control over their own research and teaching as well as the selection of administrators and other important aspects of university governance. Senior faculty in Germany elected not only their own deans but also the rector, who presided over the university as a whole. Just as the *Lehrfreiheit*, or academic freedom of German professors as it applied to teaching and research, provided an ideal that newly professionalizing faculty in the United States sought to emulate, so, too, did the degree of faculty control German professors exercised over the appointment of academic administrators and in other academic matters serve as a standard that many American faculty hoped to adapt to American higher education.[12]

The founding of Johns Hopkins University in 1876 represented the most direct effort to emulate the German model of a university devoted to graduate education and specialized research, but developments at already established schools such as Harvard, Columbia, and the University of Michigan, as well as at other newly founded institutions, such as Cornell and the University of Chicago, signaled a new stage in the development of the American university and in the increasing professionalization of American faculty. None of these institutions, not even Johns Hopkins, sought simply to replicate the German university model, but they all incorporated a German-influenced vision of the importance of research and a highly qualified faculty enjoying a major role in governance and the protections of academic freedom.[13]

One of the clearest indications of the growing professionalization of American faculty members was the increasingly common requirement of a PhD to obtain a faculty appointment at a university and at many colleges. William James in 1903 complained that the holding of the degree had become virtually a fetish in the selection of faculty. He observed that a candidate's holding a PhD took on more importance than any other consideration in the appointment of new professors, so that even at small colleges, the maxim of "No Instructor who is not a Doctor" had resulted in what he disparagingly called "the Doctor-Monopoly in teaching."[14] James undoubtedly exaggerated the extent to which the insistence on faculty members holding a doctorate had spread throughout all sectors of the highly diverse system of American higher education. Nevertheless, whatever the possible pitfalls in the new system may have been, in comparison to teachers at even the best American colleges of the antebellum period, many faculty members at the turn of the century had gone through a far more specialized form of training and were making a longer-term commitment to college teaching as a career. In addition, especially at the emerging universities, many professors were engaging in original research. Faculty could also now join such specialized disciplinary associations as the American Economic Association, the American Statistics Association, and the American Historical Association, all of which were founded in the 1880s, and which were soon joined by numerous other disciplinary organizations that contributed to a growing sense of professional identity for their members.[15]

Just as doctors and lawyers in the last decades of the nineteenth century were asserting their right to govern themselves based on their possession of an esoteric body of knowledge acquired through an extended period of formal training, a growing number of professors were also beginning to claim a similar responsibility for evaluating colleagues and for other aspects of academic decision making.[16] The particular requirements of college teaching and conducting research would also become the basis for the faculty's claims about the necessity of academic freedom in order to fulfill their mission as professionals. At the end of the nineteenth century, however, academic freedom and faculty governance were still largely aspirational ideals rather than widely instituted norms. Not all faculty members had developed a clear sense of themselves as professionals requiring a substantial degree of autonomy to carry out their responsibilities. The principles of academic freedom and faculty governance also often came into conflict with the views of the businessmen who had come to dominate college and university governing boards. Moreover, although the most influential university presidents of the late nineteenth century became highly visible public figures by advancing the cause of an expanded mission for American higher education and by touting the growing expertise and professionalism of American faculty, these men oscillated between autocratic and collaborative methods in trying to implement their vision of the new American university. In the end, however, by recruiting strong faculty members committed to an ideal of professionalism, the powerful presidents of the late nineteenth century planted the seeds for the reduction of unilateral administrative authority.[17]

Case Studies in the Rise of the Modern American University, 1868–1900

Historians often cite the founding of Johns Hopkins University in 1876 as marking the beginning of the age of the modern university in the United States, but the opening of Cornell University in 1868 was already a harbinger of many of the changes that were coming in American higher education, including an expanded role for faculty in institutional governance. Andrew Dickson White, the founding president of Cornell, had studied in Germany and been on the faculty at the University of Michigan under Henry Tappan. Having played a key role as a New York state senator in getting legislative approval for the establishment of a new land-grant university in Ithaca, which would also benefit from a substantial endowment from businessman and fellow state senator Ezra Cornell, White was in a unique position to shape what he hoped would become the first truly comprehensive American university, "where any person can find instruction in any study."[18] Whereas the vast majority of all college presidents before the Civil War had been clergymen, White was a layman with academic credentials who envisioned building a nonsectarian university that would be staffed by professional scholars regardless of their religious views and would be open to students regardless of their race or gender.

He recognized that he would not be able to recruit the most eminent scholars in the country to his new and somewhat remote campus, but in his original plan of organization for the institution, White asserted that he hoped to assemble a young and ambitious faculty who would be engaged in the pursuit of new knowledge, since "the power of discovering truth and the power of imparting it are almost invariably found together."[19] White was eager to build an institution with a broad range of both undergraduate and graduate courses in practical fields such as law, architecture, agriculture, and engineering, as well as in the liberal arts. From the outset, Cornell joined what was then the small number of American institutions of higher learning offering the PhD degree. White's highly publicized experiment in university organization began operations in 1868 with a remarkably large entering class of 412 students and 21 professors.[20]

White, along with trustee Ezra Cornell, whose interest in practical education had led him to endow the new institution, assumed expansive powers in shaping the university. White was solely responsible for identifying the first faculty members. However, White noted in his autobiography that he had learned from previous experience and observation that in many American colleges "a fundamental and most injurious error was made in relieving trustees and faculty from responsibility, and concentrating all in the president." Consequently, after he had selected the first faculty members, White "insisted that the faculty should not be merely a committee to register the decrees of the president, but that it should have full legislative powers to discuss and to decide university affairs."[21] As at the University of Michigan, where White had earlier served as a faculty member, regular meetings of the entire faculty, or academic senate, took place for "conducting the general administration of the institution and memorializing the Trustees, [and] discussing general questions of educational policy."[22] At its first meeting, the senate established an executive committee to help it fulfill its responsibilities. Faculty also met in departmental meetings, though in Cornell's early years these meetings were presided over by the president or a dean and not by a department chair.

White assigned to the faculty complete control over student discipline and the awarding of degrees. As a consequence, even though White initially proposed having a single degree designated for all graduates, regardless of their field of study, he accepted the judgment of the faculty, who rejected the idea. White was clearly the dominant figure in shaping Cornell, but in recruiting professional men of ability whose expertise he respected, he established a form of institutional governance that entailed a larger role for the faculty than was common at the time in American higher education. As at other institutions, however, faculty involvement in governance did not extend to fiscal matters, including appointment and promotion, construction of buildings, or any other action involving the expenditure of money. Although White retained the authority to make faculty appointments during his nearly two decades as president, near the end of his term in office he proposed that the faculty be entrusted with the authority to nominate new professors.[23]

The still tenuous basis for faculty involvement in governance was demonstrated in 1881, while White was on leave from the presidency of Cornell to serve as United States minister to Germany. In that year, over White's objections, the board of trustees summarily dismissed acting president William Channing Russel and several other faculty members because of what trustees considered their questionable religious views. In response to the dismissals, both Russel and physics professor William Anthony raised objections to the trustees' treating faculty as "hired servants doing the will of a master." Anthony asserted that the trustees should not interfere with the right of the faculty to "nominate its own members and initiate proceedings against them if necessary."[24] Russel also defended a view of faculty as professionals deserving of autonomy in carrying out their responsibilities: "[Universities] are not business enterprises, nor are professors clerks or servants, nor have the Trustees any right to look down on them, ignore their claims, or treat them summarily. . . . They must be free. No one near being a first-class man will work long under a whip, nor can any professor do a University his best service while he feels in danger of losing his place in spite of success in his department and good conduct. The professors move this University."[25]

In the year following the controversial firings, Waterman Thomas Hewett, a professor of German at Cornell since 1870, published an article in *Atlantic Monthly* offering a comprehensive examination of the issue of "University Administration." Hewett concluded that in order for a university to carry out its teaching and research functions, "all questions relating to courses of study and the bestowal of degrees, as well as the nomination of professors, should be entrusted to the appropriate faculty body for decision." He argued that just as it would be "absurd to trust the decision of an important legal question to a body of artists," it would be equally absurd "to confer the control of educational questions upon a corresponding body of lawyers." Professors, in other words, were professionals whose expertise was the basis for their claim to be largely self-governing with regard to academic matters. He also contended that proper university administration required faculty representation on governing boards, suggesting that the faculty ought to be authorized to elect its own representatives on an annual basis.[26]

Ironically, in 1889, under White's successor as president, Charles Kendall Adams, the Cornell trustees, who less than a decade earlier had ignored faculty concerns in dismissing a president and several faculty members, took the initiative in creating a university senate composed of the president and all full professors. The senate was charged with the responsibility of making all future professorial nominations and advising the board on questions of educational policy. This action was taken despite Adams's opposition. Subsequently, a dispute between the president and the board led to Adams's resignation and the appointment of Jacob Gould Schurman, a leader of the faculty's push for greater power, as Cornell's third president. Two decades later, with Schurman's active support, Cornell would become the first American university to provide for faculty representation on its governing board. At the same time, Cornell would also establish elected faculty advisory committees for each of its colleges that were authorized to meet with the president and governing board committees to discuss educational policies.[27]

Cornell's White was certainly a national figure, but Charles W. Eliot, who became president of Harvard in 1869, may have been the most prominent higher education reformer in the United States during the last decades of the nineteenth century. While most noted for introducing the elective system to Harvard, he also became instrumental in advancing the professional status of the professoriate. Eliot was trained as a scientist and had engaged in some original research while he was a young professor in Harvard's Lawrence Scientific School. Like Andrew Dickson White, Eliot had studied in Germany and was one of the first laymen to be appointed president of a major American institution of higher learning. Not coincidentally, just before being named president of Harvard, Eliot had published an article in the *Atlantic Monthly* criticizing "lawyers and men of business," who in "their capacity of trustees" were "constantly putting clergymen in the highest post of the profession of education, which is thus robbed of its few prizes, and subjected to such indignity as soldiers feel when untried civilians are put over their heads." He noted, however, that "fortunately for the country, education is getting to be a profession by itself," so that colleges could, in the future, turn to men from academic backgrounds to serve as presidents.[28]

Even before he became Harvard's president, Eliot had argued that advanced academic training beyond undergraduate studies was crucial to the development of a more professional faculty, as well as to proper preparation for the other learned professions: law, medicine, and the ministry.[29] Soon after becoming president, he supported the establishment of a graduate department with the authority to grant the PhD degree because he thought that graduate education was necessary to transform a person entering college teaching from being an "accidental product" to becoming "a well-equipped professional man, systematically produced in and for the higher institutions of education."[30] In his first years as Harvard's president, in part because he assumed that there was still a shortage of available professionalized teachers, Eliot usually made new faculty appointments more on the basis of personal loyalty than of professional credentials. However, once confronted with competition for prestige from the newly established Johns Hopkins (which tried to lure away many of Harvard's most distinguished faculty members), Eliot resolved to appoint and promote men with solid professional credentials. By the early 1890s, both the junior and senior members of the Harvard faculty were more likely to have advanced degrees, be engaged in scholarly research, and have served at least several years in teaching or research apprenticeship positions before being appointed than had been the case a quarter century earlier.[31]

Eliot's own experience as a faculty member at Harvard's Lawrence Scientific School made him more sensitive to the growing desire of faculty to be treated as professionals who needed a significant degree of autonomy and academic freedom to function effectively. Consequently, Eliot became a leading public proponent of the principle of academic freedom and supported Harvard's long-standing policy of what amounted to de facto tenure. Faculty appointments were "held without express limitation of time," though professors were subject to "removal for inadequate performance of duty, or for misconduct." Eliot was not averse to making use of this authority, and he did so without any formal process of peer review, but in also introducing an early pension plan and sabbaticals for Harvard professors, Eliot was contributing to the growing professional status of his faculty.[32]

At the same time that Eliot established the graduate department, he assigned to the academic council, consisting of all professors and assistant professors from all the faculties of the university, "the power to regulate the studies for, and recommend candidates for" advanced degrees.[33] By 1890, Harvard's growing size led to the establishment of faculty committees charged with responsibility for specific tasks, such as admissions and student discipline, though proliferating deans and other academic administrators soon took over some of these responsibilities.[34] Eliot's respect for faculty authority over the curriculum was demonstrated when he accepted the faculty's rejection of his proposal in 1901 to establish a three-year course of study as the norm for the AB degree. Instead, the faculty voted to raise the standards required for the awarding of the degree. By virtue of their growing prestige, the Harvard faculty gained greater influence over the university's academic decisions, but serious limits to faculty governance remained. As at Cornell, budgetary matters remained completely outside the purview of the faculty, and Eliot always retained for himself the power to choose new faculty, though in the later stages of his forty-year term as president, he did usually seek the approval of the faculty in the affected department.[35]

Like Harvard, Columbia University was one of the nation's oldest institutions of higher learning, having been founded as King's College before the American Revolution. It, too, underwent a significant transformation in the late nineteenth century to become a modern university. As part of this process, an increasingly professional faculty came to play a more prominent role in institutional governance. During the 1890s, under the presidency of Seth Low, Columbia developed discipline-based departments and a greater emphasis on faculty research. The number of full-time faculty increased from 45 in 1890 to approximately 250 in 1900, with many of the new recruits being prominent scholars. By 1900, many considered Columbia the country's leading university. Unlike most of the other presidents in the late nineteenth century who were successful in putting their schools in the front ranks of American universities, Low was a nonacademic who came to Columbia's presidency as a businessman and former mayor of Brooklyn. At the time of his appointment as president in 1889, he had been serving on the university's board of trustees. Recognizing his own limited knowledge of academic matters, Low concluded that as an essential part of his effort to transform Columbia into a true university, he would need to rely on the professional judgment of its faculty in matters of educational policy.

Consequently, not only did Low allow each college or school faculty at Columbia to elect its own dean, but soon after taking office he also created a university council, consisting of the deans and one other elected representative from each of the university's nonprofessional faculties, to make decisions about issues involving more than one university faculty and to advise the president on the academic operations of the university. At least until Low's retirement in 1902, the faculty in practice, as well as on paper, exercised substantial control over academic policies and the recruitment and appointment of new colleagues.[36]

While Cornell, Harvard, and Columbia were becoming modern universities with more highly qualified faculty playing an expanded role in institutional governance, the establishment of Johns Hopkins University in 1876 was to have an even greater impact on the nationwide development of a more professional faculty asserting its need for autonomy and academic freedom. Financed by a bequest from Quaker businessman Johns Hopkins that was virtually without strings and that was then the largest donation ever made to an American college or university, the new university was organized primarily as a graduate institution devoted to the promotion of original research.[37] Johns Hopkins quickly produced more PhDs than any other school in the country, granting during its first decade of operation nearly as many doctoral as bachelor's degrees.[38] In the late nineteenth and into the early twentieth century, many of these graduates, and the ambitious young faculty recruited to the Baltimore campus, would play a critical role in defining the professional rights and responsibilities of American professors.

As the founding president of Johns Hopkins, Daniel Coit Gilman played a role in shaping the new institution similar to that played by Andrew Dickson White at Cornell. Gilman and White had been classmates as undergraduates at Yale and after their graduation had gone together to Europe, where both men spent some time studying in Germany. Before being selected Johns Hopkins's first president, Gilman had been a faculty member at Yale's Sheffield Scientific School and then president of the University of California.[39]

When it opened in 1876, Johns Hopkins was not nearly as large as Cornell had been at its start. Johns Hopkins initially had a faculty of eighteen, of whom only six held the rank of professor, and just seventy-seven students, of whom fifty-four pursued graduate studies.[40] However, as the first American university to offer fellowships for advanced study in fields other than law, medicine, or theology, it was able from the start to attract a very able group of graduate students who were interested in pursuing academic careers. The trustees of Johns Hopkins had in fact initiated the fellowship program to help foster the development of a "new profession" committed to the pursuit of new knowledge in the arts and sciences. Johns Hopkins further contributed to the development of academic professionalism by pioneering in the publication of American scholarly journals that became an important means for professors to establish their academic credentials.[41]

Johns Hopkins may have had a small faculty, but Gilman from the outset had planned for the faculty to play a significant role in institutional governance and for departmental organization to provide an important foundation for a decentralized system of authority. The board of trustees supported Gilman's approach, and it formally resolved in the institution's first year of operation that "the Board does not interfere with the scholastic arrangement of the University." Although Johns Hopkins differed in a number of respects from a German university, especially in its combination of undergraduate and graduate coursework and its status as a private institution, Gilman adopted as part of his original plan of organization the German system of appointing one head professor for each department and then assigning that professor substantial autonomy in the running of his department, including the appointment of assistants. This small group of full professors met frequently with the president to discuss the development of the new institution's educational policies, and by one account the group operated in the fashion of a Quaker meeting, arriving at decisions by consensus.[42] In 1880, the board of trustees formally recognized the president together with the full professors of the university as the academic council and granted to the council substantial authority in guiding the university's internal affairs.[43] As at Cornell and Harvard, however, such authority did not extend to any issue directly related to the "financial management" of the institution.[44]

Johns Hopkins's early form of institutional governance, which was substantially influenced by the German system, gave significant power to the small number of head professors, but it raised issues regarding the governance role of faculty below the rank of professor, who at all times constituted a majority of the teaching staff. The question of which members of the teaching staff should be included in institutional governance processes has continued to spur debate on American campuses to the present day. Hopkins's academic council initially rebuffed the efforts of instructors and assistants to gain a voice in institutional governance but relented in 1882 and 1883 by creating two new governance bodies that provided for at least a limited role in governance for those below the rank of professor. The concession, however, was more symbolic than real in recognizing the right of junior faculty to participate in shaping the policies of the universities.[45]

Although Gilman voiced support for "the certainty of official tenure, and the expectation of a pension" as means of enhancing the professional status of faculty, he settled for a system of indefinite appointments that was similar to Harvard's and, because of financial constraints, was never able to implement the pension system that the trustees had approved in principle in 1881.[46] He was successful, however, in establishing an environment that was more conducive to academic freedom in teaching and research and to the furtherance of the professional status of his faculty than was typical of most late-nineteenth-century institutions of higher education in the United States.

The University of Chicago, which opened its doors in 1892, quickly came to rival Cornell, Johns Hopkins, and Columbia as a center for research and the development of an expanded notion of professional rights and responsibilities for faculty. Funded in large part by money provided by oil tycoon John D. Rockefeller, the new university began operations with nearly 750 students, of whom about one-fourth sought advanced degrees, and a teaching staff of 147, 77 of whom were at the rank of instructor or above. By 1909, the University of Chicago had more than five thousand students, making the still very young university one of the largest in the country.[47] William Rainey Harper, the founding president of the University of Chicago, was only thirty-five years old when he left a professorship at Yale to head the new institution. In spite of his youth, he was already a highly regarded scholar, having obtained his Yale PhD at the age of eighteen and then quickly gaining a reputation as a leading expert on the Old Testament.[48] His vision for the University of Chicago was similar to that of Andrew Dickson White for Cornell, as he sought to create a multipurpose institution with a research-oriented faculty enjoying academic freedom and offering a wide variety of undergraduate, graduate, and professional programs.

Harper instituted a system of governance that had much in common with that practiced at Johns Hopkins and Cornell. In his original plan of organization, he assigned to head professors virtually total control over their departments, though Harper expected that heads would at least consult with their instructors about courses and textbooks. Historian Richard Storr observes that "of departmental democracy there was no other hint." Harper did plan for each of the colleges and schools of the new university to hold regular faculty meetings and for the establishment of a university council, composed of the president, the deans, one elected representative from each of the faculties, and several other academic administrators, but all decisions of this body were to be subject to a veto by the president.[49]

Harper was eager to recruit men with established reputations to serve as head professors, and he discovered, even before the university opened its doors, that such professors would demand to play a role in university governance that would go beyond the confines of their own departments. His first two selections as head professors, J. Laurence Laughlin and William G. Hale, had to be enticed to leave Cornell, and they agreed to become founding members of the University of Chicago faculty only after Harper consented to the establishment of a senate consisting of the president and all head professors to serve as "the supreme legislative body in the realm of academic affairs." With the establishment of the senate, Harper's plans for a broad-based university council were dropped, and instead the same title was applied to a body made up solely of academic administrators but that had no legislative authority. Teaching staff other than head professors were organized into several separate faculties, which had regular meetings, but faculty governance still primarily meant governance by only a small portion of those engaged in teaching and research. A more inclusive advisory body, the Congregation, was established in 1896 to make recommendations on issues affecting the entire university. In addition to all faculty above the rank of instructor and all administrators, all those who had earned a PhD from the university could sit on the new body.[50]

Although Harper's new university provided a greater degree of faculty governance than was common in American higher education in the 1890s, by 1902 Laughlin and Hale, the two head professors who were most responsible for the establishment of the University of Chicago's senate, had become unhappy with the governance arrangements of the university and supported a proposal in the Congregation that would have placed further limits on administrative authority over educational policy by devolving greater powers onto the faculties of the various colleges of the university. Because of Harper's opposition, however, the reform ultimately failed to gain the support of a majority of voters in the Congregation.[51]

The University of Chicago's record on academic freedom was also uneven during its early years. Harper often spoke eloquently of academic freedom as a professional requirement for those involved in university teaching and research. In 1899, with Harper's approval, the Congregation promulgated an important statement affirming the principle of academic freedom, which complemented Harper's support for continuing appointments as a means of providing a "feeling of security from interference" in a professor's teaching and research. Harper subsequently declared that he believed professors on permanent appointment could be dismissed only for incompetence or immorality. Yet only a few years earlier Harper had been involved in a highly publicized case that seemed inconsistent with a commitment to academic freedom. In 1895, Harper did not renew the term contract of Edward W. Bemis, an economist in the Extension Division of the university. While Harper cited incompetence as the reason for Bemis's nonreappointment, the young economist's outspokenness in siding with labor against the railroads during the highly publicized Pullman strike of 1894 was undoubtedly a factor. Harper always coupled the issue of academic freedom with what Storr describes as "solicitude for the institution." Although Harper, as one of the nation's most prominent college presidents, can be credited with helping to explain to a larger public why academic freedom was necessary for universities to carry out their mission, in practice his commitment to the principle had its limits.[52]

The Growth of the Professional Ideal in Liberal Arts Colleges

Although America's emerging universities led the way in the process of faculty professionalization and professors' demands for a greater role in institutional governance, similar developments soon occurred at many smaller traditional liberal arts colleges, with long-established New England institutions generally taking the lead. While remaining committed to undergraduate education and a cohesive sense of community, these colleges also began to adopt for their own educational purposes some of the reforms being pioneered by America's fledgling universities, including greater academic specialization among their faculties and departmental organization based on discipline. Newer faculty members were better trained and began increasingly to identify with what Bruce Kimball describes as the "true professional ideal," including an insistence on greater autonomy and self-government.[53]

As early as 1872, Williams College professor John Bascom (who would go on to become president of the University of Wisconsin) expressed this new faculty identity when he declared at the inauguration of the college's new president:

> There are two conditions on which able and independent men—such as are the Faculty of Williams College . . . will cordially labor; first, that they shall have the ordering of the forms and conditions of their own work; second, that they shall have influence in that general control which includes their own work with others. . . .
>
> It is not strange that [a professor] should covet the right to be heard in [college] concerns, since these concerns are his concerns. . . . The college is

intrusted [*sic*] to the control and wisdom of grave and unimpassioned men. The president is a leader among equals, the weight of whose words is more that of wisdom than of authority.[54]

Before the late nineteenth century, many small colleges had been what historian Bruce Leslie describes as "multifunctional" institutions that could survive only by offering secondary or preparatory education to go along with their collegiate offerings. At institutions such as Swarthmore, Franklin and Marshall, and Bucknell, subcollegiate enrollments in 1870 actually exceeded the number of students enrolled in college-level studies.[55] Under such circumstances, it is not surprising that the faculties at these institutions were not fully professionalized.

As many traditional liberal arts colleges came to focus more exclusively on baccalaureate education to prepare students for postgraduate study in the professions or careers in business, and as American universities began to produce larger numbers of prospective college teachers with graduate degrees in particular disciplines, there was a noticeable increase in the qualifications and professional orientation of faculty at many of the nation's four-year colleges. Just as had occurred somewhat earlier at the larger research universities, greater academic specialization by faculty and departmental organization by discipline, which was increasingly occurring at America's liberal arts colleges by the beginning of the twentieth century, led to more insistent demands by faculty for greater autonomy and self-government.[56]

The experience of Dartmouth College is illustrative of the way the educational backgrounds and professional aspirations of faculty at many liberal arts colleges changed dramatically toward the end of the nineteenth century. In 1851, six of the college's eight professors had some training in theology and served as ministers or preachers while also teaching at Dartmouth. None had obtained advanced discipline-based training or studied abroad. They were generally uninterested in original research and publication and were oriented much more toward their local community than toward their academic peers at other institutions of higher learning. By 1881, however, of the twenty-four faculty members then teaching at Dartmouth, less than one-third had ministerial training, while nearly one-quarter had done specialized graduate work in Europe. Especially among those appointed after 1875, the change in background and orientation was even more striking. In contrast to faculty members before the Civil War, in 1881 many of the recently appointed professors participated in new professional associations, such as the American Association for the Advancement of Science or the American Philological Association, and were active researchers publishing in their particular disciplines.[57]

The increasingly professional identity of the Dartmouth College faculty led to a crisis in college governance in 1881 that reflected the desire of younger faculty members to have academic decisions based on expertise rather than on deference to hierarchical authority and conformity to traditional values. In that year, sixteen of the twenty-three resident faculty members signed a letter to the institution's governing board asking for the resignation of President Samuel Bartlett. The trigger for this faculty rebellion was the president's appointment of a new professor of Greek against the wishes of the faculty. While Bartlett based his selection primarily on the candidate's good character, the faculty objected to the appointee's lack of scholarly credentials, particularly his lack of scholarly publications and failure to establish a reputation among peers specializing in the study of Greek. Although the trustees ultimately decided to retain Bartlett as president, they did so only after holding what amounted to a highly publicized "trial" in which faculty, students, and alumni voiced their concerns about the president's unwillingness to move Dartmouth away from its traditional emphasis on Christian values and deference to authority toward a more cosmopolitan and modern conception of the college's mission and need for a more appropriate system of governance.[58]

The faculty rebellion that took place at Dartmouth in 1881 was not unique. At Union College in New York, faculty discontent over President Eliphalet Nott Potter's "exercise of arbitrary power" led the faculty to demand "new laws and regulations so that the college might be governed by the President and faculty, instead of being governed by the President." Potter's failure to initiate meaningful reforms resulted in seven members of the faculty informing the college's governing board that they had "lost confidence" in the president and then successfully getting the board to conduct a public investigation in 1882 that closely paralleled the trial at Dartmouth a year earlier. Potter was able to cling to the presidency for two more years, but before the decade was over, the leader of the faculty rebellion had replaced him as president of the college.[59]

Concerns about the paternalistic and autocratic rule of a president led to a similar faculty revolt at Hamilton College. There, too, faculty demands for a president's resignation led the school's governing board in 1884 to conduct a public hearing to consider complaints about President Henry Darling's approach to governance. As in the cases of Dartmouth and Union, the president was able to retain his position, but taken together, these incidents indicated not only a new faculty assertiveness but also the breakdown of a paternalistic form of authority that denied faculty members a significant role in institutional governance. In his study of six New England colleges, George Peterson concluded that the years from 1880 to 1895 were a period of crisis that marked the beginning of a significant change in college governance that would be felt more fully after the turn of the century.[60]

Developments at Amherst College in this period further exemplify the changing character of liberal arts college faculties and their growing insistence on a more active role in institutional decision making. Amherst College was founded in 1821 largely to prepare students for the ministry. Throughout much of the nineteenth century, the college had a small faculty with limited professional credentials, and the school remained committed to the ideal of cultivating character and Christian values in its students. By the early 1880s, however, the character of the faculty had begun to change. By then, one-third of the faculty had received training in Germany, a ratio that only increased in later years. A more professionally oriented faculty eventually sought to move the college well beyond its traditional mission and to challenge its conventional system of governance.[61]

A conflict in the mid-1890s that began as a dispute between President Merrill Gates and history professor Anson D. Morse over teaching assignments ultimately led not only to the departure of the president but also to Amherst's trustees' approving a formal policy granting each academic department complete autonomy in decisions about teaching and course assignments.[62] By 1912, the college had grown to have nearly five hundred students and forty-eight faculty members. In that year, for the first time in Amherst's history, the faculty sought a role in the selection of a new president, communicating to the board of trustees its preference for a candidate who rejected the idea that the college's primary mission was the moral development of its students. The board failed to select the faculty's favored candidate (choosing instead Alexander Meiklejohn), but the incident was the product of a new assertiveness by a faculty that was committed to what it understood to be professional values.[63]

Princeton University, which until 1896 was still called the College of New Jersey, represented something of a bridge between the traditional liberal arts college and the newly emerging research universities. As an institution that continued in the late nineteenth century to focus on offering undergraduate education and maintaining its collegiate identity, Princeton clearly lagged behind some of its Ivy League rivals, such as Harvard and Columbia, in developing significant graduate programs and transitioning into a research university.[64] In his study of the evolution of American liberal arts colleges in this period, historian Bruce Leslie, in fact, grouped Princeton with Bucknell, Franklin & Marshall, and Swarthmore, although Princeton was a substantially larger institution. Under Woodrow Wilson's presidency of the university in the early twentieth century, Princeton upgraded the quality of its faculty and modernized its curriculum, but Wilson carried out his reforms by asserting his own authority to shape the institution at the expense of the power of both the trustees and the faculty. However, the same trend that was beginning to appear in other leading institutions toward greater faculty influence in academic decision making as a natural outgrowth of professionalization soon became apparent at Princeton. John Grier Hibben, who in 1912 succeeded Wilson as president, immediately instituted a number of reforms that recognized the professional expertise of the faculty by greatly enhancing their involvement in governance. Hibben allowed the faculty to appoint all of its own committees, established an elected faculty advisory body to meet regularly with the trustees to discuss curricular matters, and, most important, created an elected faculty advisory committee on appointments and advancement that came to exercise significant authority.[65]

In sum, stirrings of change in the role of faculty in institutional governance may have first been most prominent in the nation's newly emerging universities, but by the early twentieth century the same process of professionalization of faculty members that led to faculty demands for a greater role in academic decision making was already becoming evident at many of the nation's more traditional liberal arts colleges. As growing numbers of those taking up positions as college teachers gained experience in graduate study either abroad or at American universities, they brought with them new expectations about what it meant to be a professor, including the right to professional autonomy and the importance of peer evaluation.

Growing Concerns about Academic Freedom and Institutional Governance, 1895–1915

The dismissal of economist Edward Bemis at the University of Chicago in 1895 was only one of a number of notable cases around the turn of the century in which professors who publicly espoused positions that challenged dominant corporate interests lost their jobs. Academic freedom became a rallying cry for many professors whose role began to change from simply passing on accepted truth and moral values to include becoming involved in the quest for new knowledge and in playing a more active role in public policy debates. While Americans in the 1880s and 1890s attempted to confront the problems created by rapid industrialization and the widening gap between rich and poor, academic social scientists became involved in highly publicized controversies about the best solutions to these new problems. Often, these controversies involved corporate donors to universities demanding the dismissal of professors who challenged conventional thinking. Key figures in the professionalization of American social science, including labor economist John R. Commons and sociologist Edward A. Ross, as well as Edward Bemis, all lost their academic positions in celebrated academic freedom cases between 1894 and 1900.[66]

In this context, faculty came increasingly to defend academic freedom as "the distinctive prerogative of the academic profession, and the essential condition of all universities."[67] It was not simply another term to describe "freedom of speech" as guaranteed under the First Amendment, which in a limited way protected the speech of all citizens from direct government suppression, but rather a more specific safeguard of the right of faculty at both public and private colleges and universities freely to teach in a manner they thought appropriate, to engage in research of their own choosing, and to publicize the results of that research.[68] The more rigorous and specialized postgraduate training required to become a faculty member at America's emerging universities provided a basis for claiming both the right to, and the need for, a more robust form of academic freedom than had been known in America's antebellum colleges. Expertise was thus a crucial component of the emerging concept of academic freedom. Richard T. Ely, a well-known economist and the driving force behind the establishment of the American Economic Association, nearly lost his position at the University of Wisconsin in the 1890s because of his defense of labor's use of strikes and boycotts, but he successfully defended his right to speak out on controversial public issues of the day by arguing that his specialized training as an academic economist meant that if the "science of economics is not humbug," then the economist "must know more about industrial society than others."[69]

By the early years of the twentieth century, the rise of the modern American university and the growing professionalism of many faculty members had led to increased demands by faculty, especially at America's leading institutions of higher learning, for a greater role in institutional governance and for recognition of academic freedom as a prerequisite for carrying out the professoriate's professional responsibilities. However, the newly emerging conceptions of faculty governance and academic freedom remained highly contested ideals after the turn of the century. Challenges to academic freedom, which often went hand in hand with assertions of administrative authority and a rejection of the idea of faculty self-governance, did not end with the turn of the century and the beginning of what came to be known as the Progressive Era. Dismissals and threats of dismissal of outspoken professors continued after 1900. In the early years of the twentieth century, some of the recently formed disciplinary associations, including the American Economic Association, the American Sociological Association, the American Political Science Association, the American Psychological Association, and the American Philosophical Association, participated in frustrating and generally unsuccessful efforts to intervene in several highly publicized academic freedom cases.[70]

At the same time, the increasing influence of business interests on governing boards, which was already drawing criticism from proponents of faculty governance in the last decades of the nineteenth century, led to more systematic and comprehensive calls for applying corporate management techniques to the administration of colleges and universities. Such calls represented a defi-

nite threat to the idea of faculty enjoying a large degree of professional autonomy. The Carnegie Foundation for the Advancement of Teaching and the
General Education Board (funded by John D. Rockefeller) led the way in promoting greater efficiency and standardization in ways that often challenged
faculty expectations about their role in institutional governance.[71] In 1910, the
Carnegie Foundation sponsored the publication of a study by noted management
expert Morris Llewellyn Cooke entitled *Academic and Industrial Efficiency.*
Applying the principles of Frederick Taylor's scientific management to academia, Cooke concluded that there were "two fundamental weaknesses" in
university governance: "departments have too much autonomy," and "the heads
of the institution and of the various departments lack the essentials of real authority." Cooke's approach to university governance was based on "the belief that
there is one best way to do any one thing and that usually this best way can be
determined by scientific methods if people will use them."[72] He was highly
critical of the system of "committee management" that was becoming more
common in American colleges and universities, arguing that committees were
an inherently inefficient method of administration that was not likely to come
up with the one best way of doing things. Cooke also contended that committee
work unnecessarily diverted faculty from their primary responsibilities of teaching and research. Moreover, he criticized tenure for faculty members, claiming
that colleges and universities, like business organizations, ought to be able to
retain a professor only so long as "he remains the best man obtainable" for his
position.[73]

In response to such arguments, advocates of faculty self-governance such as
well-known economist Thorstein Veblen and psychologist James McKeen Cattell expressed grave concerns about the commercialization of higher education
and the attempt by governing boards and presidents to impose what Veblen and
Cattell saw as inappropriate business standards of efficiency on American colleges and universities. Although Veblen's biting attack on the corporatization
of the university, *The Higher Learning in America,* was not published until 1918,
he had written most of the book more than a decade earlier while he had been on
the faculty at the University of Chicago. Much of his criticism of the authority
of university presidents—whom he labeled "captains of erudition"—and of
what he saw as the use of faculty committees "chiefly to keep the faculty talking
while the bureaucratic machine goes on its way under the guidance of the executive and his personal counselors and lieutenants" was based on his view of
William Rainey Harper's administration.[74]

Veblen's account of the business influence on American colleges and universities was more satire than a fully articulated prescription for reform. In contrast, Cattell offered a comprehensive and widely publicized plan for reforming
institutional governance. Cattell was a prominent psychologist who had earned

a PhD in psychology in Germany and had taught at Cambridge before coming to Columbia in 1891. In 1894, he became the editor of *Science*, the official journal of the American Association for the Advancement of Science, and by the early years of the twentieth century he began to use the pages of that journal to promote his ideas concerning the need for reform in the governance of American institutions of higher education.

Just as Veblen's analysis of university governance was inspired at least in part by his personal experience with the administration of President William Rainey Harper at Chicago, Cattell's views were clearly affected by his experience as a faculty member at Columbia under another powerful president, Nicholas Murray Butler. Cattell had been recruited to Columbia in 1891 by Butler, who had recently been elected by his faculty colleagues as the first dean of the newly constituted Faculty of Philosophy. During the 1890s, Cattell was part of a faculty that enjoyed a larger degree of self-government than did faculties at most other American colleges and universities. However, after Butler became president of Columbia in 1902, he quickly began to introduce changes to Columbia's system of governance. As a consequence, Cattell became increasingly critical of Butler's weakening of the system of faculty authority that Butler's predecessor, Seth Low, had put in place. Butler ended the election of deans by their faculties and then created the position of assistant dean for each college, with each assistant dean serving on the university council, thereby diluting the power of the elected faculty on that body. The president also limited the authority of departments to elect their own chairs. Cattell not only became an outspoken critic of Butler's changes but also developed a comprehensive set of proposals for reforming university governance at all institutions of higher learning.[75]

Like Veblen, Cattell was sharply critical of what he described as the "bureaucratic or department-store system of university control," with a powerful president responsible only to a board of trustees usually dominated by a business perspective. In its place, he called for restructuring governing boards so that they would include faculty representation and for eliminating the office of university president as it then existed, replacing it with a faculty-elected president whose salary would not exceed that of the highest-paid professor. He also proposed allowing faculty to elect their own deans and department chairs and to have the principal role in the selection of colleagues. To cap off his system of faculty self-governance, he supported the establishment of an elected senate to legislate on matters of university-wide concern.[76]

Such a plan may have seemed utopian in pre–World War One America, but Cattell sent copies of his proposal to nearly three hundred leading scientists across the country to elicit their reactions. At the time, the extensive responses he received and subsequently published in full in the book *University Control* represented the most extensive survey of faculty attitudes about the state of college and university governance ever conducted in the United States.[77] The developments in American higher education of the previous generation had helped to foster a far more professional faculty eager to claim the authority and responsibility that seemed to go with its new status. However, the growing size and complexity of American colleges and universities, together with the increasing influence of business ideals, also led to the adoption of new administrative approaches and structures that resulted in a contradictory picture of institutional governance.

Professors, especially at America's larger and more prestigious universities, were beginning to exercise more influence over some aspects of institutional decision making. However, the results of Cattell's survey demonstrated that at least among the nation's leading scientists, faculty dissatisfaction with the state of college and university governance on the eve of World War One was widespread. Eighty-five percent of those responding favored changing the existing system of governance to provide for greater faculty control, with a clear majority generally supporting Cattell's own radical proposals for reform. The written responses to Cattell's plan revealed that the issue prompting the greatest concern among the respondents was not direct interference by trustees but autocratic rule by presidents. In a separate essay included in *University Control,* University of California psychology professor George Stratton (who like Cattell had studied in Germany with the pioneering psychologist Wilhelm Wundt) expressed a sentiment reflected in many of the letters written to Cattell. He observed that university government in the United States had "assumed a form that we might have expected to see in a land accustomed to kings," while "European universities have a constitution that might have come from some American political theorist."[78] Not all those responding to Cattell favored faculty election of the president as a desirable reform, and many thought his proposal for completely revamping the composition of governing boards unrealistic. However, an overwhelming majority of respondents supported a greater role for faculty in selecting a president and favored devolving far greater authority onto faculty at the department and college level.

Faculty responding to Cattell's survey appeared most concerned about determining the selection of colleagues and curricular decisions. In generally accepting the authority of trustees and administrators to exercise overall control of finances, they echoed the view of Cornell philosopher J. E. Creighton: "The working theory as to the division of authority between the faculty and trustees has been that to the former belongs jurisdiction over all the educational matters, while the latter have the right of control over all the questions involving the expenditure of money. Now, this enunciation of the respective powers of the two bodies has proved the bulwark of our liberties, and has served to prevent the direct interference of the trustees with the work of teaching." Nevertheless,

Creighton did go on to observe that "educational questions, and questions regarding the proper expenditure of money, can not be dissociated." Consequently, he argued that faculty ought to have the opportunity to have at least some influence on "the apportionment of funds among the different colleges and departments."[79]

The Growth of Faculty Professionalism and the Formation of the AAUP

A growing determination among leading academics to define and defend the principles of academic freedom and to assert the importance of a collegial form of governance as a professional norm led to the formation of the American Association of University Professors (AAUP) in 1915. It is not surprising that senior professors from the country's leading research universities, whose status and expertise gave particular legitimacy to their calls for faculty autonomy, were instrumental in the call to form a national professional organization. In 1913 eighteen full professors from Johns Hopkins signed the initial invitation sent to faculty members at a select number of universities to attend an organizing conference. The leaders of the fledgling professional association that subsequently developed, who included Cattell, John Dewey, Roscoe Pound, and A. O. Lovejoy, came from such prestigious institutions as Johns Hopkins, Cornell, Michigan, Yale, Harvard, Chicago, and Columbia—institutions that generally provided for a greater role for faculty in institutional governance than existed at smaller colleges with less well-qualified faculty. The initial letter sent out by Hopkins professors soliciting participation in a conference to consider forming a national organization made it clear that the concerns behind the call extended beyond protecting academic freedom and included defending the role of the faculty in institutional governance more broadly: "The university professor is also concerned, as a member of the legislative body of his local institution, with many questions of educational policy which are of more than local significance; he is a member of a professional body which is the special custodian of certain ideals, and the organ for the performance of certain functions essential to the well-being of society."[80]

From the AAUP's beginnings, serious debate occurred about what kind of organization it was to be. In initially seeking members primarily among the nation's professorial elite at America's most prestigious universities, and in attempting to gain legitimacy in the eyes of college presidents and governing boards for their calls for academic freedom and faculty governance, the leadership of the new organization emphasized that the AAUP was to be a professional association of distinguished scholars, not a trade union affiliated with the American labor movement.[81] A. O. Lovejoy directly addressed this issue in his 1919 presidential message. He argued that trade unions focused primarily on obtaining economic objectives for their members, whereas the AAUP was intended, first and foremost, "to enable the profession, and the institutions in which its members are associated to discharge their distinctive function ... with the highest possible degree of competency and serviceableness."[82]

One of the first acts of the new AAUP was to adopt a resolution directing John Dewey, the organization's initial president, to establish a special committee to develop a report on the general problem of academic freedom. This committee was chaired by noted Columbia University economist Edwin R. A. Seligman and included such other prominent faculty as Lovejoy and Roscoe Pound of Harvard. Richard Ely of the University of Wisconsin, whose threatened dismissal twenty years earlier had become a cause célèbre in the developing debate over academic freedom, was also a member of the committee.[83]

Although concerns regarding academic freedom were certainly central to the AAUP both at the time of its formation and in its subsequent history, from the very beginning these concerns were inextricably linked to the defense of faculty involvement in college and university governance. In essence, both these concerns were expressions of the new professional identity that many professors, especially those at the country's most prestigious institutions, were seeking to establish around the turn of the century. The earliest AAUP statements on the subject of academic freedom demonstrate the importance that the new professional association placed on faculty governance as the necessary means of establishing an institutional basis for defending the faculty's right to academic freedom on the one hand and for identifying the appropriate boundaries for the exercise of that freedom on the other. Like doctors and lawyers, professors, too, were beginning increasingly to claim primary responsibility for evaluating colleagues and for other aspects of professional decision making.

Peer review became an essential element in the academic profession's claim that faculty, not laypeople, should have the responsibility for determining the legitimacy of charges that a professor had engaged in behavior not protected by the principles of academic freedom. In one of the first academic freedom cases for which the newly formed AAUP authorized a formal investigation, the dismissal of radical economist Scott Nearing from a position at the University of Pennsylvania, the investigating committee report affirmed its belief that those "who were in the best position to judge" the "professional qualifications" of an academic were "colleagues ... who were also specialists in his own department of knowledge."[84] The committee further elaborated on its view of the significance of faculty peer review as a necessary means of safeguarding academic freedom:

> It is the opinion of your committee that such recommendation [for the retention of Nearing] from the responsible and accredited representatives of the educational staff of a university—especially when, as in this case, no question of

moral unworthiness or neglect of duty is involved—should be disregarded by governing boards of laymen only on grave occasions, and after definite charges have been brought against the teacher concerned, and opportunity for judicial hearings has been afforded; and that the grounds for removal should be clearly stated and communicated to the faculties concerned. Summary action in such cases, and in circumstances such as attended the action of the Pennsylvania trustees, is not directed solely or most significantly, against the individual teacher affected; it is directed also against the local faculty as a body, and against the academic profession at large. For it is an instance of lay intervention in what is essentially a professional question.[85]

Several months before the University of Pennsylvania report was published, the special committee appointed by AAUP president John Dewey issued its landmark "1915 Declaration of Principles on Academic Freedom and Academic Tenure."[86] In developing both a definition and a defense of academic freedom, the special committee made a point of explaining what it saw as the "nature of the academic calling" that justified the faculty's right to claim a distinctive form of freedom that was by definition "academic." Putting particular emphasis on the professional status of faculty, the declaration proclaimed that the "conception of a university as an ordinary business venture, and of academic teaching as a purely private employment," demonstrated "a radical failure to apprehend the nature of the social function discharged by the professional scholar." That function, the committee explained, "is to deal at first hand, after prolonged and specialized technical training, with sources of knowledge; and to impart the results of their own and of their fellow-specialists' investigations and reflection, both to students and to the general public, without fear or favor." In carrying out their critical service to society, faculty might well be appointed by university trustees, but they were not "in any proper sense the employees" of those trustees, because "once appointed, the scholar has professional functions to perform in which the appointing authorities have neither competency nor moral right to intervene."[87]

The drafters of the AAUP statement of principles recognized that professors did not perform their duties outside an institutional context and that they could not ignore professional standards. The committee, therefore, announced: "It is, in short, not the absolute freedom of utterance of the individual scholar, but the absolute freedom of thought, of inquiry, of discussion, of teaching, of the academic profession, that is asserted by this declaration of principles." Consequently, the statement affirmed the notion that in matters relating to the carrying out of the faculty's academic endeavors it would be "unsuitable to the dignity of a great profession that the initial responsibility for the maintenance of professional standards should not be in the hands of its own members."[88]

In the AAUP's initial statements regarding the still-evolving concept of academic freedom, the question of the faculty's role in college and university governance was posed most directly in terms of the need for peer review in the retention or dismissal of a faculty member. Yet from the beginning of its existence, the AAUP applied the same logic to the need for faculty involvement in other areas of academic decision making. The first investigative report ever issued by the AAUP concerning an institution charged with violating the principles of academic freedom, published in the first year of the new organization's existence, also addressed more general issues of academic governance.[89] The report condemned the administration of the University of Utah for improperly dismissing two longtime associate professors without just cause or appropriate peer review and cited the resignation of seventeen faculty members in protest of the administration's actions as evidence of a crisis situation at the university. However, the report noted "with much satisfaction" that in an effort to resolve the crisis that had developed at the University of Utah, the faculty had proposed, and the administration had accepted, a plan of administration for the creation of a new system of shared governance.

The plan called for the establishment of an administrative council with the president and deans of the schools serving as ex officio members and with faculty electing from their own ranks representatives who would hold two more seats than the ex officio members on the council. The duties that were spelled out for the administrative council reflected a formal recognition of the appropriateness of faculty involvement in all areas of academic decision making: "The Administrative Council shall determine, subject to the approval of the Board of Regents, all matters pertaining to the educational policy and educational administration of the University. Examples of these matters are—requests for appropriations, apportionment of funds, the appointment, promotion, demotion, removal, or failure to recommend for reappointment, members of the teaching force, and such other matters as may be referred to the Council by the President, Board of Regents, or the Faculty." The AAUP committee that investigated the situation at Utah observed that such a "scheme of organization . . . might, in the Committee's opinion, be considered and imitated with advantage by many other universities and colleges."[90]

The AAUP's Committee T on Place and Function of Faculties in University Government and Administration first began to confer in 1917, but it was not until 1920 that the committee issued its first substantive report. In his introductory remarks to that report, committee chair J. A. Leighton, a professor of philosophy at Ohio State University, might well have been referring to Thorstein Veblen when he described how the growing size and consequent bureaucratization of American universities were contributing to problems of governance: "Critics further say that the type of organization at present prevailing seems designed for quantity production in credits and degrees, and that the result is that we have too large a proportion of mediocre and mechanized teachers engaged in turning out ever increasing numbers of graduates without any clear sense of, or respect for, the nature and value of scholarship and thoughtfulness. They attribute this situation largely to the autocratic type of university organization."[91]

Leighton was highly critical of governing boards that attempted to "interfere in the internal conduct of the universities," in spite of their having only a "slight acquaintance with educational problems." At the same time, the committee's report implicitly recognized that the lay governing boards of American universities had no clear parallel in German universities, in which no layer of administration existed between state officials and the faculty, and that it was necessary to develop a system of "joint responsibility and control, with the distribution of emphasis on responsibility and control varying with the particular aspect of the whole matter of the conduct of university affairs which may be uppermost in a given situation." The report acknowledged that American university governing boards were ultimately responsible for the well-being of the universities under their care, and that, therefore, both as a matter of law and as a matter of right, the "trustees should be primarily the custodians of the financial interests of the university, and as such they should have the consenting voice in the final determination of its educational policies." However, the report went on to argue that, based on a proper understanding of joint responsibility, "in the matter of the determination and carrying out of educational policies, the members of the faculty *are the experts*, and should usually have the principal voice in the decision" (emphasis added).[92]

While recognizing that institutions needed to establish "a recognized mode of procedure for the joint determination, by trustees and faculties, of what is included in the term *educational policies*," the AAUP's Committee T offered what it considered to be a minimum list, which included "standards for admission and for degrees; determination of the proper ratio between numbers of students, of courses and of instructors, respectively; numbers of teaching hours; the establishment of new chairs and departments of instruction, of new curricula and courses; the organization of new administrative units; the promotion of research; provision for publication; the abolition of any established form of educational or research activity; the distribution of income between material equipment and personnel."[93]

The report included as an appendix the results of a survey sent to more than one hundred colleges and universities to determine the "actual status of faculties in university government and administration." Although summary responses from only two-thirds of the institutions contacted were included in the published report, this survey provides the broadest picture available of the state of college and university governance in the early twentieth century.[94]

One key issue on which the survey sheds some light is the way in which institutions defined membership in the "general faculty" and hence eligibility to participate in formal governance processes. The majority of institutions limited direct governance responsibilities to full professors. The AAUP itself, at the time of its founding, extended membership invitations only to "persons of full professorial rank" who were "distinguished specialists" at institutions that had a minimum of five such distinguished scholars on their faculty. The AAUP soon expanded eligibility for membership, but it is clear that the major push for faculty governance initially came from, and was on behalf of, the academic "elite" that had the most obvious claims to asserting its professional prerogatives as recognized experts.[95]

Every institution responding to the survey indicated that faculty participated in the control of "educational policy." However, in nearly two-thirds, such participation was by "custom" rather than as a result of "constitutional or statutory provision." Formal faculty involvement in the appointment of new colleagues occurred at fewer than 30 percent of institutions reporting. Appointment by department heads, deans, or presidents without formal faculty consultation was the far more common practice. Even a college president as sympathetic to faculty participation in setting educational policies as Amherst's Alexander Meiklejohn opposed formal involvement by faculty in the selection of their colleagues, arguing that it often led to the selection of men of lesser quality.[96]

Not surprisingly, faculty participation in budget making was considerably less common than involvement in educational policy. Although a small number of colleges and universities, including Harvard and Johns Hopkins, provided for faculty committees to participate in the budget-making process, to the extent that faculty had any say in budgetary decisions, such influence was normally exercised through department heads or deans. This area of governance was of particular concern to the members of Committee T. With only one dissenting voice, committee members proclaimed their belief in the "fundamental principle . . . that in all cases the faculty should have a recognized voice in the preparation of the annual budget." The committee thus recognized that the allocation of resources was directly linked to the determination of educational policies and priorities, as well as to the evaluation and remuneration of individual faculty members. Committee members differed, however, on how that voice ought to be expressed.[97] These differences carried over to the membership as a whole, so that when the AAUP officially endorsed the concept of shared governance by adopting a series of resolutions at its annual meeting in 1921, no specific statement on the faculty role in budget making was included.[98]

The AAUP survey confirmed the perception of many contemporary critics that universities were still largely run in an autocratic fashion. Only rarely did faculty members play a direct role in the selection of academic administrators. Just one-fifth of the institutions responding reported having departmental faculty significantly involved in the selection of department heads. Typically, such appointments were made by either the dean or the president without consultation with the entire teaching staff of a department. Faculty involvement in the nomination of deans was similarly rare. Formal faculty participation in the selection of a president was reported at only six institutions: Grinnell, Kentucky, North Dakota, Oberlin, Ohio Wesleyan, and, most interestingly, given its recent history, Utah.[99]

The survey documented a wide variety of governance practices in American institutions of higher education, but the committee report concluded that the results revealed

> a growing tendency in the better class of institutions to accord to the faculty official participation in the selection and promotion of its own members, in the nomination of deans and president, and in the preparation of the budget, as well as in the determination of educational policies. Often trustees who are accustomed to autocratic methods in business and industry oppose a larger faculty participation in university and college government. In every case where faculty self-government has been tried out for a term of years and under fair conditions, as notably for example at Oberlin and Reed Colleges, it has proved a signal success.[100]

The resolutions adopted at the AAUP's annual meeting in 1921 in response to the report of Committee T represented what was then the first important effort to establish professional norms in the area of governance. One resolution declared that "the formal consent of the Faculty directly or through its elected representatives should be prerequisite to all changes in educational policy." The annual meeting also called upon all colleges and universities to establish "an officially recognized medium of communication between the Trustees and the Faculty other than the President" and to provide for "periodic conferences on matters of educational policy or institutional conditions between Governing Boards and Faculties or their elected representatives." Two other resolutions affirmed the faculty's primary role in appointing and promoting members of the teaching staff and in assuming the "corresponding responsibility to take initiative in removing from the teaching staff incompetent as well as unworthy members." The AAUP also expressed its support for faculty being "officially consulted" in the selection of deans and the president of the institution.[101]

However, as the AAUP's own survey demonstrated, when these resolutions were adopted by the AAUP in 1921, the practices of shared governance were still in an early stage of development, and the principle of primary faculty responsibility for academic decision making was not yet widely accepted throughout American higher education.

CHAPTER THREE

The Development of Faculty Governance, 1920–1940

Both the expansion of American higher education and the professionalization of American faculty continued apace in the two decades after World War One. On the eve of World War Two, American universities had not yet achieved the level of international prominence they would after the war. However, ongoing trends in American higher education enabled American research universities, in the words of Jonathan Cole, to be "poised to become the greatest in the world."[1] Among these trends was the continuing growth of an increasingly well-qualified professoriate enjoying more firmly established protections of academic freedom and greater responsibility for academic decision making throughout American higher education.[2]

Although salaries for college teachers may not have kept up with the salaries of other professionals in this period, public esteem for college professors was probably greater than it had ever been.[3] A survey conducted in 1925 found that professors were held in higher regard than any of the other traditional professions.[4] Subsequent studies in the 1930s and at the beginning of the 1940s found that only medical doctors consistently ranked ahead of professors in status as measured by public opinion surveys.[5]

At many institutions in the years between the two world wars, faculty began to play a more important role in college and university governance, but advances in this regard were uneven. The idea that faculty should exercise primary responsibility for most aspects of academic decision making did not gain as widespread acceptance in practice in this period as did the principle of academic freedom and the recognition of tenure as a means of protecting that freedom. Thus, for example, in his presidential address to the Modern Language Association in 1925, Smith College president W. A. Nielson criticized the AAUP's advocacy of greater faculty control on the grounds that involvement in governance would distract professors from fulfilling their primary responsibilities of teaching and research:

> The granting to the teaching staff of even consultative powers on the large variety of administrative matters that has been claimed as coming within the sphere of their rights would mean a most serious invasion of the time now at their disposal for study. My own experience leads me to believe that there is at present in our colleges and still more in our universities much more discontent over the demands made on the time of a professor by administrative offices and committees than there is over the autocracy of the president or the trustees. What most scholarly teachers want is more time to attend to their business of learning and teaching. . . . The question, in sum, seems to me not so much one of democracy versus autocracy, as of the division of labor and the avoidance of waste.[6]

On the other hand, as early as 1925, the AAUP and the Association of American Colleges (AAC), which represented institutions focusing on undergraduate education, jointly endorsed model guidelines on tenure and academic freedom. These guidelines recognized that professors' professional status entitled them to special protections in order to carry out their responsibilities in behalf of the common good. Although few governing boards initially adopted the 1925 policy recommendations in full, before the United States entered World War Two, the AAUP and the AAC jointly formulated a new document, the *1940 Statement of Principles on Academic Freedom and Tenure*, which helped institutionalize tenure as a safeguard for academic freedom at most American colleges and universities.[7] In contrast, it would not be until 1966 that the AAUP, the Association of Governing Boards of Universities and Colleges, and the American Council on Education would succeed in jointly drafting a *Statement on Government of Colleges and Universities* that recognized, at least in general terms, the desirability of affording the faculty a major role in institutional governance.

During the interwar period, American colleges and universities expanded significantly in size and grew in prestige as increasing numbers of Americans sought a college education and the country gained a fuller appreciation of the importance of the research being performed on college campuses. Financial support, especially for research universities, from both private and public sources increased dramatically.[8] The percentage of the population aged eighteen to twenty-one attending college doubled between 1920 and 1940, while the total number of students enrolled increased from just under six hundred thousand to nearly one and a half million. As a consequence, not only did the number of faculty in the United States increase by roughly 300 percent between 1920 and 1940, but the number of PhDs being granted by American universities increased by well over 500 percent as the doctorate became even more widely required for entry into the professoriate.[9]

The trend toward ever-larger institutions of higher learning also accelerated in this period. Whereas in 1909 there had been only six universities with more than five thousand students, by 1939 there were forty-three such institutions, thirteen of which had enrollments of more than ten thousand. Similarly, in 1909 only three schools in the entire country had teaching staffs of more than five hundred; in 1939 the number of such schools had soared to forty, with eight reporting more than one thousand instructional staff members. Even many traditional liberal arts colleges grew significantly larger in this period. Antioch, Carleton, Lafayette, and Williams, for example, all had more than eight hundred students in 1939; Oberlin and Swarthmore had teaching staffs of one hundred or more.[10]

The explosion in the size and complexity of American institutions of higher learning went hand in hand with the growth of a more specialized professional faculty and a growing recognition of the need to develop new mechanisms for governing American colleges and universities. Not only did the number of administrative positions increase quite dramatically, but so, too, were there increasing efforts to devise new means of making faculty involvement in governance more effective. American colleges and universities had typically provided for periodic meetings of the "general faculty," which in some cases included all members of the teaching staff and in others were limited to full professors. Such means of expressing faculty opinion had allowed faculty in some instances to shape institutional policies, but in many cases meetings of the general faculty were infrequent and lacked real influence. After World War One, more institutions began to experiment with the establishment of elected faculty senates that could serve as representative bodies to express faculty views on educational policies. Departmental governance also became an increasingly debated issue, as university departments at some schools grew to be larger than most of the colleges that had existed a half-century earlier, and the increasing specialization of faculty teaching and research meant that informed decisions about appointment and promotion required input from departmental faculty. While a formal role for faculty in the choice of academic administrators was still not the norm in 1940, there was a slow but steady trend in which more institutions began in the interwar years to provide for such input.

Three Governance Controversies in the
Immediate Postwar Period

Incidents at three very different types of institutions of higher learning in the immediate postwar period symbolized both the continuing obstacles to a larger role for faculty in governance and the progress that lay ahead in this area. Well-publicized controversies over faculty governance issues occurred between 1919 and 1922 at Washburn College, a liberal arts college in Kansas with an enrollment of about eight hundred students; at Clark University, a small but prestigious institution that was America's first school devoted solely to graduate education; and at the University of California, then probably the largest public university in the country, with an enrollment that by 1929 would approach twenty thousand.

In 1919, John Ervin Kirkpatrick was a professor of history and political science at Washburn College. Kirkpatrick had earned a master's degree from Yale and a doctorate from the Hartford Theological Seminary, and over the next decade he would become one of the nation's leading advocates of faculty self-government, publishing articles on the subject in *School and Society*, the *Nation*, the *New Republic*, and other journals, as well as a widely cited book, *The American College and Its Rulers*, that offered both a historical account of the development of college governance and a call for democratizing the way American colleges were run.[11]

Washburn College, which was founded in 1865 as a Congregational Church–supported school, had an instructional faculty of only forty-six in 1919 and had not yet developed any constitutional mechanisms for faculty participation in college governance. The faculty had, however, traditionally met periodically as a body, and at least until 1915 the president of the college generally respected its advice. The appointment in that year of a new president who had virtually no previous academic experience eventually led to protests from the faculty that President Parley Paul Womer was arbitrarily dismissing faculty members and was not allowing the faculty to have sufficient influence on college policies. Kirkpatrick played a leading role in these protests and with some of his faculty colleagues advocated a three-point plan to reform the college's system of governance. They proposed the establishment of an elected five-person faculty committee to advise the president, the devolution of authority over more routine matters of administration from the president's office onto the dean and the faculty, and the formation of a joint faculty, trustee, and alumni committee to draft a college constitution. Womer responded to faculty pressure by accepting the implementation of a college constitution with a provision for the establishment of a committee, including two elected representatives of the faculty, that would advise the president on "all questions involving the academic interests of the institution."[12] Just four days after Womer announced his acceptance of the new advisory committee, however, Washburn's governing board summarily dismissed Kirkpatrick from the faculty, setting off a controversy that gained national attention.

Kirkpatrick's dismissal led to the appointment of an AAUP investigating committee headed by prominent Johns Hopkins philosopher A. O. Lovejoy. The AAUP's investigating team concluded that the administration had dismissed Kirkpatrick largely as a result of his efforts "to bring about changes in the form of government of Washburn College" that would have resulted in the powers then exercised by the president being "limited and a larger measure of responsible faculty participation in the government of the institution and in the determination of its educational policies" being "assured." In taking up Kirkpatrick's case, Lovejoy's committee argued that retribution for speech related to intramural issues of governance was "not less serious than a charge of unwarrantable restriction of freedom of teaching. If leadership in the attempt to alter existing conditions and to introduce a greater degree of representative government into the organization of a college or university is to be punished by dismissal—as is alleged to have occurred in this case—the processes making for reform in the internal constitution of American colleges are threatened at their point of origin, and the teaching profession is deprived of the right of even urging changes which it may believe to be needful."[13]

Three years after reporting on the situation at Washburn, Lovejoy chaired another AAUP investigating committee that gave further evidence of the still tenuous basis for faculty governance even at one of the nation's most prestigious institutions. Clark University opened in 1889 as the country's first solely graduate institution and under the leadership of pioneering psychologist G. Stanley Hall had gained a national reputation as a center of research by recruiting distinguished faculty in a limited number of disciplines, with psychology being the most prominent.[14] By the end of Hall's twenty-year presidency, however, Clark confronted serious financial problems. Never a large institution, Clark by 1920 had only seventy-five students and twenty-three faculty (eleven of whom were professors), and it had become clear to its governing board that some measures of reorganization and concentration of resources would be required to keep the institution afloat. In appointing W. W. Atwood, a Harvard geographer, as Hall's successor, Clark's trustees made a commitment to establish a new school of geography as a means of attracting additional students and restoring the university's high standing. Unbeknownst to the faculty at the time, Atwood envisioned the need to eliminate or downgrade most of the existing graduate departments in order to free up the necessary resources to make Clark a center for the study of geography.

By 1922, the faculty was in open revolt against the new president's efforts to build up geography at the expense of virtually all the other programs offered at the university. A majority of the faculty signed a memorial addressed to the board of trustees complaining about the board's appointment of a new president and approving the establishment of a new graduate school of geography "without consultation or advice with their Faculty." The letter went on to argue: "A professor cannot feel or exercise responsibility when he is given no opportunity to advise in the formulation of the major policies which concern his work and in which he is supposedly a specialist."[15] By spring 1923, of the eight graduate departments that existed in 1920, six had either been discontinued or were targeted for discontinuance; eight of the eleven professors who had been on the faculty in 1920 had left or were about to leave as a result of resignations, retirements, and, in one case, suicide. The controversy over Clark's future had boiled over into the pages of the Boston press and led some faculty and alumni to call on the AAUP to investigate.

In its report about the situation at Clark, Lovejoy's committee of inquiry declared: "That matters of educational policy should not be decided by a lay governing board of a university without ascertaining the opinion of the educational staff or of its representatives is, the committee believes, a usually accepted principle."[16] Such a belief had helped justify the formation of the AAUP less than a decade earlier, but it was clear in the early 1920s that not all American colleges and universities put the principle of shared governance into practice or even subscribed to it in theory.

However, events taking place immediately after World War One at another prominent institution, the University of California, were a significant harbinger of the coming trend toward more widespread acceptance of a larger role for faculty in institutional governance. The University of California, founded in 1868, had by 1919 become one of the nation's premier public universities. The legislative act creating the university established an Academic Senate consisting of the president, all professors, lecturers, and instructors, and assigned to it responsibility for "conducting the general administration of the University." However, only the president and professors had voting privileges in the senate.[17] In the early years of the university, the senate exercised a good deal of control over the internal affairs of the institution, but following the appointment of Benjamin Ide Wheeler as president in 1899, the faculty role in governance became severely limited. Wheeler successfully presided over the growth in size and prestige of the university, but he did so in an autocratic manner, unilaterally appointing and dismissing professors, deans, and department chairs, presiding over the senate in an imperious way, and selecting by himself the members of all senate committees. The increasingly well-respected faculty that Wheeler recruited began to show signs of restiveness at his autocratic governance and attempted unsuccessfully in 1916 to reclaim some of the senate's former authority. When Wheeler retired in 1919, what ensued came to be known as the "Berkeley Revolution of 1919–1920," or the "great revolt."[18]

At a meeting of the Academic Senate following Wheeler's retirement and before a new president had been named, an overwhelming majority of the faculty voted to petition the board of regents to discuss with representatives of the faculty a series of proposals for reforming the university's system of governance. These proposals went far beyond the modest suggestions for reform that had contributed to Kirkpatrick's dismissal from Washburn. The senate recommended that all deans be elected by the faculty, with the senate itself choosing the dean of the faculties, who would serve as the senate's presiding officer, and that department chairs also be elected by the members of the departmental faculty, including instructors who had at least two years of experience. The faculty proposal would also have afforded such instructors voting rights in the Academic Senate. In addition, the list of suggested reforms called for one or more representatives to be elected by the senate to sit as advisors with the board of regents and for the senate to be consulted in the choice of a new president.

After months of discussions between the faculty and the regents, the university's governing board issued a new set of standing orders that marked an important milestone in the development of faculty governance in American colleges and universities. While delegating to the president the authority to make recommendations to the board of regents on all appointments and promotions, the new regulations directed the president to make such recommendations only "after consultation with properly constituted advisory bodies of the academic senate," which the president was also to consult "regarding changes in the educational policy of the university." While these guidelines fell well short of what the faculty had originally proposed, in a crucial concession to the faculty the board declared that the Academic Senate "shall determine its own membership . . . [and] shall choose its own chairman and committees in such manner as it may determine." Voting rights in the senate were subsequently extended to instructional faculty with at least two years of service, and an elected senate Committee on Committees quickly became an essential part of the new governance system. In addition to granting the senate authority over admissions, courses of instruction, and student discipline, the standing orders also declared that the "academic senate is authorized to select a committee to advise with the president concerning the budget." At the departmental level, the new governance guidelines allowed each faculty to establish its own operating rules and provided for chairs to be appointed annually based on nomination from the faculty.[19]

The Berkeley Revolution certainly did not institutionalize a system of complete faculty control over institutional governance. Faculty members were consulted but did not have ultimate authority over the selection of deans and department chairs. The newly established budget committee also had only advisory powers, and the faculty were still not allowed to play any formal role in the selection of the presidents who subsequently operated under the new guidelines. Nevertheless, by granting the faculty the right to choose their own representatives on university committees and diluting the president's power to name deans and department heads without consulting the affected faculty, the new standing orders represented an important step in the development of shared governance that would eventually be emulated by many other institutions of higher education in the United States.

New Initiatives in Expanding Faculty Governance, 1920–1940

During the interwar years, the development of formal mechanisms for faculty involvement in institutional governance was uneven across the country, but a number of other prominent colleges and universities initiated significant reforms similar to those adopted at the University of California, which afforded the faculty a larger role in institutional decision making. In 1930, the University of Illinois was the state university with the second-largest student enrollment, behind only California.[20] Founded in 1867, Illinois, like many other colleges and universities, was slow to develop comprehensive constitutional guidelines for institutional governance. At the beginning of the 1930s, however, the university's governing board finally adopted statutes that formally established mechanisms to clarify and enhance the faculty's role in governance.[21] The board's action came after two decades of thorough and heated debates on campus about governance issues that had begun in 1911, when then president E. J. James convinced the trustees to appoint a Committee on Organization and Efficiency. This committee took four years to make its final report, and despite years of further discussion of the issue, the committee's recommendations were never enacted. Illinois had long had a university senate that included all full professors, but faculty influence over institutional decision making, especially at the departmental and college level, had remained quite limited until the establishment in the early 1930s of what came to be known as the "executive committee system."[22]

Under this system, department heads, deans, and the president continued to exercise decision-making authority, but at all levels of the university, advisory bodies with elected faculty representatives were established that, in most cases, enjoyed significant influence. A President's Council that included three faculty representatives elected by the senate was formed to provide advice on the preparation of the budget. At the college level, the statutes called for the establishment of an executive committee with two or more members holding the rank of associate or full professor to be elected each year by all faculty members in the college at the rank of instructor and above. This committee was empowered "to advise the Dean in the administration of the College" and was to be consulted biennially by the president in the appointment or reappointment of the dean. While not required by the statutes, these executive committees in most of the colleges also became involved in advising on appointments and promotions. In the small number of departments that opted to have a rotating chair system, the new rules called for the creation of executive committees elected by all faculty members at the rank of instructor and above. These committees were involved in virtually all aspects of departmental administration. In the much larger number of departments that retained a head rather than moving to an elected chair system, an advisory committee consisting of all tenured faculty was to be consulted by the head "in regard to the departmental policies." However, there was no requirement that such consultation extend to the budget or to appointments.

Classics professor and AAUP activist W. A. Oldfather, who later wrote an account of developments at Illinois, observed that the reforms instituted in the early 1930s resulted in "superior morale in the entire faculty and administrative staff." Although he acknowledged that there were still instances where the input of faculty was not being solicited, on the whole he thought "the faculty really has . . . about as much democracy as it deserves, and probably just a little more." In rankings derived from information gathered from a survey completed in 1940 of AAUP chapters at more than two hundred institutions, the University of Illinois was tied for second on an index of the extent of faculty self-government.[23]

The University of Washington was another rapidly growing state university where the movement toward greater faculty involvement in academic decision making produced a notable change in governance practices. As at the University of Illinois, many years elapsed between the initial agitation for reform and the adoption of new constitutional provisions allowing for greater faculty involvement in institutional decision making. Before World War One, President Thomas Kane had supported faculty desires to take on a larger role in governance, but Kane's position met strong resistance from Washington's trustees, who, according to historian Charles Gates, believed that "the government of the University should be sharply focused rather than diffuse. In their way of thinking the president should not act as the leader of a constitutional republic but as the head of a large corporation."[24] Kane's support for faculty governance contributed to his dismissal in 1913 by Washington's governing board, which concluded that his deference to faculty opinion made him a weak administrator.

However, a quarter century later, a new generation of university trustees had come to accept the appropriateness of a greater faculty role in shaping institutional policies. In 1938, the board of regents approved a new administrative code that extended voting rights on the general faculty to all instructors and lecturers with three years of service and recognized the general faculty's authority over all educational policies. In addition to giving the faculty the authority to appoint standing committees, the new code also established an elected university senate to serve as "the deliberative and policy-forming nucleus of the general faculty."[25] Although the president of the university presided over the senate, an elected faculty committee was charged with preparing the senate's agenda. The move toward more faculty self-government also extended to the departmental level. The faculty members of each department were empowered to establish their own procedures and regulations for dealing with such matters as appointments, promotions, and budgets.[26]

Many small colleges continued to rely on meetings of the general faculty—rather than on representative senates—as the principal mechanism for faculty to express their views on matters of institutional governance, but as colleges and universities grew in size, there was a clear trend toward establishing some form of representative senate, even as virtually all schools retained a more inclusive body often referred to as the "general faculty." At almost the same time that the University of Washington was establishing its senate, schools as diverse as Southern Illinois State Normal University (now Southern Illinois University), the University of New Hampshire, Temple University, and Union College were all creating senates or university councils with elected faculty representatives.[27] An AAUP survey to which more than two hundred colleges and universities responded between 1938 and 1940 showed that 60 percent reported having some form of senate, though in nearly half of these cases, the senate was appointed or had only ex officio members.[28]

At one time, general faculty or senate voting privileges were often restricted to senior professors, and even as late as 1940, some institutions where the faculty played an important role in institutional governance, such as the University of Illinois and Reed College, still largely restricted that role to full professors.[29] However, the extension of voting rights at both the University of California and the University of Washington to all full-time teaching staff with some minimum length of service was indicative of a larger trend toward expanding involvement in institutional governance to include more—though by no means all—faculty members.

Michigan State College of Agriculture and Applied Science (now Michigan State University) was another school that took such a step at the end of this period. State law in Michigan had defined the faculty at Michigan State as consisting only of professors and associate professors. However, as the institution grew rapidly in the interwar years, by 1940 the number of junior faculty without voting rights had come to equal twice the number of professors and associate professors. In response to this situation, and at least until the state law could be changed, the administration and voting faculty of the college in

1942 agreed to establish "divisional faculties" in the college in which all instructional, research, and extension staff above the rank of graduate assistant would have a vote.[30]

In the early 1920s, an AAUP survey of 176 institutions revealed that more than one in ten limited voting rights to only full professors and that half had restrictions that disenfranchised many full-time members of the teaching staff.[31] By the end of the 1930s, however, it had become even rarer for institutions to restrict membership in the general faculty to full professors. In another survey conducted by the AAUP that was completed in 1940, only 5 out of 222 institutions reported such a restriction. Moreover, in about two-thirds of the institutions in which the "general faculty" was a recognized body, all ranks of instructional faculty were included, though full-time employment and one to three years of service were normally required for voting rights.[32]

Several institutions during the 1920s and 1930s engaged in governance experiments that went well beyond the establishment of representative senates that acted in an advisory role to presidents or boards of trustees. One of the most exceptional experiments in shared governance took place at the California Institute of Technology, where the office of the president was in effect replaced by an executive council on which faculty and trustees were equally represented. Caltech was founded in 1891 but underwent a dramatic administrative reorganization in 1921 after noted physicist Robert A. Millikan was selected to head the institution. As a faculty member at the University of Chicago, he had supported a move away from a powerful department headship system to a system of elected chairs and had developed a general belief in the advisability of broadly dispersed administrative responsibility. When Millikan was offered the presidency of Caltech following his wartime service as vice-chair of the National Research Council, he accepted only after he received assurances that he need "not allow administrative duties to interfere with" what he considered to be his "primary job of trying to build an outstanding department of physics."[33]

Millikan and Caltech's governing board agreed to a governance system "based on the postulate that the field of higher education differed radically from the field of military operations or the field of business in that in it *wisdom* was vastly more important than *action*, and that *wisdom only comes from the joint, independent judgments* of a group of able and informed men" (emphasis in original). Consequently, Millikan and the trustees established an executive council consisting of four trustees and four faculty members who would exercise the authority normally assigned to a college president. The faculty members were not elected by their colleagues but were named by the board of trustees. However, the faculty members selected throughout the interwar years continued to be productive scholars and were highly regarded by their colleagues. Because of the relatively small size of the institution (just over two hundred instructional and research staff members in 1929), the faculty members serving on the executive council were easily accessible to the rest of the staff. Millikan chaired the council, but he considered himself only as one among equals, not the final voice of administrative authority. Whenever important issues affecting a particular department were discussed at council meetings, senior members of that department were normally invited to discuss the matter. Moreover, the council delegated jurisdiction over the curriculum to the faculty and also assigned much of the routine administrative work of the institution to fifteen standing faculty committees. The council's actions on appointments, budgets, and other matters were subject to approval by the full board of trustees, but such approval was pro forma during Millikan's quarter century as nominal president of Caltech.[34]

Before 1920, Caltech, which until then had been known as the Throop College of Technology, had not been among the nation's leading institutions of higher learning and research. However, by the end of the 1930s, the institute had become one of the premier centers of research in the natural sciences and attracted students with the highest standardized test scores of any school in the nation. Roger Geiger has observed that one of the many factors contributing to Caltech's sudden rise was that the "collegial style of managing the institute and its laboratories made it, more than any other research university, an institution truly run by scientists."[35]

Caltech may have been unique in virtually eliminating the position of president in its administrative system, but Antioch College was another prominent institution that assigned primary responsibility for institutional decision making to a committee with significant faculty representation. Antioch College traced its origins back to 1853, but by the end of World War One the institution was on the verge of collapse before Arthur E. Morgan became president in 1920. Morgan succeeded in transforming the college by imbuing it with a broad and practical ideal of general education that included a work-experience requirement and close contact between students and faculty. By 1930 Antioch had gained a national reputation for its unique approach to college education and saw a fourfold increase in its enrollment. With 650 students and 52 instructional staff, Antioch was fairly average in size for a liberal arts college, but it had become well known nationally for innovation in various aspects of college life and administration.[36]

Initially, Morgan completely dominated college governance, having sole responsibility for appointing new faculty and shaping the revamped curriculum, but in 1926 he agreed to the establishment of an Administrative Council (Ad Cil) as an advisory body to the president, which would have faculty representatives that he himself would appoint. As Morgan increasingly spent time off campus and then finally left Antioch in 1933 to take a position with the newly established Tennessee Valley Authority, the Ad Cil quickly became much more than an advisory body to the president.[37]

In 1930, Antioch's governing board amended the college charter to give constitutional sanction to the Ad Cil, which was then to be composed of the president, the college dean, three faculty members elected by their colleagues, and three faculty members selected by the president. In addition to advising the president on "the general management of the educational and other functions of the college," the newly constituted governance body was given the unprecedented power of electing by majority vote one-third of the members of the board of trustees.

Once Algo Henderson became president in 1933, the Ad Cil took on even greater responsibilities and became less subject to domination by the institution's president. According to one observer, the council "served in effect as the peak committee of the faculty and in turn of the administration, blending the two."[38] It appointed college committees, was directly involved in the entire budgetary process, and made appointment, tenure, and dismissal decisions. In 1940, the power of the Antioch faculty was further strengthened when the governing board approved changes in the college charter to allow for all faculty members on the Ad Cil to be elected and gave more explicit sanction to the council's dominant governance role.[39] By any standard, Antioch during the 1930s had developed one of the strongest forms of faculty governance of any college in the country.[40]

Reed College, which was founded in 1911, followed a path toward creating a substantial role for faculty in institutional governance that was, in many ways, remarkably similar to Antioch's. Under its founding president, William T. Foster, Reed sought to become "a Johns Hopkins for undergraduates," setting rigorous academic standards and recruiting professors with outstanding academic credentials.[41] Only a few years after Reed's founding, A. A. Knowlton joined what was still a very small faculty after having been fired at the University of Utah in the controversy that led to the AAUP's first extended defense of the principles of shared governance. President Foster's familiarity with the Utah experience served as a backdrop to his agreeing to the drafting of a formal constitution for Reed. The constitution established both a "welfare committee," consisting of two trustees, the president, and two members of the faculty elected by their colleagues, and a council headed by the president with eight members elected annually by the faculty. Any recommendations that the president might want to make to the board of trustees would first have to "come before the council for discussion."[42]

As at Antioch, the potential for faculty influence on institutional decision making that was established by a visionary president was not fully realized until the college was firmly on the road to realizing that president's vision and a subsequent generation of college leaders came into office. Under Foster and his immediate successor, a strong president in essence dominated the system of governance. However, by the late 1920s, the faculty advisory council had come to control the making of educational policy at Reed, and it would retain this power well into the future. Although the governance system at Reed became faculty dominated, it was not fully inclusive. Not until after 1945 would Reed provide for a rank of associate professor. Foster had believed that only junior faculty who had demonstrated sufficient merit to be promoted directly to the position of full professor ought to be permanently retained by the college. As a consequence, the college experienced a good deal of turnover in the junior ranks of instructor and assistant professor, and faculty governance at Reed became what higher education scholar Burton Clark has characterized as an "oligarchy," with only senior professors exercising real authority.[43] With that very important qualification regarding the system's lack of inclusiveness, Reed still had what Clark describes as one of the strongest schemes of faculty governance of any college in America.[44]

With their systems of strong faculty governance, by the eve of World War Two Antioch and Reed had solidified their positions among the most highly regarded liberal arts colleges in the country. It is probably no coincidence that many of the other most prestigious liberal arts colleges of this era also entrusted faculty with a strong role in institutional governance, as evidenced by the results of the AAUP's 1940 governance survey. Oberlin College, which had a long tradition of faculty governance, received the highest score of the more than two hundred institutions responding to the survey, while Grinnell, Vassar, Wellesley, Mount Holyoke, Wesleyan, Amherst, and Bryn Mawr also scored very well.

The City College of New York (CCNY) was a very different kind of institution from Reed or Antioch. However, together with its sister colleges, Hunter, Brooklyn, and Queens, CCNY also experienced a dramatic transformation in its system of institutional governance in the late 1930s that placed it in the forefront of colleges and universities that were expanding the role of faculty in decision making. City College was established in 1847 under the authority of the City Board of Education and is among the nation's oldest urban institutions of higher learning. Hunter (1870), Brooklyn (1930), and Queens (1937) Colleges were later established as additional city colleges and came under the authority of a separate Board of Higher Education that New York City created in 1926. Each college also had its own governing body that enjoyed considerable autonomy. By the end of the 1930s, the entire system had approximately forty thousand students and more than seventeen hundred faculty.[45]

In most respects, the system of governance at New York's city colleges in the mid-1930s was highly autocratic. One governing board member even referred to the college presidents and department heads as having the powers of "Mussolinis and teeny-weeny Mussolinis."[46] Faculty did for the most part exercise control over courses of instruction, as evidenced by a faculty-initiated revision of the entire curriculum in the late 1920s, but they generally had little power to influence other aspects of institutional decision making. Moreover, especially after the onset of the Great Depression, the colleges came to rely more heavily on underpaid tutors and instructors who had no job security and played no role in college governance. Some individual departments operated in a collaborative fashion, but most department heads exercised unilateral authority on day-to-day issues and were beholden to the dean and president for continuation in office.

In this situation, the nonrenewal in 1936 of an English tutor who had been teaching at City College for eight years proved to be the spark that ignited what Abraham Edel—a participant in and later historian of the events—describes as the "1938 Revolution." By the early 1930s, low pay and job insecurity had already prompted junior faculty members at the city colleges to create their own independent organizations, separate from the campus AAUP chapters then in existence. In 1935 many of these junior faculty members spearheaded the formation of a local of the American Federation of Teachers. Although the union did not act as a collective bargaining agent able to sign a contract, it soon played a leading role in reversing the dismissal of the English tutor and getting the New York Board of Higher Education to establish a more secure system of tenure.[47] The union local then established an Educational Policies Committee that cooperated with the AAUP chapters at the municipal colleges to develop a full set of proposals for reforming CCNY's system of governance and strengthening and clarifying the tenure system the board had recently approved. The governance proposals focused especially on departmental organization and substituting elected chairs and collective decision making for autocratic rule by presidentially appointed heads but also called for a formal role for elected faculty representatives in the selection of presidents and for an even greater role for faculty in the selection of deans.

In 1938, a new Board of Higher Education, influenced by the rising tide of progressivism in New York and supportive of a reform agenda, adopted most of the key faculty proposals. New bylaws addressed the organization of colleges and schools, as well as individual departments, at each level expanding faculty participation in institutional governance. Faculty status was extended to nonprofessorial staff who were employed on an annual salary basis and who had served more than three years, though instructors had to wait an additional two years before enjoying full voting rights. In all colleges or schools with more than one hundred teaching staff, the new bylaws provided for the establishment of a faculty council consisting of the president, deans, directors, and three delegates from each department (the department chair, a representative of the professorial ranks, and an instructor, the latter two to be elected by the eligible voting faculty in the particular rank). Each college was also required to set up a Committee on Faculty Personnel and Budget made up of the president as chair, the deans, and all the department chairs. Although no role for the faculty in the selection of new presidents was spelled out, in the appointment of new deans, the regulations declared that the board "shall have the advice of the Presidents and the Committee on Faculty Personnel and Budget."

The most important provisions of the new bylaws represented a revolution in the way departments operated. Chairs were henceforth to be elected to three-year terms by all members of the departmental faculty, while "the educational policies of the Department" were also to be established by a vote of all department members with faculty rank, subject to the approval of the college faculty or faculty council. Each department was also required to elect a committee on appointments, consisting of the chair and "equal representation from each available instructional rank included in the faculty." Before a department chair could make a recommendation on a new appointment, such a recommendation had to be approved by the departmental committee on appointments, which also had to approve promotions to the rank of instructor. In the case of promotions in the professorial ranks, a majority vote of all departmental faculty with a rank above that of the person being considered was required.[48]

The new governance system may not have fully lived up to faculty hopes regarding a more transparent and participatory budgetary process, and presidential powers did not prove to be as circumscribed as many reformers had anticipated. Nevertheless, the institutionalization of an elected department chair system supported by clearly delineated procedures for involving departmental faculty in both appointment and promotion decisions and in the determination of other departmental policies marked a significant advance in faculty self-government. Ordway Tead, the chair of the Board of Higher Education who played an instrumental role in the adoption of CCNY's governance reforms, explained that the governing board "did expect to create a new awareness of faculty power and of faculty duties" and that he and his colleagues saw the changes they instituted as representing "the way college government must in principle move."[49]

The developments at New York's city colleges raised two significant questions that would have ongoing importance in future debates across the country about college and university governance. The first was the relation of unionization to winning acceptance for the professional ideal of faculty governance. As noted in the previous chapter, the early leadership of the AAUP viewed unionization as more appropriate for "employees" seeking to advance their own strictly economic interests than for "professionals" who saw themselves acting not out of self-interest, but on behalf of the public interest. For decades to come, faculty associated with the AAUP continued to define their organization as a professional association devoted to the development of professional norms that would gain universal acceptance rather than as a trade union with direct ties to a larger labor movement. The CCNY faculty who turned to the American Federation of Teachers in the 1930s, however, did not see the pursuit of economic security and efforts to institutionalize greater self-government for faculty as being in conflict. At a time when enabling legislation for public-employee collective bargaining did not exist, CCNY faculty did not actively pursue a traditional collective bargaining approach that would have resulted in negotiating a formal contract. However, in the context of the intense unionization drives taking place throughout the nation in the 1930s, these faculty members saw union affiliation as an effective means of trying to establish a greater role for faculty in institutional governance, as well as a means of improving the job security and economic conditions of faculty. In later decades, as unionization spread to higher education, the relationship between collective bargaining and academic governance would gain a great deal of attention, and the AAUP itself would ultimately change its position and accept collective bargaining as a means of advancing the professoriate's professional goals.

A second, and not totally unrelated, issue that was highlighted by what happened at CCNY concerns the way reformers among the faculty justified their desire for greater authority in institutional governance. It is revealing that Abraham Edel, who served as chair of the union's Educational Policies Committee that first developed the proposals for reforming the college's governance system, and who much later wrote a history of the events that took place at CCNY, entitled his account *The Struggle for Academic Democracy.* Historically, most proponents of faculty participation in institutional governance, including the leadership of the AAUP, had not relied primarily on an appeal to "democracy" to support their cause. Instead, they based their argument on the desirability of utilizing the professional expertise of faculty to make informed decisions about educational matters, including appointments, promotions, and dismissals. The faculty advocating change in the system of governance at CCNY did not reject such arguments. But in emphasizing the need to limit "autocracy" and advance the cause of "democracy," they appealed more to the progressive antifascist spirit that was prevalent in New York in the late 1930s than to a more strictly professional ethic. A certain tension between arguments based on professional expertise and those putting more emphasis on purely democratic values would continue in discussions about college and university governance to this day.

Assessing Overall Trends in Governance, 1920–1940

While several institutions experienced quite dramatic advances in faculty governance between 1920 and 1940, the question remains as to how widespread the growth of faculty involvement in institutional decision making was. An AAUP survey of governance practices that was completed between 1938 and 1940, with the participation of nearly one thousand AAUP members at more than two hundred institutions, provides the best source of information regarding this question. The survey included questions that asked respondents to report on certain basic structural characteristics of governance at their institution, as well as some questions requiring more subjective judgments about the state of governance.

One of the more than twenty questions on the survey asked AAUP chapter leaders if they perceived a trend toward more or less faculty self-government at their own institutions. Among respondents who saw a clear change taking place, four times as many chapters reported that the change was in the direction of a greater role for faculty in governance as those that saw a decline in the faculty's authority. Only twenty-five responding chapters saw a trend toward less self-government, while ninety-nine reported a trend toward more. Eighty-eight chapters saw no discernible trend. However, Paul Ward, the chair of the AAUP's Committee T on Place and Function of Faculties in College and University Government, noted that among those that reported no trend were several institutions that had previously established a significant governance role for faculty, so in some cases the report of no trend might have meant that substantial faculty authority had already been established and was continuing to be respected.[50] The AAUP survey, which was sent only to those institutions with an AAUP chapter, may not have included a truly representative sample of all American colleges and universities and obviously involved subjective judgments on the part of respondents. Relying solely on AAUP chapters for responses may well have somewhat skewed the results, since later surveys that included non-AAUP members as well as administrators as respondents showed that AAUP leaders were inclined to apply a stricter standard when judging the extent of faculty authority in academic decision making. Even with these caveats, however, the AAUP survey remains the most comprehensive source we have about the state of governance in American colleges and universities on the eve of World War Two.

An examination of the survey results is most useful in considering the four specific issues of governance that had been identified in the AAUP's first governance committee report as particular areas of faculty concern: (1) opportunities for direct faculty communication with trustees; (2) faculty involvement in the selection of administrators (president, dean, department chair or head); (3) faculty exercise of primary responsibility for appointing and promoting colleagues; (4) meaningful faculty participation in the budgetary process. Faculty authority over the curriculum had become a fairly well-established principle even before the AAUP was formed in 1915. Thus, in the 1940 AAUP survey, 78 percent of chapters responding reported that faculty at their institution enjoyed "legislative powers" regarding "educational" policies. However, prior to World War One, few American colleges and universities had made significant provision for faculty involvement in other aspects of institutional decision making.

Although the AAUP had supported establishing formal lines of direct communication and consultation between faculty members and trustees since 1920, it was still uncommon in 1940 for faculty to have such a mechanism for expressing their views to an institution's governing board. Less than one-quarter of the AAUP chapters responding to the governance survey reported that their institution had a definite plan for faculty exchange of opinion with trustees, though nearly 40 percent acknowledged that faculty did have occasional social or improvised contacts with trustees. In 1916, Cornell University had been the first school to experiment with having elected faculty members serve as nonvoting members of its board, but only two other institutions—Wellesley and Bryn Mawr—subsequently adopted similar plans in the interwar period, and in the case of Wellesley, faculty always chose someone from outside the college to represent them. For those relatively few institutions that did provide for formal consultation, a specially designated conference committee or joint faculty-board committees on particular topics were the primary means of interaction.[51]

A second long-standing AAUP position was that faculty ought to play a role in the selection of academic administrators, with the degree of involvement increasing as one moved down the administrative hierarchy from president to dean to department head or chair. In the selection of a president, as in the case of communication between faculty and trustees more generally on questions of educational policy, only a minority of institutions followed the AAUP recommendation that faculty be directly consulted. Of the more than two hundred institutions that provided information on this question, only 29 percent reported that faculty were consulted in the choice of a new president. However, this figure represented a significant increase over the percentage of colleges and universities reporting such involvement in a previous AAUP survey conducted in the early 1920s. At that time, in a sample of 167 institutions, only 10 percent reported the faculty as having any voice in the selection of a president.[52]

Although still not the norm, several prominent colleges and universities did begin to adopt the practice of formally involving faculty, together with trustees, on presidential search committees. Cornell was the exceptional institution that had elected faculty serving as nonvoting members of its governing board, and when in 1921 the board sought a successor to Jacob Gould Schurman as president, the three faculty trustees were included on the search committee. In its next presidential search, conducted in the mid-1930s, Cornell again used what was still then described as "the somewhat unusual procedure of the Board of Trustees inviting faculty participation." Four of the nine members of the search committee were drawn from the faculty, though in this instance, the individuals, including three deans, were not elected by the faculty but chosen by the chair of the board of trustees.[53]

Another example in this period of a shared-governance approach to selecting a president occurred at the University of Michigan. In conducting its search for a new president in 1925, the board of regents agreed to equal representation for faculty and trustees on the search committee and allowed the senate council, which included deans and faculty members, to elect the three faculty representatives. The search committee then presented for consideration to the full governing board only one name, Clarence Cook Little. Ironically, Little's subsequent presidency was marked by serious conflicts with the faculty over his plans for the establishment of a University College and his ultimate resignation a little more than three years later, but the process by which he had been selected entailed a significant degree of faculty involvement.[54]

A somewhat different approach to faculty involvement in the selection of a new president was represented by the experience of Allegheny College in 1930. Instead of including faculty representatives on the search committee proper, Allegheny's board of trustees authorized the faculty to elect five of their number to serve as an advisory committee to the seven trustees who composed the formal search committee. The faculty committee, though, was responsible for sending out calls for nominations, examining candidates' credentials, and winnowing the field down to six individuals, who were subsequently invited to campus to interview with both the board's search committee and the faculty advisory committee. This process provided an unusual degree of faculty influence over the selection of a new president.[55]

Somewhat surprisingly, the 1940 AAUP survey results show that faculty involvement in the selection of deans was neither less nor more common than was faculty involvement in the selection of presidents. Only 30 percent of the institutions reporting on this question indicated any form of consultation with the faculty, either formal or informal, in the choice of a dean. However, this figure did represent an increase over the percentage of institutions reporting such consultation fifteen years earlier, when only 21 percent of schools indicated that faculty were involved in the selection of deans. While no institution provided for faculty election of its president, several schools did allow faculty to elect their own deans. Yale had started this practice as early as 1905, though on the eve of World War Two, most of the limited number of institutions that entrusted their faculty with this authority were smaller liberal arts colleges.[56] Connecticut College for Women, Grinnell, Oberlin, Vassar, and Wesleyan all reported having deans elected by the faculty.

The academic administrator who most directly influenced the daily life of faculty members was the department executive. The AAUP survey demonstrated that relatively few institutions emulated CCNY in allowing departmental faculty to elect their own chair. Only 21 out of 217 reported adopting such a practice, but many of the colleges and universities that had elected department chairs were highly regarded institutions.[57] Another nineteen institutions reported having department heads appointed by a dean or president after having some form of formal consultation with the faculty members of the affected department. Still, far and away the most common method of selecting a department executive—in more than 80 percent of institutions reporting—was appointment by a dean or president without any formal consultation with the faculty. Although a governance system with powerful heads who could exercise a great deal of control over the running of their departments was thus still the norm in American colleges and universities, the AAUP survey indicated that the power of department heads was, at least to a certain extent, beginning to be circumscribed at a growing number of institutions. Even in some schools where heads were appointed, such as the University of California, the University of Chicago, Columbia, Cornell, and Harvard, the headship had come to be for a set term and was rotated among the senior faculty of the department.[58]

At many colleges and universities, the department head still had unilateral authority over appointments and promotions and the departmental budget. However, the sharing of that authority with departmental colleagues, as was instituted under the "executive committee" system at Illinois and Michigan, for example, could be found in a substantial minority of institutions. Nearly one-third of the AAUP chapters reporting on this question in the 1940 survey indicated that in the case of appointments, promotions, and dismissals, departmental faculty or general faculty committees were consulted in the decision-making process. In the 1924 survey, less than one-quarter reported a formal mechanism for faculty to participate in the selection of new colleagues.[59] It should also be noted that in the 1940 survey less than one-quarter of the schools excluded faculty altogether from decisions about appointments, promotion, and dismissal, though in the majority of cases, faculty involvement was still restricted to the department head. Especially at the larger, research-oriented universities, there was a growing recognition by presidents and deans of the need at least to consult with departmental faculty who had the relevant expertise in order to make an informed evaluation of the credentials of individuals being considered for appointment or promotion.[60]

The appropriateness of faculty involvement in budgetary decisions had long been a source of some disagreement among faculty members, even within the AAUP leadership. However, especially in the context of the Great Depression, the question of faculty participation in budgetary decisions became more pressing, as salary reductions, appointment and promotion freezes, and program cuts all began to be considered by administrations and governing boards as responses to the financial crisis. Complete exclusion of faculty in the budget-making process was reported in only one-quarter of schools, though as was the case with faculty involvement in appointment and promotion decisions, in a substantial majority of institutions the department head was the sole representative of faculty interests in the process.

A separate study completed in 1936 by a specially appointed AAUP committee (Committee Y) to look into the impact of the Depression on the professoriate, concluded that "significant policies and practices become effective without the degree of discussion by faculty members that the importance of these policies and practices would lead one to expect. Faculties apparently speak through administrative officers: through department chairmen, the deans and the president. It is by these steps that their voice reaches the governing boards, if at all." The author of Committee Y's report, University of Minnesota sociologist Malcolm Willey, acknowledged that many factors accounted for the faculty's limited influence over budgetary decisions, including the faculty's own "timidity, inertia, and complete acceptance of the principle of administrative separatism." He also noted, however, that "the machinery for faculty discussions, especially in large institutions, is inadequate."[61]

Only 16 percent of the schools responding to the 1940 Committee T survey had faculty committees that formally participated in budgetary deliberations. However, these were again among the nation's most prestigious institutions of higher learning. The list thus included large research institutions such as Harvard, Johns Hopkins, Caltech, Columbia, Cornell, Wisconsin, California, Illinois, and Ohio State, as well as highly regarded liberal arts colleges such as Antioch, Grinnell, Oberlin, Reed, and Vassar.

In sum, in 1940 the typical American college or university still did not make available means for faculty to communicate directly with their governing board or to have any formal role in the selection of a president, dean, or department head and provided for faculty consultation on appointments, promotions, dismissals, and budgets only through department heads or chairs. Yet there were clear indications that across the country, the faculty role in institutional governance had increased over the previous quarter century and that, as evidenced by the AAUP's governance survey, there was a definite correlation between the reputation of an institution and the extent to which its faculty enjoyed a measure of self-government. Not only were many of the nation's most prestigious research universities and liberal arts colleges among the highest scorers on Committee T's faculty self-government index, but teachers colleges and small church-controlled schools, where faculty were less likely to have significant professional status, dominated the lower end of the rankings.[62]

Moreover, the developing consensus in American higher education after 1915 about the need for professors to enjoy academic freedom in order to carry out their service to the public good was grounded in a recognition of the professional status of college faculty members and the appropriateness of relying on their professional judgment in evaluating the conduct of their colleagues. Both the 1925 statement adopted by the Association of American Colleges and the AAUP and the subsequent 1940 *Statement of Principles* developed by these two organizations declared that any termination for academic incompetence of a faculty member on permanent or long-term appointment should require a hearing before a faculty committee, which would be in the best position to pass judgment on the professional fitness of a faculty member.

In 1935, the president of the AAC Commission on Academic Freedom and Academic Tenure, James L. McConaughy, went even further in recommending that the faculty role in peer review should extend beyond the case of dismissals to include involvement in decisions about appointments and promotions. In his commission report that year concerning discussions that led eventually to the 1940 *Statement*, McConaughy observed: "We believe in the value of faculty committees, usually elected by the faculty itself, to advise with the President regarding appointments, dismissals, and promotions; colleges having such committees report quite generally that they promote closer cooperation between faculty and President in such matters."[63] In the late 1930s, the Commission on Institutions of Higher Education of the North Central Association of Colleges and Secondary Schools became probably the first regional accrediting agency to take at least some notice of faculty governance in its standards for accreditation when it proclaimed that it would give consideration "to group organization of the faculty, to faculty meetings, and to faculty committees."[64]

In the next several decades, American higher education would become the envy of much of the rest of the world. The tremendous resources a rich and powerful postwar America could devote to higher education certainly played a key role in the growing predominance of American colleges and universities, but so, too, did the expanding system of shared governance that allowed faculty to build on many of the precedents that had been developed in the interwar years.

CHAPTER FOUR

The Developing Consensus on Shared Governance, 1940–1975

The years from the beginning of World War Two to the mid-1970s witnessed both the rise of American universities to a position of global preeminence in the world of higher education and the development of a broad consensus on the desirability of significant faculty involvement in institutional governance.[1] The greater authority exercised by faculty in governance reflected not only the increased leverage professors had as a result of the significant growth in the demand for faculty but also a further increase in the professional status and identity of those engaged in college and university research and teaching. One reflection of the growing professional identity of faculty was the rapid postwar expansion in AAUP membership, which went from a little over 15,000 in 1940 to nearly 44,000 in 1955. By 1972, membership exceeded 91,000.[2] Competition among schools for students and funding led to a growing emphasis by administrators on research and graduate education because these were the principal measures of status in the world of higher education. This emphasis among a widening circle of colleges and universities strengthened the demand for highly qualified faculty, who were, in turn, in a better position to insist on a significant role in academic decision making.[3]

American colleges and universities in this period experienced dramatic growth, not only in the numbers of students and faculty, but also in the resources available for the support of teaching and research. While the number of institutions of higher learning almost doubled, reaching three thousand by 1975, the total number of students mushroomed from 1.5 million in 1940 to 11.2 million in 1975. The coming of age of the baby boom generation was a major factor in this tremendous upsurge. Equally important, greater national prosperity and the perception that a college degree had become an essential prerequisite to economic success resulted in the percentage of those eighteen to twenty-four years old attending institutions of higher education increasing by more than 400 percent. The huge increases in enrollments led to a burgeoning demand for additional faculty, so that by 1975 there were approximately 628,000 instructional faculty members in the United States, with unprecedented numbers having earned doctorates. The increased demand for qualified professors resulted in a rise in the number of doctoral degrees being awarded in the United States from a little over 3,000 in 1940 to just under 34,000 in 1975. Revenues in current dollars went up even more dramatically than the numbers of students and faculty. Whereas current fund revenues for all American colleges and universities in 1940 totaled $715 million, by 1975 this figure had risen to over $35 billion.[4]

Although the principles of shared governance were slower to win general acceptance in academe than the principles of academic freedom and the institution of tenure, the joint formulation by the AAUP, the Association of Governing Boards (AGB), and the American Council on Education (ACE) of the 1966 *Statement on Government of Colleges and Universities* reflected a broadening agreement over the desirability of recognizing a significant role for faculty in institutional governance. A report by the Carnegie Commission on Higher Education published in 1973, for example, referred to the "consensus" that had been reached by the mid-1960s on the advisability of granting faculty primary responsibility for making most academic decisions.[5] The survey data discussed later in this chapter further confirm the trend in the postwar decades toward more faculty authority in various aspects of academic decision making.

By the end of this period, however, several countervailing forces were beginning to take shape that would challenge and ultimately undermine the growing power of faculty. These included an increasing role for state legislatures and the federal government in university affairs as public funding for both state and private institutions rose significantly. The development of multicampus systems and state coordinating bodies for public higher education also took decision-making authority away from individual campuses, where faculty had the greatest opportunity for influencing decisions. The change in the nation's economic situation in the 1970s, characterized by the new problem of stagflation (a combination of two conditions—inflation and rising unemployment—that were previously believed to be incompatible) and by tightened budgets, signaled the end of the era of almost unrestrained growth in funding for American colleges and universities. As a result of new economic pressures, by the middle of the 1970s signs had already begun to appear of what would become an increasing tendency of institutions of higher education to appoint part-time and non-tenure-track faculty, whose participation in governance was problematic. This was the case not only from the standpoint of administrators who did not want to recognize governance activities as part of the work assignment of contingent faculty but also from the standpoint of many tenured and tenure-track faculty who feared that faculty members on contingent appointments would be more subject to administrative pressures and less likely to have a long-term commitment to the institutions at which they worked.[6] The increasing use of contingent faculty would become part of a larger trend toward the corporatization of American colleges and universities in which business models of management provided an alternative to the shared-governance approach that had risen to prominence in the 1960s. The significant growth in the number of two-year institutions, in which faculty generally enjoyed less prestige and professional status and hence were less likely to be able to gain authority over academic decision making, also served to limit the practices of shared governance in a rapidly expanding sector of American higher education.[7] Finally, the emergence of demands for student power introduced a new claimant for a right to be involved in institutional governance.

Nevertheless, even with the emergence by the mid-1970s of many of these trends, faculty in the postwar decades came to enjoy a more prominent role in the governance of American institutions of higher education than ever before. The heyday of shared governance coincided not only with the achievement of greater professional status by the American professoriate but also with a global recognition of the unsurpassed quality of American higher education. These two developments were closely linked. Virtually all commentators on governance in higher education in this period agreed that the nation's most highly regarded colleges and universities were the institutions that were most likely to grant faculty a primary role in academic decision making.[8] Sociologist Burton Clark contended that institutions at which faculty authority was strong were better able to recruit highly competent faculty. Moreover, faculty control also helped colleges and universities retain their commitment to protecting the "traditional values" that were "central to the cultural heritage" of society.[9] While governing board members or others not steeped in academic culture often viewed college largely as a place for job preparation or the creation of practical knowledge to benefit the economy, faculty members were more likely to champion a role for higher education that also included the cultivation of cultural literacy and preparation for students to participate in society as informed citizens.

World War Two and Its Aftermath

Although the initial impact of US involvement in World War Two was to re-
duce the number of students enrolled in American colleges and universities
and to divert resources away from higher education,[10] the long-term consequences of America's involvement proved highly beneficial both to the prestige
of America's institutions of higher education and to their ability to attract increasing numbers of students and additional resources. In mobilizing the nation's scientific and technical resources for the war effort, the federal government's Office of Scientific Research and Development, under the leadership of
former MIT dean of engineering Vannevar Bush, relied primarily on developing contractual relationships with leading research universities instead of recruiting scientists to work directly for the government. This pattern of reliance
by the federal government on American universities to carry out research and
development work would provide the basis for the dramatic increase in federal
dollars that helped fuel the postwar rise to preeminence of American higher
education.[11] The role university researchers played in such technological break-
throughs as the development of the atomic bomb was also a significant factor
in the increased prestige enjoyed by the American professoriate after the war.
The passage in 1944 of the GI Bill, which included generous benefits for veterans who chose to pursue higher education, greatly contributed to the explosion
in college enrollments after the war's end. In the five years after the return of
peace, more than two million veterans made use of the GI Bill to go to college,
and competition among institutions of higher education developed to attract
these and other new students.[12] One element of this competition was an effort
by schools to hire the best qualified and most professional faculty. World War
Two, in sum, had the result of accelerating prewar trends that already posi-
tioned American higher education to play an increasingly important role in
the life of the nation and allowed faculty to claim a larger role in institutional
governance.

Faculty's Expanding Role in Governance, 1945–1960

A 1953 survey conducted by the AAUP's Committee T on Place and Function
of Faculties in College and University Government confirms the postwar trend
toward greater faculty involvement in academic decision making.[13] Although,
like earlier AAUP surveys, this postwar survey represented subjective judgments by respondents and did not constitute a fully representative sample of all
institutions of higher education, since only schools with AAUP chapters were
included and only AAUP leaders were responsible for filling out the questionnaires, it is by far the most comprehensive source available on specific governance practices at the time. Moreover, the inclusion of the majority of the na-

tion's most prestigious universities and liberal arts colleges meant that the results do reveal trends that were occurring in the development of professional norms.

Among the questions to which responses were received from AAUP chapters at more than three hundred institutions across the country was one that asked whether faculty involvement in the determination of institutional policies at the respondents' own school was increasing, staying the same, or declining. While only one in ten chapters reported a decline in the level of faculty self-government, six in ten reported an increase in faculty participation. Using the same format as the 1939 survey conducted by Committee T, the 1953 survey provided the basis for scoring the degree of faculty self-government at an institution on a 28-point scale. Although such scores represented the perceptions of the AAUP leaders doing the rating rather than some objective reality, the use of the same format as in the earlier survey allows for a meaningful measure of comparison with earlier conditions. Of the more than two hundred colleges and universities responding to the 1939 survey, 172 were also included in the 1953 survey results. More than twice as many of these institutions registered gains in their governance scores as those that experienced declines. While declines or increases of one or two points may not hold much significance, changes of ten points or more in either direction are certainly worthy of note. Only a single institution, Occidental College, saw a decline of ten or more points. In contrast, eighteen schools reported increases of ten or more points.[14]

While many of the nation's leading research universities and premier liberal arts colleges had already established some degree of faculty self-government prior to World War Two, most of the institutions reporting dramatic gains in shared governance did so as part of an effort to upgrade their standing in the world of higher education. Many were state institutions that had been undergoing a transition into becoming large research-oriented universities. The University of Oklahoma was representative of this group. Created in 1890, before Oklahoma became a state, the university did not grant its first PhD until 1929. On the eve of World War Two, the school had fewer than two hundred faculty members and about six thousand students. As an institution of higher education that was still striving to become a major research university in the late 1930s, Oklahoma had a system of governance that one close observer, director of the university's press Savoie Lottinville, described as "conservative, hierarchical, and authoritarian."[15] The university president did not govern single-handedly, since the academic council made up of the school's deans exercised significant authority. However, the faculty collectively had very little say in determining institutional policies. In 1939, on the AAUP's 28-point scale for faculty governance, the AAUP chapter leaders at Oklahoma gave their institution a score of 3.[16]

With the appointment of Joseph A. Brandt as president in 1941, the situation at Oklahoma began to change. Although Brandt acted unilaterally in revamping the curriculum—much to the chagrin of the faculty—he set the stage, according to Lottinville, for the subsequent development of a system of shared governance by introducing "the campus to academic democracy by fiat, a course for which its previous half century of development had prepared it scarcely at all."[17] Brandt did away with the system of department heads with indefinite terms and instituted a system of rotating department chairs. He also supported, and the board of regents approved, the establishment of an elected university senate that replaced the academic council to become the chief legislative body responsible for the development of university policy. In recognition of the growing importance of research by an increasingly more professional faculty, the university also created a research institute and the new position of "research professor" that was awarded to some of the school's most outstanding faculty.[18]

Brandt's tenure in office was short lived. Facing opposition from the deans and department heads, as well as from many faculty members who resented his unilateral imposition of a new curriculum, Brandt resigned in 1943 to become the director of the University of Chicago Press. Once Brandt left office, however, the University of Oklahoma did not reverse course in granting greater recognition of the professional status of its faculty and in allowing them a larger role in institutional governance. In an unprecedented move for the university, the regents, following a recommendation from the alumni association, created a presidential selection committee that was elected by the new university senate. The man who was subsequently chosen as president, George Cross, not only supported the enactment of the university's first formal tenure system, with provision for faculty review in cases of dismissal, but also referred to the senate for consideration both the new curriculum Brandt had introduced and the possibility of making revisions to the system of rotating nonrenewable chairs that Brandt had imposed on the departments. Cross later recalled that he "knew well that any plan I might devise would be viable only if it had the approval of the university faculty."[19]

By fall 1946, the University of Oklahoma had not only greatly expanded with the influx of veterans taking advantage of the GI Bill, so that its enrollment exceeded ten thousand, but it also had established a solid basis for a system of shared governance. This latter development was reflected in the governance score reported in 1953 by the chapter leaders of Oklahoma's more than two-hundred-member AAUP chapter. Whereas the score of 3 reported by chapter leaders in 1939 placed the school near the bottom of institutions responding to the AAUP survey, the score of 18 the university earned in 1953 placed it in the top 10 percent of institutions reporting.

A similar pattern of evolution occurred at the University of Nebraska in the immediate postwar period. Founded in 1869, the university by 1940 had become a fairly large institution with an enrollment in excess of seven thousand students and more than four hundred faculty members.[20] However, on the eve of World War Two, under Chancellor C. S. Boucher, the faculty played little role in institutional governance. AAUP chapter leaders in 1939 reported that faculty had no effective influence in most areas of academic governance, giving their institution a score of only 2 on the AAUP's 28-point self-government scale. In a few short years, however, the situation would be substantially changed.

The immediate trigger for a faculty revolt against the existing system of governance was Boucher's failure in 1945 to ask the state legislature for salary increases to offset the inflation that had occurred during the war. With the local AAUP chapter taking the lead, an ad hoc faculty committee was established to appeal directly to the board of regents to modify the budget for the coming year in order to address the problem of faculty salaries. This committee then successfully lobbied the legislature to approve a revised budget that included salary increases. Following this significant victory, the faculty voted to create an ongoing executive committee to oversee the budget and the university's administration. The faculty revolt led to Boucher's resignation and to the establishment of a faculty advisory committee that played a major role in the selection of a new chancellor.

Coming into office in 1946 with the support of the faculty, the new chancellor, Reuben Gustavson, recognized the legitimacy of the faculty committee that had been responsible for getting revisions to the previous year's budget by making it a permanent advisory body to consider "any matter concerning the operation or general welfare of the University." He also further strengthened the faculty role in governance by relying more heavily on other university committees on which faculty served.[21] The transformed system of shared governance at Nebraska was reflected in a dramatic change by 1953 in the institution's rating on the AAUP's faculty self-government survey, which went from a lowly score of 2 in 1939 to 19. This score was exceeded by only fourteen other schools that participated in the survey.[22]

During the war and in the immediate postwar period, significant gains for faculty in professional status and greater involvement in institutional governance were not restricted to emerging public research universities that served as flagship institutions in their states. Illinois State Normal University (now Illinois State University) was an example of a less prestigious institution that was also undergoing a transformation in its system of governance as it attempted to enhance its academic reputation. Illinois State traced its origins back to 1857 and had developed primarily as a teacher training school, reaching an enrollment of just under two thousand students in 1939.[23] According to John Freed, a longtime Illinois State faculty member and author of a history of the institution, Raymond Fairchild, who was appointed the university's president in 1933, had a "management style" like "that of a school principal or a superintendent of schools. He failed to grasp that when a Ph.D. became the requisite terminal degree for faculty members, it became necessary to treat them as professionals who needed to be consulted rather than as subordinates." Faculty discontent at such treatment led to the formation of an AAUP chapter in 1935 and to Fairchild's making the grudging concession of establishing a university senate in the same year. The senate, however, consisted of deans, division directors, and department heads and no full-time teaching faculty. Moreover, it had no actual policy-making authority. AAUP chapter leaders in 1939 gave their institution a score of 3 on Committee T's faculty self-government scale.[24]

A growing AAUP chapter began in the late 1930s to press for the establishment of a formal tenure system at Illinois State similar to what was soon to be recommended in the 1940 *Statement of Principles on Academic Freedom and Tenure* and for a reform of the institution's governance system that would allow for a greater faculty voice. By 1950, the Illinois State chapter numbered 169 members, and its agitation in behalf of governance reform helped lead the university's governing board to direct the president to "make every effort to bring full faculty cooperation to the administration of the school" and to delegate many of the administrative duties that had been long centralized in the president's office. This directive resulted in the establishment in 1951 of an elected university council that was authorized "to make recommendations on curriculum, campus planning, scholarship, the budget, and the appointment, promotion, and tenure of staff members."[25] In the 1953 governance survey, AAUP leaders gave their institution a score of 16, a substantial change from the prewar rating.

Franklin & Marshall College in Pennsylvania represented still another kind of institution that experienced a significant increase in the role of faculty in academic decision making in these years. Founded in 1787, Franklin College merged with Marshall College in 1853. The institution remained a relatively small undergraduate-oriented liberal arts school into the twentieth century. On the eve of World War Two, the college had a little more than nine hundred students and forty-five faculty members.[26] The college's historian notes that even before the war, "one sign of the emerging professional consciousness within the faculty was the 1933 organization of a campus chapter of the American Association of University Professors." Although the chapter soon signed up nearly half of all faculty members at the college, divisions among the faculty between those who had long ties to Franklin & Marshall but lacked significant academic credentials and newer faculty, many of whom had recently obtained PhDs from prestigious Ivy League schools and were thus more likely to identify with AAUP principles, helped to prevent a substantial change from taking place in the college's traditional governance practices. This adherence to traditional hierarchical governance practices was reflected in the meager score of 1 point that the AAUP chapter gave the college in Committee T's 1939 survey.[27]

In the years following World War Two, Franklin & Marshall, like many other institutions of higher learning in the United States, experienced an academic revolution as it evolved into a more selective college that gave an increasingly professionalized faculty more time to conduct research, even though teaching remained the college's highest priority. Membership in the AAUP jumped from nineteen in 1940 to sixty-two in 1950. Of more direct relevance to the governance system at Franklin & Marshall, the entire faculty in 1947 voted to create an elected budget committee to advise the president. In addition, a five-person Committee on Appointments, Promotions, and Dismissals came to play an important role in selecting the many new faculty members who joined the college in the immediate postwar years. President Theodore Distler acknowledged the desirability of the faculty's playing a larger role in the appointment process because their specialized expertise was needed to evaluate the credentials of candidates. Complementing these changes in the governance system was the trustees' approval of AAUP tenure guidelines.[28] Consequently, when AAUP chapter leaders evaluated the state of faculty governance at Franklin & Marshall in 1953, they gave the college a score of 14, which, while ranking somewhere in the middle for all institutions reporting, was, nevertheless a significant increase over the score of 1 the college had received in 1939.

The most dramatic gains in faculty governance in the postwar decade were most likely to take place at emerging institutions that were striving to improve their standing among American colleges and universities. However, there were also instances of significant change at some of the nation's already well-regarded institutions of higher learning. The University of Pennsylvania was one of the nation's oldest institutions of higher education, having been founded in the colonial era. By the mid-twentieth century, Penn had grown into a major Ivy League university with nearly twenty different colleges. Before 1952, however, it lacked an institution-wide, faculty-controlled governance body. A university-wide Educational Council did exist, but it was dominated by administrators, so that, according to philosophy professor and former second vice president of the national AAUP Glenn Morrow, "There had been a rather widespread feeling that, in the organization and operation of the University, faculty influence had been notably absent." This changed in 1952, when the president and board of trustees agreed to a faculty proposal to establish a university senate consisting of all the voting members (assistant professors and above) of each of the college faculties. The new senate quickly gained the right to play a role in the appointment of administrators and in the formulation of the budget. In reviewing the state of governance at Penn, Morrow concluded that "it can hardly be denied that the Senate has played an enormously effective part at the University in increasing the faculty's participation in University decisions."[29]

While many institutions, especially state universities that were aspiring to improve their standing in the world of higher education, were introducing a greater degree of faculty involvement in institutional governance, it is important not to exaggerate the gains that were made during the 1940s and early 1950s. At some schools where the faculty's role in institutional governance expanded during the war and the immediate postwar period, the changes did not always survive the coming to power of a new administration. The experience of the College of William and Mary is one example. Like the University of Pennsylvania, William and Mary was established in the colonial period. Until the 1930s, the college had a strictly hierarchical form of governance. During the 1920s and early 1930s, faculty members feared publicly criticizing the authoritarian leadership of President Julian A. C. Chandler. After Chandler's death in 1934, subsequent presidents John Stewart Bryan and John E. Pomfret gradually introduced governance reforms giving the faculty more authority, so that the college's score on the AAUP self-government index increased from 3 in 1939 to 13 in 1953. However, following the appointment of Julian Chandler's son, former navy admiral Alvin D. Chandler, to the presidency in late 1951, the college administration slowly set about reducing the authority the faculty had come to exercise as Chandler returned the college to the management style of his father's day.[30] While the trend in college and university governance across America was toward greater faculty involvement, much still depended on the individual personality and leadership approach of the individual who sat in the president's chair.

Certain types of institutions of higher learning were also less likely to participate fully in the growing trend toward greater faculty involvement in governance. Many small historically black, as well as religiously affiliated, colleges continued to maintain hierarchical systems of authority. Two-year colleges, or institutions that were only recently evolving from two-year into four-year institutions, did not consistently recognize the professional status of their instructors and hence denied them a significant role in academic decision making. Sociologist J. Victor Baldridge has argued that the lack of professional autonomy enjoyed by two-year college faculty was directly related to certain "environmental pressures," such as "financial dependency" stemming from a lack of endowment funds and tuition revenue, open enrollment policies established by law rather than by the faculty, and the direct control over institutional policies exerted by external political bodies. All of these factors contrasted sharply with the circumstances in which more highly regarded institutions of higher education functioned. As a result, far greater environmental constraints existed on the degree of self-government and academic freedom enjoyed by faculty at two-year institutions, which often had more in common with public high schools than research universities.[31]

Not coincidentally, the AAUP's first formal investigation of faculty-administrative relationships at an individual institution involved a college that had only recently evolved from a two-year to a four-year school. Monmouth College in New Jersey was established in 1933 to offer postsecondary classes at the local high school; in 1947 New Jersey gave it authority to grant associate in arts degrees. The Middle States Association of Colleges and Secondary Schools then accredited Monmouth as a junior college in 1952, but by 1956 it had begun to operate on its own campus as a four-year college. Rapid growth soon followed. From a total faculty of only 36 and a student enrollment of 1,101 in 1956, Monmouth by 1959 had a faculty of 91 and an enrollment of 2,639 students. However, even as the school grew, its hierarchical and administration-dominated form of institutional governance under longtime head Edward G. Schlaefer changed little from the time Monmouth had been an extension of the public school system.[32] Student and faculty unrest led not only to a formal investigation by the AAUP in 1960 but also to a scathing report the previous year by the accrediting committee of the Middle States Association that resulted in a delay in reaccreditation.

The Middle States accrediting committee observed that Monmouth's system of governance had not evolved to keep up with its growth in size and academic mission: "As a junior college administrator the president was a wise and unselfish authoritarian. By long acceptance, this became the rule. Now, however, this would appear no longer tenable, both because of the expansion in number, curricula and plant, and the changing nature of the faculty." The AAUP's investigating committee noted that Schlaefer's rejection of meaningful faculty involvement in governance was but one aspect of his "lack of confidence in the faculty and an absence of criteria for judging professional competence in the scholarly disciplines." Requiring syllabi, texts, and examinations to be reviewed by the dean of instruction, not allowing faculty members into their offices except during business hours, and insisting that they sign in and out when coming to or leaving work all implied "a lamentably low estimate of the competence, judgment, and responsibility of men who may be considered adults of superior intelligence and education."[33]

Less than a year after the publication of its report on Monmouth College, the AAUP acknowledged the growing importance and problematic nature of governance at two-year institutions when the organization's annual meeting adopted the following resolution:

> [The AAUP] regards the faculty members of junior and community colleges as valued colleagues in higher education, and encourages their efforts to achieve responsible participation in the governance of their institutions. It regrets that the emergence of many of these colleges from the public school system has often posed legal inhibitions which seriously limit faculty participation in governance of such institutions, and urges appropriate legislative action be taken to accord junior and community college faculty members the same status as is normally accorded faculty members in other institutions of higher education. It hopes that, in those colleges not so restricted by law, the professional role of the faculty can be advanced through the combined efforts of faculty members, administrative officers, and board members.[34]

Another factor that limited the development of a more robust system of faculty governance was the continuing, though narrowing, divide between tenured and nontenured faculty members. Faculty governance in American colleges and universities had initially been advocated most forcefully and effectively by established senior faculty members at America's most prestigious institutions of higher learning. Internal conflicts between tenured full professors and junior nontenured instructors and assistant professors, who generally felt excluded from institutional decision making, had appeared at least as early as the late nineteenth century. However, the trend over the first half of the twentieth century was for greater, if often still limited, inclusion of junior faculty in governance. This trend continued in the immediate postwar period. Among those schools reporting to the AAUP's Committee T that they had an organized "general faculty" governance body, the percentage of institutions indicating that this body included all ranks of the teaching faculty increased between 1939 and 1953 from sixty-eight to eighty-nine. In 1953, only 4 out of 271 institutions with a general faculty organization limited membership to full professors (compared to 5 out of 195 in 1939).[35]

The University of Minnesota was an example of an institution that during this period expanded its governance system to make it more inclusive and, not coincidentally, saw its score on AAUP governance rankings go from 3 to 13. In 1954, after a lengthy period of consultation and deliberation, the university moved from a senate consisting of all full and associate professors that typically met only once a quarter to a representative senate that was elected by all the faculty, including instructors and assistant professors. However, while one senator was elected for every ten full and associate professors, one senator was elected for every forty assistant professors and instructors. The predominance of senior faculty carried over to membership on senate committees. In perhaps the only published study of its kind for this period, Ruth E. Eckert examined committee membership at the University of Minnesota between 1945 and 1958 and found that the percentage of full and associate professors actually increased in these years, from 74 percent to 80 percent, and on the most important senate committees, the percentage was considerably higher.[36] Although public discussions of governance issues still focused primarily on faculty relationships with presidents and trustees rather than on internal divisions within the faculty itself, in later years these divisions, especially over the appropriate role for what would later be called "contingent faculty," would gain greater prominence.

The responses to specific questions on the AAUP's 1953 survey make it clear that in some areas of academic decision making not much had changed since 1939. Whereas before the war, only 23 percent of institutions reporting indicated that they had a formal means by which faculty could communicate directly with trustees, this figure had risen to only 25 percent by 1953. Similarly, consultation with faculty on the formulation of the budget was reported at just 25 percent of institutions in 1939. By 1953, that number had risen by only 2 percent. According to survey results in 1939, department executives had been appointed without consultation with the faculty at 78 percent of schools. That number had gone down only slightly to 76 percent in 1953. The percentage of institutions reporting having a senate remained virtually the same, actually declining very slightly from 57 percent in 1939 to 56 percent in 1953.

In several important areas of institutional governance, however, the faculty did experience significant gains. Although the proportion of schools with senates did not increase, the nature of faculty representation on those senates that did exist changed substantially. Not only were more senates open to participation by junior faculty but more also provided for election rather than appointment of senators. In 1939, fewer than half (44 percent) of institutions responding indicated that some or all of the senators were chosen by election. By 1953, 71 percent of institutions that reported on this question indicated that at least some senators were elected.

Faculty participation in the selection of administrators also increased. Whereas only 28 percent of schools reporting in 1939 indicated that the faculty played any role in the selection of a new president, in 1953 that number had risen to 46 percent. A similar increase took place in faculty involvement in the selection of deans. From 29 percent in 1939, the number of institutions reporting such involvement went up to 53 percent in 1953. Some type of formal consultation with faculty on appointments, promotions, and dismissals also increased from what it had been before the war, though the increase was not very large. In 1953, 17 percent of chapters reported that faculty had no role at all—down from 23 percent in 1939. Moreover, whereas in 1939 only 33 percent of institutions provided for formal faculty input beyond the role played by the department executive in hiring and promotion, in 1953, 39 percent of institutions allowed for such faculty input.

A comparison of the 1939 and 1953 survey results in one other area shows a dramatic change that had a potentially strongly positive impact on faculty participation in governance. Protections for academic freedom through the offering of formal contracts and the establishment of a tenure system are essential for an effective faculty role in institutional governance. Without such protections, intimidation or self-censorship can be serious obstacles to faculty participation in governance.[37] This has always been one of the reasons that participation in governance by faculty holding contingent appointments has been a controversial issue. In 1939, slightly more than half the 228 institutions responding to the AAUP survey indicated that their school did not offer formal contracts to faculty members. By 1953, in part because of the widespread adoption of the guidelines outlined in the 1940 *Statement of Principles on Academic Freedom and Tenure*, only 8 percent of institutions reported faculty working without formal contracts.

At the same time that tenure and formal contracts were being introduced to more and more institutions of higher education, the postwar period also witnessed the rise of McCarthyism in the United States. As historian Ellen Schrecker has shown, the postwar Red Scare resulted in serious limitations to academic freedom on American college campuses in the realm of political discourse, especially as it applied to extramural speech.[38] Even while this troubling development was taking place, often with the collaboration of faculty governance bodies, the change from what amounted to employment at will to a system with formal contracts and tenure did provide greater protections from administrative retaliation to faculty members who became involved in campus governance issues.

It is also significant that neither the 1939 nor the 1953 AAUP survey included a specific question about the role of the faculty in determining the curriculum. One possible reason for not including such a question is that faculty responsibility for this area of academic decision making had already become so well established by this time that Committee T did not find it necessary to inquire directly about the issue. The survey did, however, include a question as to whether the faculty had any legislative powers. If any such powers existed, they most likely would have been exercised in regard to curricular matters. Even in 1939, only 18 percent of respondents reported that faculty had no legislative authority at all. In 1953, that number had declined to 14 percent.

In reviewing the results of the AAUP's governance survey, Paul Ward, the chair of the AAUP's Committee T and a professor of philosophy at Syracuse University, expressed cautious optimism regarding the expansion of shared-governance practices in the immediate postwar period when he concluded: "The implication which the data force upon us is that the general picture, so far as faculty participation in the selection of institutional policies is concerned, is somewhat better; in some spots it is a little worse, but in other spots it is very much better. A slow but pervasive shift toward more consultation of the faculty by the administration is evidently in progress."[39] Developments over the next two decades would provide further evidence of continued progress.

The Formulation of the 1966 *Statement on Government*

As early as 1957, discussions had begun among leaders of some of the nation's most important higher education organizations about the possibility of developing a consensus statement of principles on the subject of college and university governance.[40] The AAUP itself, however, first proceeded unilaterally to draft its own updated statement, expanding upon the basic set of principles first developed by Committee T back in 1920 and then reaffirmed by the committee in 1937.[41] These brief earlier statements focused, in general terms, on the primary responsibility faculty should bear for a college o███████████████ tional policies and on the appropriateness of administrat███████████ faculty on such matters as academic appointments. In 1962███████████ cil of the AAUP adopted an extended policy statement titl███████████ *tion in College and University Government* that more fully elaborated on these themes.[42]

At almost the same time, John D. Millett, president of Miami University of Ohio, as well as of the State Universities Association (which soon merged with two other organizations to form the National Association of State Universities and Land-Grant Colleges), published *The Academic Community: An Essay on Organization.* The book was a forceful call for shared governance on American college and university campuses. Millett asserted his strong belief that "a college or university has little if any resemblance to the generalized conceptions of organization which may be applicable to certain types of governmental administrative agencies and certain types of business entities."[43] Instead of "being organized upon the principles of a hierarchy of authority," he argued, "our colleges and universities are organized internally upon the principle of a community of authority."[44] Although Millett expressed some reservations about the AAUP's statement of principles on governance, asserting that the AAUP approach at least implicitly accepted a hierarchical rather than cooperative

conception of authority by focusing solely on the faculty role in academic decision making, he supported a formal advisory role for faculty in such matters as
the selection of a president, tenure and promotion decisions, and the formulation of a budget.[45]

Staff members in the national office of the AAUP read Millett's book "with
enthusiasm." An exchange of communications between AAUP leaders and
Millett subsequently resulted in the holding of a joint session in April 1963 of
the Commission on Administrative Affairs of the American Council on Education (ACE), which Millett chaired, and Committee T of the AAUP. At that
meeting, Millett raised the possibility of the two organizations formulating a
joint statement dealing not only with the role of faculties in institutional governance but also with the functions of trustees and central administrations.[46]
Negotiations between representatives of the AAUP and the ACE over drafting a statement proved lengthy and, at times, difficult. Following a suggestion
from ACE president Logan Wilson, who twenty years earlier had written the
first comprehensive sociological study of the American professoriate, the discussions were expanded in 1964 to include representatives from the Association
of Governing Boards of Universities and Colleges (AGB).[47]

The *Statement on Government of Colleges and Universities* that was finally
completed in 1966 in many respects used the 1962 AAUP statement of governance principles as a jumping-off point, even though many of the members of
the ACE's Commission on Administrative Affairs initially voiced serious concerns about giving their sanction to a statement that seemed to affirm a great
deal of faculty responsibility for most aspects of institutional governance.[48] In
the end, however, sufficient common ground was reached by all the parties to
the negotiation to allow for the drafting of a joint statement and for the ACE
and AGB officially to state that each organization "recognizes the statement as
a significant step forward in the clarification of the respective roles of governing boards, faculties, and administrations" and, therefore, "commends it" to
members. The AAUP council officially adopted the statement as policy.[49]

The joint *Statement on Government* begins with an acknowledgment that
"legislative and executive governmental authorities" were taking on an increased
role in "the making of important decisions in academic policy" by virtue of
their control over much of the funding for public colleges and universities. The
statement contends that this development made it all the more important for
the campus community to develop "its own generally unified view" in responding to these external "voices and forces." The 1962 AAUP policy statement on
governance acknowledged the "broad legal powers" of "lay governing boards"
and referred briefly to "the principle of joint responsibility of faculties, administrators, and governing boards." However, the earlier AAUP statement had
focused primarily on the responsibilities of the faculty in the making of aca-

demic policy based on their "particular competence" in educational matters. The 1966 *Statement*, in contrast, puts far more emphasis on "joint effort" and "joint action" and the "inescapable interdependence among governing board, administration, faculty, students, and others," while emphasizing the need for "communication" between and among these groups. *belongs 6 faculty!*

In the area of "general educational policy"—that is, the establishment of "the objectives of an institution and the nature, range, and pace of its efforts"— the statement observes that the interests of trustees, administrators, and faculty "all are coordinate and related" and warns that "unilateral effort can lead to confusion or conflict." Similarly, the statement calls for "joint effort" in the areas of long-range planning, including the development of physical facilities and budgeting, while still recognizing the special responsibility of the governing board for the financial well-being of the institution.[50] In a similar fashion, the document addresses the issue of the selection of administrative officers: "Joint effort of a most critical kind must be taken when an institution chooses a new president. The selection of a chief administrative officer should follow upon a cooperative search by the governing board and the faculty. . . . The president should have the confidence of the board and the faculty." The statement also declares that the "selection of academic deans and other chief academic officers," while the responsibility of the president, should be made "with the advice of, and in consultation with, the appropriate faculty." *too weak!!*

The selection of department heads or chairs is dealt with somewhat differently, as these administrative officers are most closely involved in the day-to-day lives of faculty members and are often considered more "the chief representative of the department" than members of the central administration. In a private communication to his fellow Committee T members, committee chair Ralph Brown expressed his "frank astonishment" that the AGB and ACE were willing to accept a statement that declared that chairs or heads "should be selected either by departmental election or by appointment following consultation with members of the department and of related departments" and that such "appointments should normally be in conformity with department members' judgment."[51] *always! usually!* *only in the sense that the chair represents the will of the dept.!! of defined & expected by the faculty!*

Unlike the earlier AAUP statement, the 1966 *Statement*, in addition to including a separate section on the responsibilities of the governing board, also contains a separate section on the responsibilities of the president, who is recognized as providing critical "institutional leadership" while serving as the "chief planning officer." The statement notes that a president requires the "general support of board and faculty" but acknowledges that a "president must at times, with or without support, infuse new life into a department; relatedly, the president may at times be required, working within the concept of tenure, to solve problems of obsolescence."

X X!

Even with such acknowledgments of board and presidential authority, the statement still closely paralleled the earlier AAUP position on what were considered faculty responsibilities: "The faculty has primary responsibility for such fundamental areas as curriculum, subject matter and methods of instruction, research, faculty status, and those aspects of student life which relate to the educational process. On these matters the power of review or final decision lodged in the governing board or delegated by it to the president should be exercised adversely only in exceptional circumstances, and for reasons communicated to the faculty."

The statement goes on to elaborate more fully on what is meant by primary responsibility in the area of faculty status, stating that "this area includes appointments, reappointments, decisions not to reappoint, promotions, the granting of tenure, and dismissal." The faculty's claim to authority in these areas, as in other educational matters, "is based upon the fact that its judgment is central to general educational policy" and because "scholars in a particular field or activity have the chief competence for judging the work of their colleagues." Expertise, in other words, is the basis for the assignment of primary responsibility to the faculty in certain areas of institutional governance. The statement reaffirms the meaning of "primary responsibility" by repeating the admonition that the "governing board and president should, on questions of faculty status, as in other matters where faculty has primary responsibility, concur with the faculty judgment except in rare circumstances and for compelling reasons which should be stated in detail."

The 1966 *Statement* also includes a brief section on "student status." A new surge of campus activism among college students was well under way as the AAUP, ACE, and AGB worked to complete their joint statement on governance, so it was hard to completely ignore the issue of student participation. However, the statement recognizes that the "obstacles to such participation are large and should not be minimized." Those obstacles include the "inexperience" of students and their "transitory status which means that present action does not carry with it subsequent responsibility, and the inescapable fact that the other components of the institution are in a position of judgment over" them. As a consequence, the statement contains only a limited recommendation regarding students: "Ways should be found to permit significant student participation within the limits of attainable effectiveness."

Student activism and demands for greater involvement in college and university governance increased in the years immediately following the issuance of the 1966 *Statement on Government.* The AAUP's Committee T itself responded by issuing in 1970 a statement titled *Student Participation in College and University Government* that supported granting students a "share in the exercise of responsible authority on campus." The statement elaborated on this principle: "Student involvement in institutional government may include membership—voting and nonvoting—on departmental committees, on college or division councils and committees, or on the university senate or any other principal legislative body and its committees." Moreover, the AAUP's Committee T also called for students to be "consulted where feasible" in the selection of administrators and faculty.[52]

Many colleges and universities responded to the student protests and demands for greater participation in institutional governance in the late 1960s and early 1970s by establishing university senates with substantial student representation, either to replace or, more frequently, to complement existing faculty senates. Both Columbia and Cornell, for example, created university senates at this time and, in the case of Cornell, allotted equal representation to students and faculty. In the large majority of cases, however, these broadly based campus senates, which often included representatives of the staff and administration, as well as faculty and students, exercised relatively little power.[53] Colleges and universities also responded to student demands for a voice in governance by including students, along with faculty, on newly established budget and planning committees. Princeton, for example, created a sixteen-member Committee on Priorities in 1969 that had six students and six faculty members, as well as four administrators.[54] Similarly, the Teachers College of Columbia University responded to student unrest in 1972 by establishing a forty-member College Policy Council that included nine students, along with eighteen faculty members and ten administrators.[55]

By 1973, the Carnegie Commission on Higher Education was referring to the "student shock" to the "governance of higher education" and observed that more students were sitting on more committees than ever before, a development for which the commission expressed general support. However, the commission also concluded that students in the United States, in spite of their "vociferous" protests and demonstrations, had actually achieved quite limited influence in American colleges and universities, especially in comparison to students in other parts of the world, and that faculty generally remained dubious about the advisability of allowing students to play a significant role in institutional decision making.[56] Even at the University of California, Berkeley, which many regarded as the fount of student activism, the faculty proved to be less willing than the administration to concede to students a significant role in institutional governance.[57] Similarly, at the University of Wisconsin, Madison, which was also a hotbed of student protest, the faculty rejected student representation in the senate that was established in place of the town meeting form of governance that had existed until 1970.[58]

Although the 1966 *Statement on Government* was only a broad statement of principles and contained very little in the way of specific guidance on how those principles ought to be embodied in particular institutional structures, it nevertheless represented a milestone in the history of college and university governance in the United States. The ACE and AGB may not have expressly adopted the statement as "policy," but their cooperation with the AAUP in formulating the statement and their willingness to commend it to their members reflected a greater degree of consensus on the desirability of entrusting faculty with "primary responsibility" for decision making about academic matters than had ever previously existed.

In the years immediately following the publication of the 1966 *Statement*, a profusion of studies on the subject of college and university governance began to appear, most placing a particular emphasis on the growing role played by faculty in institutional decision making and accepting the joint statement as a basic starting point for any further discussion.[59] Thus, for example, in its 1973 special report on governance, the Carnegie Commission on Higher Education, which was chaired by former University of California president Clark Kerr and included among its members William Friday, president of the University of North Carolina; Theodore Hesburgh, president of the University of Notre Dame; and Nathan Pusey, former president of Harvard, declared: "It is our view that faculties in most, if not all, institutions should have approximately the level of authority recommended by the American Association of University Professors. We give this a high level of priority."[60] In the late 1960s, many individual colleges and universities incorporated references to the statement in their faculty handbooks or other official institutional policies, and both the Board of Trustees of the California State Colleges and the Board of Governors of State Colleges and Universities in Illinois formally recognized the statement as providing guiding principles for institutional governance in their systems.[61]

1970 AAUP Survey of Governance Practices

Another extensive survey of governance practices at the nation's colleges and universities conducted by the AAUP in 1969–70 provided further evidence of what might be described as the slow but continuing expansion of faculty authority in institutional decision making over the previous two decades. Nearly one thousand institutions responded to what was then by far the broadest survey of governance practices ever undertaken in the United States. In contrast to previous surveys in which AAUP chapter leaders were solely responsible for reporting on conditions at their institutions, the AAUP's Committee T encouraged administrations and AAUP chapters to collaborate on preparing a joint response to a list of more than thirty questions. Such joint responses were received from almost two-thirds of the colleges and universities included in the final results. Nearly 20 percent of the institutions responding had replies from only administrators, and in another 10 percent replies came from only chapter leaders.[62]

The format and wording of the 1970 survey were different from the previous two AAUP governance surveys, and no attempt was made to replicate the faculty self-government score for each institution.[63] Nor did the survey include a question asking respondents if they thought the faculty's role in decision making was increasing or decreasing. Compared to the previous AAUP governance survey, the 1970 sample was three times as large and therefore included a much greater diversity of institutions, in large part because AAUP membership had spread to so many more schools. Consequently, direct comparisons to the 1953 survey data are not possible for many aspects of governance, and, as before, the results for many of the questions indicate the subjective judgments of those responding rather than a wholly objective description of the reality of faculty authority. Nevertheless, some comparisons can still be made between the 1953 and 1970 survey results, and they indicate continued growth in faculty influence over these years. Respondents were asked to rate the degree of faculty authority on various items in one of five categories: determination, joint action (formal), consultation (informal), discussion, or none. It was a reflection of how far the AAUP had come since its founding in 1915 on the issue of who should be eligible for inclusion in governance that the instructions for the survey contained this explanatory note: "The Full Franchise. It should be emphasized that in all elections of representatives or for a faculty vote on a particular issue the newest instructor or assistant professor must have his say and vote. This may run contrary to well-established traditions in several places where departmental matters are determined only by full professors or tenured professors. This may be judged good practice, but it is not full faculty participation."[64]

In four particular areas of decision making, the selection of a president, deans, department chairs or heads, and senate committee members, it is possible to compare the 1953 and 1970 survey results regarding the extent to which faculty members were completely excluded from any role in decision making. In 1953, 49 percent of institutions reporting indicated that faculty members were not consulted in the selection of a new president; by 1970, only 33 percent of responses indicated such a lack of consultation. In the selection of deans, there was also a decline in the percentage reporting no faculty role, although the drop was only from 36 to 31 percent. In the selection of department heads or chairs, while in 1953 40 percent of institutions reported faculty members playing no role, in 1970, just 26 percent of respondents indicated a total lack of faculty involvement. Similarly, in the choice of representatives to serve on institution-wide governance committees, whereas in 1953 30 percent of schools reported faculty members being totally excluded from the selection process, in 1970 that number had fallen to 16 percent.

In other areas of decision making covered in the 1970 survey—with the important exception of matters relating to budgetary planning and salary determination—the total exclusion of faculty from any role had become relatively rare. However, the survey authors observed that "on average, faculty participation in college and university government in the United States is viewed by faculties and administrations as being at the level of CONSULTATION, a far cry from the ideals envisaged by the 1966 *Statement on Government of Colleges and Universities*."[65] Yet in several areas of greatest concern to faculty—control of the curriculum and degree requirements and evaluation of student performance—the average of all responses indicated that faculty either exercised the power to determine the outcome or had joint responsibility with the administration. In addition, the survey results indicated that faculty had come to enjoy significant influence on departmental governance, which had the most direct bearing on the daily lives of faculty members. Even though the majority of respondents indicated that the faculty role in the selection of a head or chair was limited to discussion or consultation rather than determination or joint action, with respect to specifying what departmental committees should exist and choosing their members, the average response was that faculty participation was either determinative or involved joint action.

In sum, the survey provided clear evidence that the faculty role in institutional governance had increased over the previous two decades, even if that increase was not dramatic. The degree of faculty responsibility for educational matters still varied considerably by type of institution, and rarely, in spite of claims by some to the contrary, did faculty actually enjoy determinative authority over institutional policies.[66] Nevertheless, the change in governance practices over the previous one hundred years had been considerable.

Newly Emerging Challenges to Shared Governance

Many of the studies of the current state of college and university governance that appeared in the late 1960s and early 1970s viewed the principles set forth in the 1966 *Statement on Government* as having become the normative standard for American colleges and universities, but they also identified several newly emerging challenges to the practices of shared governance. The 1966 *Statement* was itself predicated on the notion that "legislative and executive governmental authorities" had come to play an increasing role in making academic policy and that the rise of multicampus systems had also brought new challenges to the system of shared governance that had developed within the framework of the individual campus.

Not long after the publication of the 1966 *Statement*, the Carnegie Commission on Higher Education sponsored an extensive study of the governance issues stemming from the rapid rise in the 1960s of multicampus systems.[67] By 1968, 40 percent of all students were enrolled in colleges and universities that were part of multicampus systems, and for public institutions the figure was over 50 percent. Although some multicampus systems had been in existence for many years, Eugene Lee and Frank Bowen, the authors of the Carnegie Commission report, observed that "not until the 1960s did the multicampus university as an educational and organizational concept truly come of age."[68] In a subsequent report published in 1973, the Carnegie Commission declared: "External authorities are exercising more and more authority over higher education, and institutional independence has been declining. The greatest shift of power in recent years has taken place not inside the campus, but in the transfer of authority from the campus to outside agencies."[69] In addition to pressures stemming from increased governmental attention to the day-to-day operations of higher education, the growth of multicampus systems lessened the authority of individual campus executives, who now had to report to a system-wide chancellor or president. This development also meant that faculty senates had less influence, as planning and other key decisions were shifted to a central authority in which the faculty voice was either nonexistent or less effective.[70]

Lee and Bowen examined nine multicampus systems: the Universities of California, Illinois, Missouri, North Carolina, Texas, and Wisconsin; the City University of New York (CUNY); and the two largest systems in the country, the State University of New York (SUNY) and the California State Colleges (now California State University). Only two of these, the Universities of California and Wisconsin, had well-established system-wide faculty governance bodies. Two others, the California State Colleges and SUNY, had system-wide faculty organizations that had been in existence for several years, and two others, CUNY and the University of North Carolina, had very recently established such systems. The University of Illinois had a faculty body to coordinate the work of the separate campus senates, but no system-wide faculty senate. The Universities of Missouri and Texas had no system-wide faculty organizations of any kind.[71]

Most commentators at the time agreed with the assessment of an American Association for Higher Education–National Education Association (AAHE-NEA) task force on governance that faculty governance institutions had not kept up with the growth of multicampus systems and that this worked to the detriment of faculty influence on college and university decision making.[72] Lee and Bowen, however, offered an interesting alternative perspective. While acknowledging that the faculty role in system-wide governance remained "uncertain," they claimed that a clear pattern had developed in which the flagship or dominant campus in a system set the standard for such policies as appointment and promotion that came to be followed throughout the system. The flagship campuses, such as the University of California at Berkeley and the University of Wisconsin at Madison, typically were institutions where professionalized faculty had long before established norms of shared governance. Thus, according to Lee and Bowen, campuses that were being incorporated into broader systems and that may not have previously had "a history of faculty government are all instituting it, most often with the help and encouragement of the system administration and systemwide faculty organization."[73]

A similar argument, however, could be made with regard to colleges and universities that were not part of a larger system but still increasingly sought to emulate more prestigious institutions in order to compete for students and funding. Richard Freeland observed a pattern of such attempts to emulate more prestigious institutions in his study of the postwar development of eight quite different colleges and universities in Massachusetts, all of which except one were not part of multicampus systems.[74] J. Victor Baldridge's case study of governance at New York University (NYU) in the 1960s also revealed a comparable effort on the part of the NYU administration to upgrade the status of the institution by increasing admission standards and raising the quality of the faculty in order to compete more effectively with the expanding and much less expensive public institutions of higher education in New York. Baldridge observed that, although the transformation of NYU was initially driven by the administration—against the strong opposition of significant sectors of the faculty—the end result was the development of a more professional faculty that was insistent on a greater role in governance than faculty had ever previously enjoyed at NYU.[75]

Lee and Bowen also asserted that the decisions that were moving away from the individual campus to a central system administration were generally in "areas where the faculty has never had final authority, for example, in the establishment or location of a new school or campus," so that the net effect of the rise of multicampus systems had been that faculty authority had been "either retained or enhanced."[76] Nevertheless, Lee and Bowen, writing in 1971, recognized that with the growth of very large multicampus systems of higher education, external governmental bodies—coordinating agencies, legislatures, and governors—were "assuming a far more active interest in major educational policy than in the past. This trend poses new challenges to faculty government and casts doubt on the ability of existing structures to respond."[77]

The growing challenge to the practices of shared governance posed by the rise of multicampus systems was evidenced in two governance investigations conducted by the AAUP's Committee T in the early 1970s that involved problematic relations between a central administration and the faculty of a particular campus within a larger system. In contrast to Committee A investigations into possible violations of the 1940 *Statement of Principles on Academic Freedom and Tenure*, which were fairly frequent, the AAUP only rarely made use of the procedures that were established in the late 1950s for initiating formal governance investigations. So it is significant that two of the limited number of investigations that did take place involved issues arising in the governance of multicampus systems.

Long Island University (LIU) was founded in 1926 and opened its doors in Brooklyn the following year. By the late 1960s, now with four separate major campuses, LIU had become the fastest-growing private university in the United States, having a total enrollment of over twenty-one thousand. Not until 1964, however, did the board of trustees establish a strong central administration and appoint a chancellor to oversee the system. Although each individual campus had developed a tradition of effective faculty governance with active senates, tensions between faculty members and the central administration developed once the new governance structure was established. This was especially the case between the Brooklyn Center and Chancellor R. Gordon Hoxie. First, against the wishes of a clear majority of the faculty, Hoxie dismissed the Brooklyn Center's provost and then, in collaboration with the board of trustees, but without any faculty consultation, sought to sell the Brooklyn Center to the City University of New York. The sale ultimately fell through, and Hoxie would soon thereafter leave office. However, continuing complaints from faculty members about the university's new governance structure and the "lack of faculty participation in the appointment of administrators, the appointment and removal of department chairmen" as well as "the lack of a faculty voice in the allocation of University resources," and the question of whether it was "the prerogative of the Board of Trustees to dispose of a University center without adequate prior consultation of the faculty and student body" led to an AAUP investigation and subsequent publication of a report in 1971.[78]

Following the departure of Chancellor Hoxie and the initiation of the AAUP investigation, new university statutes were adopted with "substantial consultation and participation by the faculty." These included provisions that made the president of the university senate and the chair of each of the campus senates ex officio members of the chancellor's cabinet, as well as more explicit guidelines for faculty consultation in the appointment of department chairs. Nevertheless, the AAUP investigating committee concluded that in general, "it appears that the [University] Senate has not functioned actively or effectively, and indeed for a protracted time was unable to muster a quorum, perhaps because a large portion of its membership find it extremely inconvenient to attend meetings not held on their own campus."[79] Moreover, the committee observed: "Outside consultants, accrediting bodies, the Board of Trustees, and the central administration of the University have tended to favor centralization. . . . The faculty and local administrative officers of each campus have tended to favor a high degree of autonomy, maintaining that the distinct characteristics and role of each center require separate treatment."[80] In spite of what seemed to be an improved situation at the time of the report's publication, the situation at Long Island University demonstrated the potential challenges to faculty authority that were a product of the expansion of central administrative control in rapidly growing multicampus systems.

In 1973, the AAUP conducted another governance investigation involving issues stemming from tensions between an individual campus, the University of Texas at El Paso (UTEP), and the central administration of a multicampus system.[81] UTEP was founded in 1914 as the Texas School of Mines and Metallurgy and since its creation had been part of the University of Texas. By the early 1970s, UTEP had an enrollment of approximately eleven thousand students, over one-third of whom were Hispanic, and four hundred faculty members. The trigger for the AAUP governance investigation was the appointment in 1972 by the system chancellor and board of regents of a new president for the El Paso campus without any consultation with the UTEP faculty. The appointment of Arleigh B. Templeton followed several other high-level administrative appointments at UTEP the year before without faculty consultation and, according to local faculty members, at the instigation of the system's central administration. Ironically, Logan Wilson, who was instrumental in the drafting of the 1966 *Statement on Government*, had earlier served as chancellor of the system, and as recently as 1967 a professor at UTEP had published an article discussing the positive potential for faculty governance in the newly expanding statewide "super-boards" and coordinating agencies that were being created across the country.[82] The University of Texas board of regents' own standing rules at the time of the controversial appointments actually endorsed "the principle of reasonable faculty and student consultation in the selection of administrative officers." However, the rules did not require such consultation and made no explicit provision for institutional representation in the composition of search committees for campus presidents. While other factors, including highly publicized recent protests by Chicano students who were increasingly pressing for greater attention to their concerns, also entered into the situation at UTEP—and were cited by the system leaders as the reason for a precipitate appointment of a new president—the increasing power of the central administration at the expense of the individual institutions in the multicampus University of Texas system contributed significantly to the problems at the El Paso campus.[83] The situations that arose at both LIU and UTEP were thus early indications of the way the growth of multicampus systems posed new threats to the recently developed practices of shared governance.

Another development that gained force in the early 1970s and threatened to undermine the consensus that had developed in the 1960s around the model of shared governance was the change in the nation's economic situation. One of the factors that had contributed to the growth of faculty influence in institutional decision making in the postwar decades was the high demand for qualified faculty made possible by a strong national economy and a well-funded and rapidly expanding system of higher education. Professors gained leverage not only in pressing their demands for better salaries and fringe benefits, which rose more significantly in the 1950s and 1960s than at any other time in the history of American higher education, but also in asserting their demands for professional autonomy and self-government.[84]

However, the onset of inflation in the late 1960s, followed by the appearance of the new phenomenon of "stagflation" in the 1970s, led the Carnegie Commission on Higher Education in 1973 to observe that the "Golden Age" for American higher education, which it described as lasting from 1945 to 1965, had given way to a "Time of Troubles." Instead of enjoying the unique prosperity of the immediate postwar decades, American colleges and universities had returned to "the genteel poverty" they had known through much of their history.[85] As early as 1971, Earl Cheit had titled another Carnegie Commission report *The New Depression in Higher Education*. The problem, according to Cheit, was not so much an absolute reduction in revenues for colleges and universities but the developing gap between the rate of growth in expenditures per student—which had risen at an annual average of 8 percent between 1959 and 1969—and the rate of growth in revenues, which had begun to slow markedly after 1967.[86]

The consequences for faculty of the new economic circumstances included not only a decade of relative decline in economic status, as salaries failed to keep up with inflation and the supply of qualified faculty began to outpace the demand,[87] but also new efforts by external governing bodies and campus administrations to cut costs in ways that challenged faculty responsibility for the determination of educational policies.

A poll of 599 chairs of governing boards conducted for the AGB annual meeting in 1974 revealed a growing concern among governing board members that too much authority had been ceded to faculty. There was "widespread agreement" among those polled that "trustees should assume a bigger role in handling such issues as faculty workload, tenure, and even the content of the curriculum." As one trustee put it: "If we are to maintain the vitality of institutions of higher education—someone must be accountable in the basic areas of academic substance and academic methods. The trustees themselves must either exact this accountability or see to it that somebody else does and reports to them."[88]

By the early 1970s, more than eight hundred colleges and universities were participating in the National Center for Higher Education Management Systems, which the federal Department of Health, Education, and Welfare had helped to establish in the late 1960s. Among other projects, the center sought to develop "a series of output measures" and methods of analyzing "faculty activity," which, according to William H. Danforth, then chancellor of Washington University in Saint Louis, not only threatened to "put in quantitative form areas of human activity that we do not understand fully or that may be inherently unquantifiable," but also might cause "the locus of decision making" being "pushed away from individual campuses, further from the faculty and campus-based administrators."[89]

One notable development that would in coming decades become what Jack Schuster and Martin Finkelstein describe as "the single most dramatic redeployment of academic staff" was the growing use of part-time non-tenure-track faculty who bore little if any responsibility for institutional governance. While the percentage of all faculty holding part-time appointments had declined during the 1960s, between 1970 and 1975, the increase in part-time appointments rose four times faster than the increase in full-time appointments.[90] Economic concerns also accelerated the trend toward centralization of authority as state coordinating agencies and system-wide governing bodies sought to achieve greater efficiencies in the use of more limited resources. In order to improve "productivity," governing boards in both multicampus and single- campus institutions became more involved in such matters as determining curricular offerings and teaching loads. These new challenges to faculty governance and to the quality and multipurpose nature of American higher education would become even more pronounced in later years and are discussed more fully in the next chapter.

The Rise of Faculty Unionism

The changing economic context was also an important factor contributing to another development, the growth of faculty unionism, which rapidly gained momentum in some sectors of higher education in the late 1960s and early 1970s. The sudden emergence of faculty collective bargaining posed difficult questions for those advocating the model of shared governance that had guided the formulation of the 1966 *Statement on Government*. These years witnessed intense debates within academia, and especially within the AAUP, over the degree to which collective bargaining was compatible with the notion of professionalism that had long provided the foundation for faculty claims to a key role in institutional governance. These debates raised the question of whether faculty senates, which ideally operated within a context of joint faculty-administration responsibility for institutional policies, could successfully coexist with faculty unions, which typically adopted a more adversarial approach to relations with administrators and governing boards. One contemporary supporter of faculty unionization, one-time candidate for the American Federation of Teachers (AFT) presidency Myron Lieberman, in fact, questioned the legitimacy of faculty senates and the ideal of professionalism that was central to the notion of shared governance. He argued that faculty senates were akin to company unions, which had been outlawed by the 1935 National Labor Relations Act because of their lack of independence, close association with management, and consequent inability effectively to represent the interests of employees. Lieberman thus argued that only independent unions had the means to protect faculty members' full range of interests and that the notion that senates could achieve the same results represented a naïve and illogical belief in the willingness of administrations voluntarily to accept faculty assertions of professional prerogatives.[91]

Before the mid-1960s, collective bargaining by unionized faculty was virtually unknown in American higher education. Although there had been some attempts at faculty unionization before the 1960s, the AFT achieved the first lasting organizing success at an American college or university in 1964, when it won the right to represent the faculty at Olympia College in the state of Washington.[92] While the AFT and the National Education Association (NEA) had some organizing successes immediately following the breakthrough at Olympia, at the end of 1967 only twenty-five campuses had unionized. By 1975, however, 430 campuses, representing more than 20 percent of all full-time faculty in the United States, had adopted collective bargaining.[93]

Faculties at different types of institutions responded quite differently to the prospect of unionization. Although very few of the nation's leading research universities or selective liberal arts colleges had unionized by the mid-1970s, unionism spread rapidly among the nation's public two-year institutions and, to a lesser extent, among public universities devoted more to teaching than to research. At this time, two-year colleges represented more than 60 percent of institutions—and 30 percent of all faculty members—engaging in collective bargaining, even though only 15 percent of all faculty members nationwide taught at two-year colleges.[94] Unionization remained rare at private institutions, especially since before 1970, the National Labor Relations Board had not considered private institutions of higher learning to be covered by federal labor law. At state institutions, which also were not covered by federal labor law, unionization was dependent on state enabling legislation that allowed public employees and, in particular, faculty, to engage in collective bargaining.

Because fewer than half the states in the country had such legislation as of 1975, faculty unionization was largely restricted to states such as Michigan, New Jersey, New York, and Pennsylvania, where unions in general were strong and exercised considerable political influence.[95]

Contemporary observers cited several factors they believed contributed to the rise of faculty unionism in this period. Most agreed that the worsening state of the nation's economy created economic pressures that spurred faculty to consider unionization as an option. Even prior to the economic downturn of the late 1960s, community college faculty, who were the most likely of all faculty members to opt for collective bargaining, had the lowest pay and fewest benefits and may, therefore, have seen unionization as the best means of improving their economic situation and gaining greater parity with their colleagues at four-year institutions.[96] Governance issues, however, also played a significant role in determining which faculties were most attracted to collective bargaining through union representation.[97] In fact, an American Association for Higher Education (AAHE) report on faculty discontent published in 1967—right at the beginning of the emergence of faculty unionism, but before economic problems had become acute across the country—found that "economic considerations" were "not of primary importance among the factors giving rise to faculty discontent." Rather, "the enhancement of the economic and social status of the professor" that had occurred in the 1950s and first half of the 1960s led to a situation of "rising expectations" and demands by faculty members for "the full prerogatives of professionalism," including "direct participation in the formulation of the policies and rules that govern the performance of their duties."[98] Community colleges and less prestigious four-year public universities may have been most likely to feel the immediate impact of the economic downturn that subsequently occurred in the late 1960s and early 1970s, but they were also the institutions furthest removed in practice from the shared governance model set forth in the 1966 *Statement on Government*. Faculty members at research universities typically played a greater role in institutional decision making, enjoyed considerably higher salaries, and were far less likely than their colleagues at two-year schools to see the need for new approaches to pressure administrations to recognize their professional claims to a role in governance or to improve salaries and ensure job security.[99]

The potential relationship between weak faculty governance and the appeal of unionization is indicated by developments at three of the institutions that were the subjects of the small number of AAUP governance investigations in this period. Monmouth College, Long Island University, and St. John's University had all turned to unionization by 1974. Monmouth, in fact, became, in 1971, the first private college in the country to adopt collective bargaining.[100] At several other institutions where frustrations about their lack of influence in institutional decision making led faculty to consider unionization, administrations sought to strengthen traditional faculty governance mechanisms on their campuses as a means of countering the appeal of collective bargaining.[101]

Faculty members at institutions that were part of multicampus systems in which decision-making authority was increasingly being centralized were also more likely to see unionization as a necessary means of responding to the new environment. Especially given the general weakness of existing system-wide faculty governance bodies at most institutions, many faculty members in multicampus systems saw centralized collective bargaining as the most effective way of protecting their interests. Thus, two of the largest systems in the country, the State University of New York and the City University of New York, were among the first major universities to adopt collective bargaining, and the California State Colleges system would follow a decade later.

The California State Colleges represent an interesting case study in the complex dynamic between the growing appeal of collective bargaining for faculty and the development of the ideal of shared governance expressed in the 1966 *Statement on Government*. In the mid-1960s, although California had not yet passed public-employee collective bargaining legislation, the AFT began to mount a serious campaign to win bargaining rights for the faculty of the eighteen campuses of the California State Colleges system. In a statewide vote in June 1967, a bare majority of 274 out of more than 5,000 voters opposed choosing the AFT as the faculty's exclusive bargaining agent. In the election, a majority of faculty at four of the six largest campuses in the system voted in favor of unionization.[102]

In response to the growing threat of faculty unionization, the board of trustees of the system later that year adopted a resolution declaring that it favored "the development of its institutional governance on the basis" of the 1966 *Statement on Government*. The resolution went on to state that "these principles support the continued growth, strengthening and development of the statewide and local senates" and that should such senates desire "to utilize some form of council for the purpose of exchanging views with the Chancellor and the Board of Trustees prior to the development of economic matters for submission to the Legislature, the Board of Trustees" would "cooperate with such a procedure." The board's resolution stated explicitly that it offered such support as an alternative to the possibility of unionization and affirmed its opposition to "the application of collective bargaining to the problems of governance of the colleges in economic and other matters."[103]

The AAUP praised the board's action as a "landmark" in the history of university governance in the United States. Just before the vote of the California State Colleges board on the resolution opposing collective bargaining and supporting the principles of the 1966 *Statement*, Bertram H. Davis, the AAUP's general secretary, had communicated to the board his "full agreement" with the "basic position that it is not desirable to order faculty-administration relationships on the basis of employee-employer patterns which have been developed to fit situations in industry." Instead, Davis argued that in "place of the adversary relationship which has been formalized in industry, a cooperative relationship built upon the principle of shared authority appears to us to be the proper basis for organizing faculty-administration relationships in higher education."[104] Several months earlier, in a memorandum distributed to all the faculty of the California State Colleges system, AAUP associate secretary Louis Joughin had expressed the AAUP's long-held view that a faculty member was not simply an "employee" but a professional with "wide managerial responsibility" whose "personal interests . . . at a good institution are often inextricably mixed with those of the members of the governing board, the administration, and the student body. All are mainly concerned with achieving the best possible operation of the educational process."[105]

At almost the same time that the question of collective bargaining was being addressed in the California State Colleges system, a task force created by the American Association for Higher Education, a department of the NEA, published a major policy statement on the issue. Headed by Arnold R. Weber, then a professor of industrial relations at the University of Chicago who would go on to become president of the University of Colorado and later of Northwestern University, the task force argued that a system of "shared authority" utilizing an academic senate or other representative faculty bodies was the best means of addressing the governance problems of colleges and universities. Weber and his colleagues also shared the AAUP's view that in developing "any scheme of campus governance," a professor's identity as a "professional," not as an "employee," should be "preeminent." The AAHE report, however, affirmed its support for the right of faculty members to unionize without fear of reprisal and acknowledged that some colleges and universities were so lacking in meaningful avenues for faculty participation in governance that unionization might be a necessary alternative.[106] While slower than the AFT to make a full commitment to organizing higher education faculty, the NEA would very soon move in that direction. The AAUP, in contrast, would undergo a major internal battle over the next several years about the appropriateness of collective bargaining for the professoriate before finally coming out clearly in support of unionization as an option for faculty.[107]

The AAUP's long-standing commitment to the view of faculty members as professionals rather than "employees" and its role in the development of the 1966 *Statement on Government*, which emphasized the need for cooperative relations between faculty, administrators, and governing boards, were the principal factors in its initial reluctance to support collective bargaining for faculty.

Although the AAUP had not ignored the economic concerns of faculty members and had in fact pioneered in the development of a comprehensive annual survey of faculty salaries, the organization's primary emphasis had always been on academic freedom and shared governance, concerns that the professional association had always argued were directly related to protecting the quality of American higher education and hence the common good. AAUP leaders' reservations about collective bargaining were also based on what they saw as threats to academic freedom posed by the idea of limiting faculty members to an exclusive bargaining agent and possibly compelling them either to join a union or pay agency fees. In addition, the idea of a faculty strike seemed to conflict with the AAUP's view of itself as advancing the common good rather than just the economic interests of faculty members.[108]

As collective bargaining took hold in some sectors of American higher education after the mid-1960s, the AAUP never issued a blanket condemnation of faculty unionism. Although initially very reluctant to join the AFT and the NEA in trying to organize faculty for the purpose of collective bargaining, the leadership of the AAUP recognized that in some extreme cases where faculty governance was virtually nonexistent, unionization might be the only means of establishing a faculty voice. Several factors, however, ultimately convinced the leadership of the AAUP to reverse its previous position generally opposing unionization for faculty members and to declare in 1971 that the organization "will pursue collective bargaining, as a major additional way of realizing the Association's goals in higher education."[109]

Undoubtedly a key consideration in the AAUP's change of position was the threat posed by the increasingly successful efforts of the AFT and the NEA to organize college and university faculty members. Not only did these efforts represent a challenge to the AAUP's traditional dominance in the field of higher education and, therefore, a threat to its membership base, but AAUP leaders also came to see a danger in standing by on the sidelines while collective bargaining for faculty members developed in ways that might prove inconsistent with AAUP principles. Some of the first contracts negotiated by the AFT and the NEA included provisions that ran directly counter to the principles and procedures set forth in the 1940 *Statement on Principles on Academic Freedom and Tenure* and also seemed to violate the guidelines laid out in the 1966 *Statement on Government*. For example, one such contract allowed for tenure decisions to be made by administrators without faculty consultation. Consequently, the AAUP's national council responded favorably to the argument that "there is a pressing need to develop a specialized model of collective bargaining for higher education rather than simply to follow the pattern set by unions in industry" and that to "the extent that AAUP is influential in the shaping of collective bargaining, the principles of academic freedom and tenure will not be negotiable, nor will the primary role of a college or university faculty in determining academic policy be undermined." The leadership of the AAUP had finally concluded that collective bargaining, when "properly used, is essentially another means to achieve" the AAUP's "longstanding programs" of enhancing "academic freedom and tenure . . . due process . . . and sound academic government."[110]

Writing in 1971, AAUP associate counsel and labor law professor Matthew Finkin could point to the collective bargaining agreement that had recently been negotiated by the St. John's University AAUP chapter as an example of the potential of collective bargaining to advance the AAUP's conception of shared governance. The dismissals of thirty-one faculty members in December 1965 had been the trigger for the AAUP to launch separate investigations into the state of academic freedom and shared governance at St. John's—the only time the AAUP had initiated such separate parallel investigations—as well as a decision by the Middle States Association of Colleges and Secondary Schools to issue St. John's a show-cause order as to why the institution's accreditation should not be revoked. These events made the subsequent developments at St. John's especially striking.[111]

Finkin noted that the union contract wholly incorporated "by reference the *Statement on Government*" and modified "existing university statutes by insuring faculty-elected committees in the academic departments and school- or college-wide committees to function in decisions on tenure and promotion." In addition, the agreement provided for "the nomination of academic deans by elected faculty search committees" and prohibited "the appointment of deans unacceptable to such committees." Unionization had thus brought to St. John's a far more robust form of faculty governance than had existed several years earlier when disgruntled faculty had sought an AAUP investigation of the institution.[112]

The collective bargaining agreement at St. John's also ensured the continuation of previously existing bodies of faculty governance and provided that any actions taken by those bodies did not subsequently modify stipulations contained in the union contract. AAUP leaders by the early 1970s had come to argue not only that unions and faculty senates could coexist on a campus but that a union could actually work to strengthen the authority of a senate in the area of educational policies, even as the union took responsibility for negotiating economic issues. Some referred to this division of responsibility as a "dual-track" system of bargaining.

During contract negotiations in 1972–73 at the City University of New York, for example, the faculty union, the Professional Staff Congress (PSC), sought to include a provision stating: "The rights, privileges, and responsibilities of the University Faculty Senate shall not be diminished during the term

of this Agreement." The union thereby sought to strengthen, or at least protect, the existing mechanisms of shared governance. It did not seek to do away
with the traditional means of faculty involvement in the determination of academic policies. However, the administration stoutly resisted the inclusion of
such a provision in the contract, even ignoring a fact finder's holding that governance procedures were part of "past practices" that could be included. In
spite of this failure, the PSC subsequently was able to cooperate with the senate
in getting the administration to roll back its attempt to establish tenure quotas
and also by requiring presidents who reversed a faculty personnel recommendation to provide reasons.[113]

The contract negotiated by the AAUP collective bargaining chapter at
Temple University in 1973 was another example of such a dual-track division of
responsibility. The contract included a provision that tenure policies could not
be changed without the concurrence of both the board of trustees and the
faculty senate. This provision gave the senate greater authority than it had
previously enjoyed.[114]

Such productive coexistence between senates and unions, however, was not
a foregone conclusion, and the claim that a clear division of responsibility between unions and senates was possible continued to be a matter of controversy.
Amid the debate over unionism within the AAUP, Queens College (a CUNY
campus) chapter president Marc Belth argued that strong senates allowed for
the creation of a "context within which the several differing conditions and
responsibilities of higher education are balanced against each other." The bal-
ancing made possible by the functioning of effective senates allowed a college
or university "to overcome the dangers attendant upon attempting to separate
the inseparable, the economic from all that is involved in the nurture of intelligence in those who learn and those who teach. To separate them is to destroy
one of them, usually the very reason for the University's existence."[115] Belth
was not alone in contending that unionization would inevitably result in the
decay of traditional faculty governance structures. Some administrators also
warned that if their faculties opted for unionization, traditional governance
mechanisms would have to be abandoned so as not to infringe on the exclusive
collective bargaining rights of the union.

In their 1975 study *Unions on Campus*, Frank Kemerer and J. Victor Baldridge argued that it was still too early in the history of faculty unionization to
render a definitive judgment on the possibilities for strong senates and faculty
unions to develop an effective reciprocal relationship. They observed that in
most cases where faculty had opted for collective bargaining, faculty governance bodies had previously been weak or even nonexistent, so there were
few examples to consider of how senate-union relations developed in a situation where faculty governance had already been a well-established tradition.

Although Kemerer and Baldridge predicted that as unions matured they were likely to expand the scope of issues they addressed, thereby rendering their relation to traditional governance structures "unstable," they still maintained that a dual-track system of bargaining held out the promise of maximizing the influence of faculty on institutional governance.[116]

The most immediate impact of collective bargaining on American colleges and universities, according to Kemerer and Baldridge, was not so much on governance as it related to the formulation of educational policies but on personnel procedures, especially appointment, dismissal, and determination of salary increases. They concluded: "*Faculty unions may help to raise standards in institutions where professional practices, peer judgments, and faculty rights have had little foothold.* Probably the most positive function of unions is supporting reasonable and fair personnel practices in institutions that have been weak in those areas"[117] (italics in original).

After the rapid spread of faculty unionism in the early 1970s, a number of developments (discussed in the next chapter) caused a noticeable slowdown in the rate of expansion of union membership. By the beginning of the twenty-first century, the proportion of all faculty members engaging in collective bargaining, which stood at around 20 percent in 1975, had increased only to 25 percent.[118] Nevertheless, the development of collective bargaining in American higher education would continue to have major ramifications for the state of institutional governance.

The State of Faculty Governance in the Mid-1970s

Even with the challenges to the practice of shared governance that had clearly emerged by the mid-1970s, American faculty exercised considerably greater influence at that time over institutional policy making and the appointment and dismissal of their colleagues than ever before. Faculty members at the nation's most respected institutions certainly enjoyed a larger role in institutional governance than did professors at less prestigious colleges and universities. However, the values of professionalism, including an insistence on a recognition of faculty expertise on academic matters, had spread widely throughout American higher education, and many colleges and universities that before World War Two had denied their faculties any meaningful role in institutional decision making had taken steps to reverse that situation.

In the postwar decades, American colleges and universities also achieved a level of distinction and global recognition for quality that far surpassed their status prior to World War Two. The preeminence of American higher education was certainly the result, in large part, of the availability of unmatched financial resources. In this period, no other country could come close to matching the prosperity of the American economy and the level of investment

Americans made in their institutions of higher learning. Financial resources alone, however, could not account for the prestige of American colleges and universities. The increasing professionalism of the faculty and the consequent growth of faculty involvement in the development of educational policies also contributed to the improved overall quality of American higher education. Not only did American universities become global leaders in many fields of research, but the standards for student learning were also raised throughout much of academia.

In coming decades, however, the challenges to the model of shared governance that had gained widespread support in the mid-1960s would increase. Economic pressures on American colleges and universities would intensify, while a market-based business model of management would gain even greater appeal with the general decline of the Great Society liberalism of the 1960s. The process of professionalization that had taken place since the nineteenth century among ever-widening circles of college and university faculty and had provided the foundation for an increased role for faculty members in institutional governance would itself be threatened by the beginning of the twenty-first century by a countertrend of deprofessionalization as more and more faculty members were relegated to contingent status. Only time would tell whether such challenges would result in the triumph of a new model of college and university governance and what effect these challenges might ultimately have on the quality of American higher education.

CHAPTER FIVE

Corporatization and the Challenges to Shared Governance, 1975–Present

By the mid-1970s the Golden Age for American higher education had clearly come to an end. Not only did government funding for public institutions continue to be problematic in subsequent years, but dismal projections for future enrollments seemed to be coming true when in 1975–76 the number of students in American colleges and universities actually fell by 175,000 from the previous year.[1] However, the last decades of the twentieth and the early years of the twenty-first centuries were marked not only by continuing economic challenges for American colleges and universities and troubling developments regarding the status of the academic profession but also by significant expansion in new directions of what was increasingly being referred to as the higher education "industry."

One significant development was the dramatic increase in the number of older "nontraditional" students, as higher education became increasingly important for success in the job market. Between 1970 and 2010, the number of students thirty-five years of age or older attending college full time increased by a factor of ten (the number enrolled in 2010 exceeding one million), while the number of such older students attending part time went up more than 400 percent, to nearly three million. Related to the growth in the demand for education by nontraditional students was the rapid rise of for-profit institutions, which catered especially to this segment of the higher education "market."[2] In 1980, for-profit colleges and universities enrolled a little more than one hundred thousand students. By 2010, enrollments exceeded two million. Attendance in two-year institutions also grew significantly, nearing eight million by 2010, so that in that year approximately 40 percent of all faculty members were employed at either for-profit or two-year colleges, two types of institutions in which faculty involvement in governance had always been most problematic.[3]

After the early 1980s, enrollments among students eighteen to twenty-four years of age also once again expanded considerably. Although the proportion of high school graduates going on to college, which reached 35 percent in 1969, actually declined slightly during the 1970s and early 1980s, the rate of college attendance since that time has substantially increased, so that by 2010 nearly one in two high school graduates (48 percent) enrolled in an institution of higher learning. In 2010, all together the nation's approximately 4,500 colleges and universities enrolled more than 21 million students, double the number enrolled in 1975.[4]

The number of instructional faculty members increased by an even larger percentage, reaching nearly 1.5 million by 2011. However, much of the increased demand for instructors was met by the hiring of part-time or full-time non-tenure-track faculty. Whereas in 1975 30 percent of all faculty members had part-time appointments, by 2011 51 percent were employed on a part-time basis.[5] Moreover, while full-time appointments off the tenure track were extremely rare in the Golden Age of academia (in 1969 constituting only 3 percent of all full-time appointments in universities), by the end of the first decade of the twenty-first century, among all degree-granting institutions, 39 percent of all full-time faculty members were in tenure-ineligible positions. When the increased use of graduate assistants for classroom instruction is also taken into consideration, more than three-quarters of all instructional staff members in 2011 had appointments off the tenure track and hence fewer protections of their academic freedom and, in most cases, less of a long-term identification with the institution at which they taught. This dramatic change in the nature of the academic profession would have major consequences for faculty involvement in governance.[6]

Although revenues for American colleges and universities grew substantially in the decades after 1975, reaching nearly half a trillion dollars in 2010 and thereby making higher education one of the most important sectors of the nation's economy, this statistic obscures significant economic problems that have continued to plague American institutions of higher learning since the early 1970s.[7] For public institutions, state support as a percentage of all revenues declined significantly as state spending on other budget items, such as health care and prisons, increasingly displaced spending on education. In 1975, spending on higher education nationwide represented 6.7 percent of all state appropriations. By 2000, that number had fallen to 4.5 percent. Even more significantly, student per capita funding in constant dollars declined by 26 percent between 1990 and 2010.[8] Public colleges and universities, consequently, became more dependent on tuition, research dollars, endowment income, and gifts. By 2010, tuition revenues for all public research institutions combined exceeded direct state support. This marked a dramatic change from even ten years earlier.[9] At some major state universities, such as the University of Virginia and the University of Michigan, state appropriations represented less than 10 percent of total revenues.[10] The decline in state support, however, was not generally accompanied by a reduced role for state authorities in efforts to impose external controls on the management of public colleges and universities.[11] As higher education increasingly came to be seen as a private investment rather than a public good, public institutions became ever more responsive to market forces, including students' "consumer" preferences and externally determined spending priorities, in order to bring in revenues.

The increasing power of market forces over colleges and universities in this era of financial constraints created a new situation that would be less favorable for faculty involvement in institutional decision making than was the environment created by the unprecedented growth in public support and resources for higher education of the postwar period. In times of expansion, when choices revolve around what programs to add or what additional faculty members to hire, faculties more readily play a significant role in curricular and personnel decisions than in times of financial stringency, when the issue is often what programs to cut or even which faculty members to let go.

In general, the uneven performance of the American economy since the 1970s, together with the rapid rise in the costs of higher education, placed serious pressures not only on public institutions but on private ones as well. For most institutions of higher learning, a variety of factors contributed to overall costs generally rising more quickly than revenues. These factors included the administrative expenses involved in complying with the increasing array of government regulations (what Howard Bowen refers to as "socially imposed costs"), growing investments in new and often very expensive technologies, and the costs of trying to attract students in an increasingly competitive marketplace, which often involved spending on activities and services that were not directly related to instruction or research.[12] Although faculty salaries, when adjusted for inflation, did not rise appreciably between 1971 and 2004, the substantial increase in noninstructional expenditures drove up the cost of a college education.[13] In addition, the heady optimism of the 1960s had led to the overexpansion of costly programs and capital construction, thus creating a financial legacy that became increasingly problematic in the following decades.[14] Ronald Ehrenberg has also highlighted the fact that nonprofit colleges and universities compete on the basis of quality rather than profit margin, so whatever revenues do become available tend to be spent, especially since faculty members who played an important role in the postwar system of shared governance have generally been focused on their institutions' academic and research priorities rather than on the fiscal bottom line.[15]

In the first years of the twenty-first century, American colleges and universities still retained the position of global preeminence they had achieved in the post–World War Two era. However, the country's entire system of higher education was confronted with an ongoing crisis of confidence, which was expressed in declining public support and increasing criticism of the cost of a college education. As a consequence, critics more forcefully called for new approaches to institutional governance and a more economical use of personnel—which often entailed the deprofessionalization of the professoriate—in order to put America's colleges and universities on a more sound "business basis."

Some recent survey evidence indicates that many full-time tenured and tenure-track faculty members believe that they continue to play a significant role in institutional decision making, especially in those areas, such as control over their own teaching and research and peer reviews of colleagues, where the primary responsibility of faculty had come to be widely recognized by the 1960s.[16] Moreover, the financial pressures of the last several decades have led to some innovative efforts to expand the role of the faculty in areas that had long been largely excluded from faculty influence, in particular by involving faculty in institutional decisions about budgets and priorities in a more meaningful way than had previously been common.

However, the growing deference to market forces, the increasing deprofessionalization of large sectors of the faculty, and mounting pressures from governing boards and legislatures for colleges and universities to use externally imposed metrics for assessing performance have resulted in an overall weakening of the practices of shared governance that had developed over the previous century. These trends threaten to undermine the academic quality of American higher education, as financial considerations increasingly override educational concerns. As higher education comes to be treated more as a private than as a public good, these developments also restrict the ability of colleges and universities to fulfill a broadly conceived democratic mission.

Experiments in Managerial Approaches, 1975–1985

Efforts to use the latest business-management techniques in the operation of colleges and universities go back at least to the beginning of the twentieth century, when Morris Cooke attempted to apply the principles of scientific management to higher education.[17] Yet the early 1970s marked a turning point in the scope and magnitude of such efforts. Inspired by federal and state government experiments in such highly touted but ultimately short-lived management fads as planning programming budgeting system (PPBS), management by objectives (MBO), and zero-base budgeting (ZBB), colleges and universities in the 1970s and early 1980s tried to borrow from government and business what seemed to be the most up-to-date methods to increase their "efficiency" in a time of budgetary constraints. In most cases, colleges and universities rather haltingly adopted these new management systems after these systems had already begun to be discredited in the private sector and in government. In subsequent years, other management experiments with acronyms such as TQM (total quality management), CQI (continuous quality improvement), and BPR (business process reengineering) would have their moment in the sun. Eventually, all of these elaborate but ephemeral management systems would practically disappear from the halls of academia, but two more general and less comprehensive approaches to management that emerged in this period did prove to have a lasting legacy.[18]

One lasting legacy of the growing acceptance of the need to be responsive to market forces of supply and demand led administrators increasingly to treat academic departments as "cost centers and revenue production units" within a system of "academic capitalism." The notion that every academic unit had to balance its expenditures with its own revenues—"every tub is on its own bottom"—was not usually applied universally within an institution. Nevertheless, even the partial adoption of such a responsibility-centered-budgeting (RCB) approach often posed a threat to traditional academic disciplines such as philosophy and literature, which frequently had difficulty using the prevailing quantitative metrics to demonstrate their cost-effectiveness. These approaches also weakened faculty control over educational matters at the departmental level, where financial considerations began to overshadow academic concerns.[19]

"Strategic planning" also developed as a less comprehensive and less well-defined approach to management than such systems as PPBS, MBO, or ZBB, but planning and the establishment of academic priorities became especially pressing issues as the economic context of higher education changed from an era of almost limitless expansion to one of budgetary constraints and the need for possible retrenchment—that is, the closing of programs and the termination of faculty appointments. Strategic planning thus came increasingly into prominence in the 1970s. While taking various forms, it then spread on college campuses in the following decade.

Emphasizing the importance of long-range planning and the setting of priorities, strategic planning was greatly influenced by George Keller's *Academic Strategy* (1983), which a *New York Times* poll found to be the most influential book on higher education in the 1980s.[20] Keller opened his book with what was becoming a familiar but nevertheless dramatic warning: "A specter is haunting higher education: the specter of decline and bankruptcy." Keller noted that some observers were predicting that "between 10 percent and 30 percent of America's 3,100 colleges and universities will close their doors or merge with other institutions by 1995." Keller described what he saw as a serious "leadership crisis" stemming from the "progressive breakdown of governance" in the postwar period that was associated with the rise of strong faculties and the consequent weakening of presidential powers. He argued that college and university governance had become too easily divorced from concerns about an institution's financial condition and future economic viability. In his view, academic matters such as curricular planning could no longer be considered in isolation from their economic impact. Keller criticized the ineffectiveness of senates and the increasing tendency of faculty members to focus on their own individual interests rather than the collective well-being of the institutions in which they worked. His basic premise was that "every major organization . . . must have a single authority, someone or some body of people authorized to initiate, plan, decide, manage, monitor, and punish its members."[21]

In language that was becoming commonplace among critics of the shared-governance practices that had gained a foothold in American colleges and universities in the 1950s and 1960s, Keller claimed that the AAUP's views on governance appeared "stuck in a historical freezer," inasmuch as they ignored the changes that were then occurring in higher education.[22] He argued that colleges and universities needed to respond in a more timely and effective manner to developments in the external environment, notably declining public support, and to market forces such as changes in student demand for certain curricula and campus amenities. One element of his proposed solution was to hold out as examples to be emulated those institutions where "administration is yielding to management."[23] In part, this meant accepting the notion that the persons best equipped to lead colleges and universities into a challenging future might be experts in management who did not necessarily have backgrounds in higher education.

Keller cited the experience of Wesleyan University in Connecticut as a model of what he believed transformative and business-savvy managerial leadership could accomplish. Wesleyan had long been among the nation's leading liberal arts colleges. During the 1960s, the institution had one of the lowest student-faculty ratios in the country, high faculty salaries, reportedly the largest per-student endowment of any college in the country, and a strong tradition of shared governance.[24] Yet, when Colin Campbell became president in 1970, Wesleyan was beginning to dip into the principal of its endowment for operating expenses and, according to Keller, faced an uncertain, even perilous, economic future. Campbell, who was only thirty-five years old when he became president, was trained as a lawyer and had worked at the American Stock Exchange before coming to Wesleyan in 1967 as executive vice president.[25] After becoming president, he quickly adopted cost-cutting measures that included raising the student-faculty ratio by reducing the number of programs and staff while at the same time seeking to increase the number of students and raising tuition to boost revenues. Keller asserted that "there was little readiness by the faculty to accept" Campbell's more "businesslike" approach to the management of the institution. The faculty, on the other hand, questioned the reasons for the school's financial difficulties and voted in 1978 for a "full and forthright accounting" to explain why Wesleyan's endowment between 1968 and 1978 had decreased by 37 percent (by nearly two-thirds in inflation-adjusted dollars). Some professors charged that the wealthy banker trustee who chaired the governing board's investment committee had mishandled the management of the endowment and engaged in a conflict of interest, since he was a director of the company whose subsidiary controlled Wesleyan's portfolio.[26]

The student government organization, as well as the faculty, expressed opposition to the five-year plan Campbell presented to the board of trustees in 1980.[27] Keller, on the other hand, approvingly quoted a Wesleyan vice president's explanation as to why the administration's plan for the institution's future was not submitted to the faculty for a formal vote: "Naturally we regretted not having faculty endorsement. But the situation is very serious, and we must move ahead. Anyway, ours by necessity is not a bottom-up planning process. It is a top-down process."[28] Keller credited Campbell with successfully putting Wesleyan on a sound financial footing and attracting more and better students to the campus, even if he did so in ways that ignored the college's tradition of shared governance.

While Keller was highly critical of traditional institutions for faculty involvement in governance, he contended that a new type of campus governance body, which would include some role for faculty and other campus constituencies, was needed to support presidential efforts to plan for the future. Although faculty senates, in his view, had become useless debating societies, he praised the establishment of what he called Joint Big Decisions Committees (JBDCs), which he described as "usually composed of selected senior faculty members and key administrators, with some junior faculty, students, or trustee members sitting in at some instances."[29] While an institution's president did not normally serve as a member, a JBDC was typically chaired by the school's chief academic officer, with its members selected by the president rather than elected by their peers. Of crucial importance to Keller, the deliberations of this new type of committee regarding the most important decisions affecting the future of the institution had to be "kept secret" and were intended to be strictly advisory to the president.

Both before and after the publication of Keller's book, a variety of colleges and universities experimented with some type of strategic planning, though not many institutions established JBDCs that were fully consistent with Keller's model. Some institutions, such as Princeton and Teachers College of Columbia University, had already begun to experiment in the late 1960s and early 1970s with priorities or budget committees that included students, faculty members, and administrators. These early efforts, however, were not so much a response to immediate economic pressures or the product of a fully developed institutional commitment to long-range planning as they were a response to student demands for a greater voice in institutional governance and to faculty desires to extend their governance role to nonacademic areas of institutional decision making. Although both Princeton and Teachers College had traditions of faculty control over academic matters, neither had an institution-wide senate when it established its variant of a JBDC. As at most other colleges and universities, the faculty at Princeton and Teachers College had historically played little role in budgetary decisions, so the establishment of new planning and priorities committees held out the promise of expanding the scope of shared governance.

At Princeton, an external review conducted in the late 1980s found that during the two decades after a priorities committee had been established in 1969 to make budgetary recommendations to the president, the body was widely regarded as having "enhanced the quality of budget decision making" at the university, while increasing the influence of faculty on the budgetary process. Faculty members held only six seats on the sixteen-person committee and were appointed by the provost, but because the faculty representatives were well regarded by their colleagues and the committee's recommendations were almost always accepted by the president, the committee won widespread support as having strengthened shared governance at Princeton.[30]

Another example of an institution at which the move toward a more formalized approach to planning actually led to an expanded role for faculty in institutional governance was Ohio University. Like Princeton and Teachers College, Ohio's first move toward involving various campus constituencies in planning and budgetary decisions was a response to student unrest and demonstrations leading to a campus strike in 1970, but a dramatic 30 percent decline in enrollments and revenues over the next several years led a new president, Charles J. Ping, to initiate a more thoroughgoing approach to planning and resource allocation. In 1977, the institution created a University Planning Advisory Council (UPAC) to advise the provost and president on the budget, staffing, and space allocation. The eighteen-member council was chaired by the provost and included the faculty senate's five-person executive committee and three other faculty members appointed by the provost, as well as three students, and a total of seven administrators. Although deliberations within the council remained confidential, its final recommendations were formally presented to the faculty, student, and administrative senates, so that the new body was closely linked to the existing governance structures. A study published in 1994 by the American Council on Education and written by Jack Schuster and others examined various campus efforts to establish mechanisms of "strategic governance" and concluded that UPAC allowed meaningful faculty input into budgetary and planning decisions for the first time in Ohio University's history and not only improved campus morale but also helped put the institution back on a sound financial and academic footing.[31]

While other schools also had at least some success during this period in establishing more meaningful mechanisms for involving faculty in budgetary planning and the setting of priorities, at many institutions such efforts were generally ineffective, even when they were introduced by presidents with great fanfare. For example, many faculty members came to see the College Policy Council established at Teachers College in 1972 as a threat to traditional faculty governance bodies, since faculty members comprised only a minority on the council, and the council was widely seen as simply rubber stamping decisions made by the administration. Schuster's study concluded that the council's impact on budgetary decisions and institutional planning was "minimal" at best. Sixteen years after the council's establishment, the body was disbanded.[32] Schuster and his colleagues also cited Northwestern University, Georgia Southern University, and the University of Montana as other examples of institutions at which the establishment of some variant of a JBDC had very little effect on actual planning efforts or on the allocation of resources.

Governance in a Time of Financial Crisis: CUNY and SUNY

On many campuses, when priorities had to be established and dwindling revenues allocated in response to immediately pressing economic problems, the practices of shared governance came under particular strain as administrations often acted unilaterally and hastily in ways that directly undercut the faculty's role in curricular and personnel decisions. The changed economic circumstances of the 1970s created particularly acute crises in the city and state of New York and, consequently, for the City University of New York (CUNY) and the State University of New York (SUNY), two of the nation's largest systems of higher education. The faculty at both institutions had also recently unionized. Although the governance situations at these schools may not have been typical for all of American higher education, many of the issues that arose during the crises at

CUNY and SUNY foreshadowed problems that would occur in the coming decades on many other campuses, both unionized and nonunionized.

Because CUNY was heavily dependent on funding from the municipal government of New York, the city's near financial collapse in the mid-1970s resulted in a drastic cut in the university's total revenues of almost 30 percent in inflation-adjusted dollars between 1974 and 1976. In the summer of 1976, the university responded by terminating the appointments of nearly one thousand full-time faculty members. During the course of the crisis, approximately five thousand part-time faculty members were also let go. Although none of those whose services were terminated was tenured, the nearly one thousand full-time faculty members who were released had already been given contracts for the coming academic year when they received only thirty days' notice that their contracts would not be honored. One immediate consequence of these staffing cuts was a drastic increase in class sizes and the curtailment of some academic programs.[33]

Key decisions about how to deal with the university's financial situation were made by the city's Board of Higher Education, which after July 1976 included the chair of CUNY's system-wide faculty senate as a nonvoting member. However, according to an investigation subsequently conducted by the AAUP, "faculty participation in all of the decisions of the central administration" during the crisis was at best "minimal."[34] Although the collective bargaining agreement with the faculty union, the Professional Staff Congress (which was then jointly affiliated with the American Federation of Teachers and the National Education Association) placed some constraints on the board's actions, the faculty was afforded virtually no opportunity to influence the way CUNY's central administration shaped its basic strategy in response to the fiscal crisis confronting the university.

The board granted to the presidents of each of the university's eighteen separate schools what the AAUP report described as "unreviewable administrative authority" to determine what constituted a "retrenchment unit" and how cuts were to be distributed among those units. Although the collective bargaining agreement guaranteed that terminations would be based on seniority and that the appointments of nontenured faculty members would be terminated before those of tenured faculty members, seniority was calculated within whatever the president defined as a retrenchment unit—a program, department, or college, for example. That power was critical in the ultimate determination of who was laid off on a given campus. One campus president acknowledged that under the guidelines established by the Board of Higher Education he could have used his authority to define retrenchment units as a means of radically reordering the institution's priorities and programs, even though he chose not to do so.[35] The AAUP investigation did not find that either the central administration or individual campus administrations actually used the financial crisis to restructure the university in any substantial way. Nevertheless, the basic decision to downsize CUNY took place in a way that involved little if any faculty involvement.

In certain respects, the situation that developed at SUNY at almost the same time that CUNY was going through its painful fiscal crisis initially appeared less dramatic. The cuts in state funding experienced by SUNY for 1976–77, which precipitated the administration's imposition of retrenchment, represented only 4 percent of SUNY's total budget, a far smaller percentage cut than the reductions suffered by CUNY as a result of decreases in city and state support. Terminations of faculty appointments on the grounds of retrenchment at SUNY's thirty-four campuses were also far fewer (165 by the administration's count) than the nearly one thousand layoffs of full-time faculty members at CUNY. Nevertheless, the events at SUNY posed an even greater challenge to the practices of shared governance. Not only were more than sixty tenured faculty members let go, but SUNY also underwent a more substantial reordering of academic priorities without meaningful faculty involvement than occurred at CUNY.[36]

As was the case at CUNY, SUNY's collective bargaining agreement with the faculty union, the United University Professions (UUP), that was in force at the time of the retrenchment sought to protect seniority rights and favored tenured over nontenured faculty members. However, it also ceded to the chancellor of the university, or to his designee, the authority to determine what constituted a retrenchment unit, thereby giving the administration virtually unfettered discretion in applying the rule of seniority. In anticipation of the need to make substantial cuts, Chancellor Ernest Boyer in 1975 issued guidelines that called upon each of the university's campus presidents to identify not only those programs that "should be reduced or phased out" but also those that "should be continued and strengthened."[37] Boyer thus expected that in response to the potential financial crisis planning on each campus might entail a reordering of priorities and redistribution of resources rather than simple across-the-board cuts or reliance on attrition through retirements and voluntary departures. The chancellor issued his list of guidelines for dealing with the likelihood of significant funding reductions, including the possibility of retrenchment, without any consultation with the university faculty senate. Only after issuing his guidelines did Boyer appoint a special University Commission on Purposes and Priorities composed of administrators, faculty members, and students to conduct a yearlong study of SUNY's programs and operations.[38] Subsequently, both the university faculty senate and the special commission endorsed the notion that selective program cuts were to be preferred to across-the-board cuts, but there was no faculty involvement in the crucial decision that the financial situation actually justified the terminations and program closures that followed. Moreover, the faculty endorsement of selective cuts did not extend to approval of redistributing resources in order to bolster what the administration regarded as existing institutional strengths.

Each president ultimately had very broad discretion, subject only to the collective bargaining agreement's vague requirement to consult with faculty as the president deemed "appropriate" in deciding how to implement cuts once the chancellor and the board of trustees had determined each campus's total budget for the coming year. In practice, this meant that faculty involvement in decisions about how to respond to the budget cuts varied significantly from campus to campus. On no campus did faculty have the opportunity to determine whether a condition of financial exigency actually existed that would justify terminations, but at least on several campuses, such as Albany, Oneonta, and New Paltz, committees with faculty representation played an important role in deciding who should be let go, though departmental and school faculties sometimes had as little as one week to respond to the recommendations of these special committees. At other campuses, such as Binghamton, Brockport, and Stony Brook, presidential decisions about whom to terminate took place with no meaningful faculty involvement.

An AAUP investigating committee found that the SUNY administration "clearly administered the retrenchments with a view to reorganization as well as to economy." Whereas CUNY's more severe financial crisis resulted in a substantial reduction in the size of the instructional staff for the entire university, though not in the termination of tenured faculty appointments, SUNY's administration cited its less critical funding shortfall to justify releasing sixty tenured faculty members, while still slightly increasing the total number of faculty members on its thirty-four campuses.[39] The administratively controlled reordering of priorities not only undermined faculty control over SUNY's academic programs but also, in the view of the AAUP's investigating committee, "produced a climate in which academic freedom is gravely endangered," since under "the circumstances that now prevail, no faculty member can be certain of his position, for it is possible for the administration . . . to so define a 'program' that a particular individual can be targeted for retrenchment." The investigating committee's report concluded: "In situations where tenure has not been honored, where faculty participation has been thwarted, and where administrative prerogatives have been graphically invoked, few will venture openly to disagree with administrative decisions. . . . In such an atmosphere, learning and the transmission of knowledge cannot be expected to flourish."[40]

Slowing the Tide of Faculty Unionization, 1975–1982

The faculties of both CUNY and SUNY had become unionized shortly before the financial crisis of the mid-1970s had a severe impact on their campuses. A tide of faculty unionization seemed to be sweeping the nation's colleges and universities in the early 1970s. Whereas a decade earlier not a single faculty was unionized, by 1975, 430 campuses and 20 percent of all full-time faculty members in the United States were engaged in collective bargaining.[41] Although successful unionizing drives did not altogether come to an end after 1975, the pace of further unionization slowed considerably, even before the Supreme Court in 1980 handed down its *Yeshiva* decision (discussed below), which virtually halted any further efforts to organize faculty at private colleges and universities. Unionization had always been more prevalent at public than at private institutions of higher learning, but the *Yeshiva* decision had the effect of greatly intensifying the contrast in unionization rates between these two sectors of higher education.

One of the factors accounting for the slowdown in union organizing at public institutions was that while the number of states adopting legislation that allowed public employees, including faculty members, to engage in collective bargaining had quickly expanded in the 1960s and early 1970s, after 1975 the spread of such enabling legislation markedly slowed.[42] Unionization was thus foreclosed as an option to those public-sector faculty members in states without enabling legislation. Even with the addition of collective bargaining for the large California State Colleges system in the late 1970s, the proportion of all full-time faculty members in the nation belonging to unions had increased to only 23.5 percent by 1982.[43]

The experiences of CUNY and SUNY demonstrated both the possibilities and the limitations of faculty unionization as a means of furthering the goals of shared governance. Since the late 1930s, CUNY had established a strong tradition of faculty involvement in institutional decision making, especially at the departmental level, where chairs were elected by the faculty. When faculty and staff unionized in the late 1960s, many faculty members saw collective bargaining as a means of further strengthening the practices of shared governance. A dual-track system developed, with the existing governance bodies maintaining their authority over academic matters and the union focusing on conditions of employment. Only a couple of years before the onset of the financial crisis at CUNY, the union had, in fact, attempted unsuccessfully to negotiate a contract provision whereby the administration would formally recognize those governance procedures and structures already in existence.[44] As subsequently approved, the union contract did provide some protections for faculty members, but the acceptance of managerial discretion in the determination of and response to a condition of financial exigency gave the administration significant authority to shape the university's handling of a situation of fiscal constraint without meaningful faculty involvement.

Most supporters of faculty collective bargaining have long insisted that a faculty union and traditional governance bodies could be mutually supportive in a dual-track system, an assumption written into California state law with the passage in 1979 of the Higher Education Employer-Employee Relations Act that permitted collective bargaining for faculty at both the University of California and the California State University (formerly California State Colleges) systems while continuing to recognize the important role of faculty senates.[45] Nevertheless, one of the recurring arguments made by administrations opposed to faculty collective bargaining has been that unionization would preclude administrators from negotiating or even discussing with traditional senates or other faculty governance bodies virtually all matters of concern to faculty, since the union would legally become the faculty's "exclusive bargaining agent." In the late 1960s, the CUNY administration had sought to discourage faculty members from voting for unionization by claiming that the faculty was already making "many decisions which, in industrial situations, are considered prerogatives of management" and consequently might be foreclosed to faculty if they opted for collective bargaining.[46]

The argument that shared governance was incompatible with collective bargaining failed to prevent the CUNY faculty, as well as faculties at many other public colleges and universities, from choosing to unionize while still retaining their existing role in institutional governance. In private institutions, however, a different situation developed. After the Supreme Court's 1980 *Yeshiva* ruling, collective bargaining was basically foreclosed as an option for faculty at any private college or university in which even a limited degree of shared governance had been established.

In the mid- to late 1970s, the most highly publicized struggle by a faculty at a private college or university to gain union recognition took place at Boston University, where John Silber became president in 1971. Silber had ambitious plans to remake the school into a major research institution, in part by using endowment funds and revenue from increased tuition rates to recruit star professors at salaries substantially above what BU paid its existing faculty members. By 1974, Silber's autocratic leadership style and unwillingness to tolerate dissent led the large and long-standing local AAUP chapter to seek recognition as a collective bargaining unit.[47] Silber strenuously opposed faculty unionization, insisting that professors were in "an incredibly favored position" and functioned not as hired help but as managers.[48] AAUP chapter president Fritz Ringer, on the other hand, later wrote that professors at BU supported unionization not only to protest the low salaries for non-star faculty members but also "to compensate for an unequal balance of power, to reestablish traditional faculty rights of participation in academic governance, and to reassert principles of academic collegiality and peer review that were being ignored by the Silber administration."[49]

Although the AAUP won a representation election in 1975, Silber initially refused to negotiate with the newly formed union. Silber's refusal led not only to an overwhelming vote by the entire faculty in 1976 calling for the president's resignation but also to a similar call from ten of the university's fifteen deans. In spite of these developments, the institution's governing board, which had become increasingly stacked with Silber's handpicked appointees, stood by the president in what historian Richard Freeland has described as the "bloodiest bureaucratic battle in the modern history of Massachusetts higher education."[50] Only after a federal court in 1978 finally ordered BU to begin negotiations was a contract ultimately agreed to, and then only after a faculty strike was called in protest of the governing board's last-minute efforts to change the terms of the contract that had been negotiated.[51]

Even after the final signing of a contract, Silber and the BU governing board continued to pursue a legal challenge to the right of the faculty to unionize. Before the university's case reached the Supreme Court, however, a challenge by another institution, Yeshiva University, resulted in a 1980 high-court ruling that ultimately upheld Silber's contention about the management status of professors at private institutions.[52] This ruling would soon result in the BU's union being decertified after the expiration of its first contract, as well as a virtual halt of the spread of faculty unionization to other private colleges and universities.[53] The *Yeshiva* case demonstrated not only the extent to which the notion of faculty responsibility for academic decision making had gained the status of a virtual truism but also the growing challenges that the recently developed standards of shared governance faced in practice.

Yeshiva University, which had an enrollment of approximately seven thousand students in the late 1970s, had granted its first baccalaureate degree in 1932. Although the private institution had strong ties to the Orthodox Jewish community, the university was officially nonsectarian and offered a broad range of academic and professional programs. In 1974, the Faculty Association of Yeshiva University petitioned the National Labor Relations Board for recognition as the exclusive bargaining agent for the full-time faculty at ten of the university's thirteen schools. Although the NLRB ruled in favor of the union and ordered Yeshiva's administration to negotiate with the Faculty Association, the administration challenged the ruling, with the result that the case ultimately went to the Supreme Court for a final judgment.

In a five-to-four opinion, the court held that full-time faculty members at Yeshiva University were excluded from coverage by the National Labor Relations Act by virtue of their being "managerial employees" who were "involved in developing and enforcing employer policy." Writing for the majority, Justice

Lewis Powell supported the court's decision by arguing that the authority of faculty "in academic matters is absolute. They decide what courses will be offered, when they will be scheduled, and to whom they will be taught. They debate and determine teaching methods, grading policies, and matriculation standards. They effectively decide which students will be admitted, retained and graduated. . . . To the extent the industrial analogy applies, the faculty determines within each school the product to be produced, the terms upon which it will be offered, and the customers who will be served." Powell also claimed that in the system of "shared authority" that prevailed at Yeshiva, the faculty's power extended "beyond strictly academic concerns," so that in cases of "faculty hiring, tenure, sabbaticals, termination and promotion . . . the overwhelming majority of faculty recommendations are implemented."[54]

Yet one of the reasons the faculty at Yeshiva voted to unionize was dissatisfaction with the role they played in institutional governance.[55] Like many other institutions of higher learning, Yeshiva in the 1970s was experiencing enrollment declines in several of its academic units. As at CUNY and SUNY, the administration responded by implementing a policy of retrenchment (though on a smaller scale) over which the faculty had very little control. The dismissal of three tenured professors in 1978 as part of an administratively mandated reorganization of the university ultimately led to an investigation and a vote of censure by the AAUP for Yeshiva's violations of the principles of academic freedom and tenure and for the "lack of opportunity for a meaningful faculty role in the decisions to consolidate programs."[56]

In his dissenting opinion in the *Yeshiva* case, Justice William Brennan had argued that the majority opinion was based "on an idealized model of collegial decisionmaking" that bore little relation to the reality of the contemporary American university. He observed: "Education has become 'big business,' and the task of operating the university enterprise has been transferred from the faculty to an autonomous administration, which faces the same pressures to cut costs and increase efficiencies that confront any large industrial organization. The past decade of budgetary cutbacks, declining enrollments, reductions in faculty appointments, curtailment of academic programs, and increasing calls for accountability to alumni and other special interest groups has only added to the erosion of the faculty's role in the institution's decisionmaking process."[57]

Moreover, Brennan echoed the argument that faculty had long made concerning the rationale for faculty involvement in institutional decision making. Far from acting as the "representative of management," the faculty made recommendations, according to Brennan, that were intended to serve the faculty's "independent interest in creating the most effective environment for learning, teaching, and scholarship," so that "whatever influence the faculty wields . . .

is attributable solely to its collective expertise as professional educators, and not to any managerial or supervisory prerogatives."[58]

As demonstrated in the majority opinion in the *Yeshiva* decision, by the early 1980s the idea of shared governance had, to a certain extent, become something of a cliché, though not necessarily a reality for many faculty members. One indication of the growing challenges to both the ideal and the practices of shared governance was a report from a major conference on the subject of governance that was held under the sponsorship of the AAUP, the Carnegie Foundation, and the Johnson Foundation one year after the *Yeshiva* decision. The report stated that the conference, which was attended by faculty members and administrators, including representatives of the AAUP and the American Council on Education, was premised on the understanding that the circumstances then prevailing in American higher education were "much more adverse" to the implementation of the principles spelled out in the 1966 *Statement on Government* than could have been envisaged when that document had first been promulgated. The main issues discussed at the conference—"the faculty role in the budgeting process; the relation between academic governance and collective bargaining; the impact of statewide boards and systems"—reflected the major challenges to shared governance that had developed since the formulation of the 1966 *Statement*.[59]

Another indication of the change in attitudes toward shared governance that had occurred by the mid-1980s, as well as the increasing attention being devoted to the subject of unionization, was a statement on governance issued in 1984 by the American Association of State Colleges and Universities (AASCU), an organization founded in 1961 to represent many of the nation's non-research-intensive public four-year schools. The AASCU statement constituted a partial retreat from the principles laid out in the *Statement on Government*. While acknowledging that "faculty cooperation in campus decision making is essential to the success of the institution's activities" and agreeing with the 1966 *Statement*'s assertion that faculty "have the primary responsibility for such fundamental areas as curriculum, methods of instruction, degree standards, research, and those aspects of student life which relate to the educational process," the AASCU statement notably omitted any reference to the faculty's responsibility for determining faculty status or to the importance of "joint effort" in the determination of general educational policies and the budget. Moreover, the statement included what amounted to a warning about the consequences of faculty unionization: "To the degree a faculty union is given exclusive authority under an agreement to deal with specific matters related to institutional governance, these same matters cannot also be the responsibility of the faculty as a whole or a faculty senate."[60]

Collective Bargaining in the Aftermath of the *Yeshiva* Decision

The basic pattern of unionization by institutional type that had been established at the outset of the union movement has continued to characterize faculty collective bargaining to the present day. At major research universities, whether public or private, faculties have rarely engaged in collective bargaining. In the mid-1990s, among the nation's top 194 institutions as measured by their share of federal funds for research, only 18 were unionized.[61] By contrast, after 1980, union membership in the two-year sector not only continued to outpace membership in other sectors of higher education but actually significantly expanded. In 2011, 60 percent of full-time faculty members at two-year institutions were represented by a union, so that approximately half of all unionized faculty members in the United States were at community colleges.[62]

Several factors account for the high proportion of unionized faculty members at degree-granting community colleges. First, since the overwhelming majority of such colleges were public institutions, few were precluded from unionization by the *Yeshiva* decision. Second, the historical links of community colleges to K–12 education resulted in close ties to what had become one of the most highly unionized sectors in the entire American labor force. Thus, in California, for example, community college faculty members gained collective bargaining rights before their state college and university colleagues by virtue of legislation passed in 1975 that was intended primarily for K–12 teachers.[63] Third, in addition to earning lower salaries than those teaching at universities, community college faculty members were often denied a meaningful role in institutional governance, including the appointment and evaluation of colleagues. Unionization, therefore, was attractive as a means of trying to achieve a greater role in institutional decision making as well as a means of winning economic benefits. One community college union activist observed that his union's collective bargaining contract had been "crucial to empowering" the faculty and to giving them, for the first time, some of the "prerogatives that are often taken for granted at four-year colleges and universities." In particular, he cited the important role of faculty in appointment decisions and peer review.[64]

In fact, the 1975 legislative recognition of collective bargaining rights for community college faculty members in California's extensive system of two-year schools—which by the early twenty-first century enrolled 2.5 million students on 108 campuses—was followed thirteen years later by legislation that sought to clarify the relationship between collective bargaining and traditional faculty governance mechanisms in the state's two-year colleges. The legislation sought to do this by treating collective bargaining and traditional governance mechanisms as complementary means of ensuring a faculty voice in institutional decision making. Assembly Bill (AB) 1725, which was signed into law by Republican governor George Deukmejian in 1988, required the board of governors of the California Community Colleges to develop "policies and guidelines for strengthening the role of the academic senate with regard to the determination and administration of academic and professional standards, course approval and curricula, and other academic matters." The law outlined the responsibilities not only of a system-wide senate but also of senates on each of the individual campuses within the system, including in the process of making appointments and granting tenure, where faculty expertise was recognized as crucial. The law required joint action by the faculty's collective bargaining agent and senate on a number of matters, while explicitly addressing the argument made by the majority in the *Yeshiva* case: "There has been a great deal of uncertainty . . . regarding whether increased faculty involvement in institutional governance and decisionmaking might subject the faculty members to legal challenges in connection with their rights of collective bargaining. This act is intended to enable faculty members . . . to avoid having to choose between collective bargaining and greater participation in these functions." The California legislature declared its intent that "the exercise of this increased responsibility shall not make these faculty members managerial or supervisory employees" under the state's collective bargaining laws.[65]

In spite of the intentions of AB 1725's authors, implementation of the shared-governance model upon which the law was based proved difficult in practice. The California system of community colleges was more like a loose confederation than a tightly controlled and centralized system. Resistance by many local campus executives and the lack of strong enforcement from the central administration, together with ongoing economic pressures and the appeal of more corporate-style approaches to management, presented continuing obstacles to the full implementation of the law's shared-governance model. An inherent conflict between unionization and the practices of shared governance, however, was not a significant factor in the often disappointing results that ensued from the implementation of AB 1725.[66]

The experiences of many colleges and universities since the advent of faculty collective bargaining in the 1960s have clearly demonstrated that unionization and traditional forms of shared governance are not mutually exclusive and can, in fact, complement each other. Nevertheless, a highly publicized controversy in the late 1990s at Miami-Dade Community College, the nation's largest multicampus, single-district community college, demonstrated that administrative claims about the incompatibility of collective bargaining and shared governance have persisted and can still have a powerful impact in shaping the climate for institutional governance on any given campus. In the late 1990s, Miami-Dade enrolled more than one hundred thousand students on six different campuses, though it had a full-time faculty of only 775 but nearly twice that number of part-timers. Established in 1959, the two-year college had early on developed a system of shared governance that, to a certain extent, set it apart from many other community colleges. Full-time faculty members enjoyed a significant voice in academic decision making through individual campus senates and a system-wide Faculty Senate Consortium. These governance bodies were composed of elected faculty representatives and were formally recognized in policies adopted by the college's governing board.

Relations between the faculty and the administration were generally harmonious, at least until the appointment of Eduardo Padrón as president in 1995. According to an investigation subsequently carried out by the AAUP, the new president quickly embarked on a program of "reorganizational engineering" that entailed a reordering of the college's priorities and making important decisions on academic policy matters, including the appointment of several academic administrators and a decision to freeze the further granting of continuing contracts (the equivalent of tenure), without consulting the faculty's elected representatives. Discontent with Padrón's bypassing of the existing system of shared governance led several of the school's current and former senate leaders to spearhead an effort to unionize the faculty. By more than a two to one margin, with more than 90 percent of the eligible full-time faculty members participating, the faculty chose to unionize in 1998.[67]

Before the union election, Padrón had warned that a favorable vote would require him to abandon the system of shared governance then in place because, in his view, virtually every action by the existing governance bodies in some way affected the faculty's conditions of employment. He contended that the administration would be barred by law from dealing with senates or other governance bodies instead of with the union that served as the faculty's exclusive bargaining agent. He made this claim in spite of the fact that the Florida Public Employee Relations Commission ruling that he cited to support his position included language that explicitly rejected the assertion that collective bargaining and traditional shared governance were mutually exclusive. Nevertheless, Padrón followed through on his threat to disband all governance bodies that existed under the policy guidelines in effect before the union vote and proceeded to establish a new administratively dominated governance system that was never submitted to the faculty for a vote of approval. While the faculty union has managed to survive and to negotiate contracts dealing with wages and working conditions, these contracts have been silent on questions of broad institutional governance, which continues to this day to operate under the system administratively mandated in 1998.

Miami-Dade's outright elimination of all established mechanisms of shared governance in response to faculty unionization was an extreme measure that did not establish a precise precedent that was subsequently followed by other public institutions. However, the reaction by the administration of the University of Akron in 2003 to a faculty decision to unionize entailed a similar but less thoroughgoing approach. Akron traced its history back to 1870 as a private institution but in 1913 became a municipally supported university and then in 1967 a state-supported school. By the late 1990s, the university had an enrollment of approximately twenty thousand students and a fairly typical system of shared governance with an active senate and various faculty governance committees. Akron had a long-standing AAUP chapter that had been founded in the 1930s and that in the 1950s already had more than one hundred members.

Subsequent to the appointment of Luis Proenza as president in 1999, concerns about what many faculty members perceived as the deterioration of shared governance on campus led the faculty in 2003 to vote in favor of making the AAUP its exclusive bargaining agent. The Akron administration responded not by totally eliminating the faculty senate but by gutting much of its and the faculty's role in institutional decision making. Without any consultation with the faculty, the governing board removed references to the senate's Planning and Budget Committee and its Campus Facilities Committee from the university's standing rules and eliminated language that provided a significant role for faculty in the selection of department chairs, deans, and the president of the university. The faculty senate was left standing, but only as a severely compromised vehicle for faculty involvement in institutional governance.[68]

Although the pace of union expansion among faculty remained slow after 1982, collective bargaining continued to be a significant factor in the public sector of American higher education in the decades after the *Yeshiva* decision. By 2011, more than one thousand campuses had unionized faculties. Nationally, 26 percent of all full-time faculty members—but only 3 percent in private nonprofit institutions and none in for-profit schools—were covered by collective bargaining agreements. Organizing part-time faculty members always posed difficult challenges for unions, but as part-timers came to play an ever-increasing role in the academic workforce, growing numbers (21 percent in 2011) also became involved in collective bargaining. By 2011, in absolute numbers, almost as many part-time as full-time faculty members were covered by union contracts.

More recently, following the state elections of 2010, collective bargaining rights for all public employees, including faculty members, came under attack in several states, as conservative Republican governors and state legislatures sought to place various limits on public-sector unions. In some cases, "reforms" represented barely concealed efforts to eliminate public-employee unions altogether. In Ohio, where faculty unionism was particularly strong—with all four-year public institutions except Ohio State University, Miami University of Ohio, and Ohio University covered by collective bargaining agreements—public-university faculties were singled out in an effort to end the right of full-time faculty members to engage in collective bargaining. Senate Bill (SB) 5 originated as an attempt to restrict, but not totally eliminate, collective bargaining rights for all public employees. However, as the bill worked its way through the legislature, the Inter-University Council of Ohio, which represented the administrations of the state's public four-year universities, was able to add an amendment to the legislation that used the logic of the *Yeshiva* decision specifically to deny full-time faculty members the right to unionize, specifying that "any faculty member or group of faculty members that participate in decisions with respect to courses, curriculum, personnel, or matters of academic or institutional policy shall be deemed supervisors or managers." Although SB 5, including the amendment denying full-time faculty members the right to engage in collective bargaining, passed and was signed by Governor John Kasich in 2011, the law was subsequently revoked by voter referendum, as the state's entire labor movement was mobilized to protect the bargaining rights of all public employees.[69]

In several other states, less drastic measures restricting the collective bargaining rights of public employees have recently been passed and still remain in effect. Nevertheless, joint AFT/AAUP organizing campaigns at two major research universities, the University of Illinois at Chicago (2011) and the University of Oregon (2012), have resulted in recent organizing successes.[70] It is unlikely, however, that these victories mark the beginning of a trend in which unionization will rapidly spread into research-intensive universities or highly selective liberal arts colleges. Nevertheless, together with the demonstrated staying power of unions where they have already established a foothold, these recent union successes would seem to indicate that faculty unionization is likely to continue as a significant factor in American higher education.

The Continuing Impact of the Market Model on Higher Education

The difficult economic situation of the 1970s and early 1980s gave way after 1983 to generally improved conditions for most of the next two decades, thereby easing some of the worst financial pressures on American colleges and universities until the Great Recession began in 2007.[71] Nevertheless, the market model of how best to manage both the economy as a whole and institutions of higher education in particular became even more dominant as a result of the conservative Reagan Revolution, and in the aftermath of America's victory in the Cold War and the collapse of communism in the Soviet Union and Eastern Europe. The apparent discrediting of state economic planning and a growing backlash against the government programs of the Great Society contributed to a greater assertiveness on the part of those heralding the benefits of a purely market-based approach to solving economic and social problems. This approach emphasized a reliance on the pursuit of individual self-interest and the workings of the laws of supply and demand, instead of purposeful efforts to determine what was in the public interest, to guide institutional decision making.

As deference to market forces grew throughout society, American colleges and universities experienced intensifying conflicts over the application of corporate models of management. Among the issues generating controversy have been the insistence by administrators on the necessity of managerial discretion over such matters as retrenchment and reorganization of academic programs to achieve greater efficiencies, control over the use of new forms of instructional technologies, greater use of part-time faculty to ensure "flexibility," and salary determination based on the varying market demand for different disciplines. Although administrators and governing boards have generally continued to acknowledge the essential role that faculty members should play in such academic decisions as appointment and promotion of tenure-track colleagues and the establishment of academic standards, many of the policies universities have actually implemented over the last thirty years have, in fact, eroded faculty control of the curriculum and authority over other academic matters.

Retrenchment and Reorganization

Although George Keller's dire predictions that a substantial number of colleges and universities would have to close their doors for reasons of financial exigency failed to materialize, since the early 1980s many institutions have cited the threat of potential future financial difficulties to justify retrenchments that administrators increasingly have used to restructure and reprioritize institutional commitments.[72] Of the more than nine hundred four-year colleges and universities responding to a 2001 governance survey, 43 percent reported department closures between 1996 and 2001.[73] This form of restructuring occurred even more frequently with the coming of the Great Recession.[74] Gary Rhoades's examination of more than two hundred union contracts from the 1990s found that more than 80 percent contained some language relating to retrenchment.[75] However, like the SUNY and CUNY contracts of the 1970s, these contracts allowed substantial managerial discretion and included only minimal requirements for consultation with faculty.

Whether unionized or not, few institutions directly linked the option of retrenchment to a formal declaration of financial exigency, which in the language of Regulation 4c of the AAUP's *Recommended Institutional Regulations* on *Academic Freedom and Tenure* (originally adopted in 1957) had long been defined as "an imminent financial crisis that threatens the survival of the institution as a whole and that cannot be alleviated by less drastic means" than the termination of tenured faculty appointments.[76] In many cases, administrators and governing boards implemented program closures and retrenchment of faculty by invoking financial considerations at the level of an individual program or department, without claiming that the entire institution was in danger of closing.[77]

In some instances, such as the program eliminations that took place at the University of Maryland in the early 1990s and the merger of Marymount College (New York) with Fordham University in 2002, retrenchment and reorganization were carried out with the full cooperation and participation of representatives of the faculty.[78] In most other cases, however, managerial discretion in the implementation of retrenchment led not only to dismissals of tenured professors but also reprioritization of programs without meaningful faculty involvement in the decision-making process. In her 1993 study of seventeen retrenchment cases from the 1980s, Sheila Slaughter concluded that administrators used the threat of financial constraints to consolidate their power:

> In addressing crises, administrators used the language of productivity, economy and efficiency, and competition, language similar to that used by business leaders. In effect, administrators used crisis to become academic executives, the CEOs of universities. However, administrative invocation of the language of the market and business competition was not elucidated in terms of educational and scholarly goals, nor in terms of institutional missions. That the parallels between colleges and universities . . . were less than exact or perhaps inappropriate was apparently not of concern to academic executives. Rather than considering the nature of higher education, administrators were intent on reshaping it. However, administrators were not engaged in retrenchment, the cutting back or reduction of institutions; rather, they were engaged in restructuring, or molding higher education through internal reallocation of resources and procurement of more resources from external sources. In short, academic executives did not want to make do with less, but to spend more on programs they identified as worth strengthening.[79]

Slaughter found that program and personnel cuts fell disproportionately on the humanities, fine arts, social sciences, and education—fields in which women faculty were most likely to be employed and that were far less likely than the hard sciences and engineering to secure external funding.

A subsequent updating of Slaughter's review of AAUP investigative reports of institutions that terminated faculty appointments for financial reasons considered all twenty-eight such reports between 1974 and 2001 and concluded that in almost all those cases "faculty involvement in decisions leading to terminations was either inadequate or nonexistent."[80] Administrators consistently claimed that faculty involvement would have produced unacceptable delays and that faculty members, at any rate, were too tied to their own disciplines to adopt the institution-wide perspective that was necessary for action in behalf of the common good, but, as Slaughter has argued, these same administrators often applied assessment measures that had little to do with the broad educational mission of their institutions.

Another form of restructuring that has occurred with increasing frequency over the last quarter century and has undermined previously accepted forms of governance has been the establishment of research institutes and centers, sometimes referred to as organized research units (ORUs). Universities have developed ORUs to take advantage of possibilities for external funding from both industry and governmental agencies as well as to foster interdisciplinary work. These units are independent of traditional academic departments. While ORUs have been established at a wide range of institutions and have been successful in bringing in billions of dollars to support research in a variety of fields, the nature of their funding and the authority structure that typically characterize these units raise serious questions concerning both the practices of shared governance and the safeguards to academic freedom.[81]

In contrast to traditional academic departments, which over the course of the twentieth century came to be governed in a collegial manner with substantial involvement of at least the tenured and tenure-track faculty, ORUs have typically been organized in a more corporate, top-down manner, with a director exercising considerably greater authority than a typical department chair. As more institutional resources and personnel have become absorbed into ORUs, what some analysts describe as the "periphery" or "suburbs" of the university have expanded in such a way that the "core" governance structures, particularly academic departments but also institution-wide faculty governance bodies, have lost influence.[82] The external funding of these centers, especially from industry, which often places restrictions on the free distribution of the knowledge thereby created, also poses a potential threat to academic freedom. Concern with the governance and academic freedom issues involved in the research frequently carried on through the ORU organizational structure led the AAUP in 2012 to develop guidelines for the establishment of appropriate academy-industry relationships.[83]

Governance Implications of New Approaches to "Delivering Education"

The market revolution in American higher education has also been expressed in the development of new ways of delivering instruction and of making decisions about the curriculum. The use of new technologies, especially those that allow for instruction to take place more readily outside the confines of the traditional classroom, has held out the promise—though not always the reality—of reducing costs, while also catering to the demands of modern-day students for greater flexibility in their study and work schedules. In addition to being responsive to student demands, however, the use of new instructional technologies in many cases has undermined faculty control over the curriculum and methods of instruction.

As early as the 1990s, Rhoades found that the issue of instructional technologies was already being addressed in about one-third of the more than two hundred union contracts he examined, but only a small fraction (5 percent) of these agreements included language calling for "faculty involvement in decisions to utilize and purchase new technologies." Rhoades observed that the increasing use of instructional technologies in American colleges and universities has often been undertaken at the instigation of administrators and that it has contributed to "the increased discretion that managers enjoy in this emergent and growing area of the curriculum. . . . Technology expands managers' flexibility not by enhancing their control over faculty in traditional curricula, but by enabling them to develop new curricular areas and hire new faculty outside the purview of traditional contractual and academic/faculty constraints."[84]

Thus, for example, in 2013 the Georgia Institute of Technology announced plans to partner with a private company, Udacity, to develop a large online master's program in computer science in which "course assistants" employed by Udacity would play a major role interacting with students. Moreover, while avoiding the necessity of adding significant numbers of new faculty members to handle what was expected to be an influx of thousands of new students, Georgia Tech agreed to hire a new class of teaching assistants who would be neither traditional faculty members nor graduate students but "professionals" who might be employed for an indefinite period. Although the new program had the support of Georgia Tech's computer science faculty, the administration bypassed the university's normal curriculum review process in reaching its agreement with Udacity.[85]

The issue of distance education may have played an important role in what became one of the most widely reported governance controversies of recent years. At the University of Virginia in 2012, the push by a corporate-minded governing board chair for a more rapid expansion of the institution's commitment to online education appears to have been a central factor in the board's sudden dismissal of a university president with strong faculty support. However, university president Teresa Sullivan was quickly restored to her position after vociferous protests by faculty, students, and alumni about her removal gained national attention. Helen Dragas, the head of the board, never fully explained the reasons for the board's dissatisfaction with Sullivan, but she did state that the board believed a "bold leader" was necessary to respond to the "transformation" that was taking place in higher education "now that online delivery has been legitimized by some of the elite institutions."[86] Although the faculty, together with students and alumni, was successful in reversing the decision to dismiss Sullivan, the incident demonstrated the growing tensions that have arisen between faculty, on the one side, and governing boards and elected officials, on the other, about not only the most effective way to introduce new technologies into instruction but also the advisability of a more corporate approach to the management of colleges and universities.[87]

The case of Western Governors University (WGU) exemplifies even more fully the potential threat to faculty governance posed by an essentially market-driven, corporate-style approach to distance education.[88] Although the institution now claims to have more than one thousand full-time faculty members, it proudly asserts that its "academic programs are developed and guided by WGU administrators working through several councils, which are composed of academicians and industry experts in the various fields of knowledge." These councils, however, are not composed of WGU's own faculty members but "experts" employed at other universities or by private-sector industries hired on a contract basis. Moreover, direct instruction is carried out largely by student and course "mentors" who do not have faculty status and who play no role in developing the courses they teach. Rather than relying on the traditional system of credit hours earned as the path toward a degree, WGU relies on a "competency-based" system of student assessment whereby testing is conducted independently of the courses a student takes. WGU, in effect, has no meaningful institution-wide mechanisms of faculty governance, so the curriculum is driven largely by administrators, not by a traditional faculty.[89]

The growing insistence by administrators, governing board members, and legislators that colleges and universities make greater use of instructional technologies is but one part of the larger movement to make higher education more responsive to market demands and to treat students more as "customers" whose desires must be satisfied rather than apprentice learners in need of guidance by a professional professoriate. By distorting the criteria used to determine what should be taught and how, such pressures can have serious repercussions for faculty control of the curriculum. Thus, for example, half of all courses taken in the early 1990s by students at four-year institutions were in business fields, though it is hard to believe that this pattern was the result of educationally based decisions by faculties about what was pedagogically most beneficial for the full development of their students.[90] At the prestigious University of Chicago in the mid-1990s, concerns about attracting more students led the president, economist Hugo Sonnenschein, to press the faculty to cut back on the school's rigorous and highly regarded core curriculum. Sonnenschein's actions led prominent faculty members to declare: "Making academic decisions on the basis of marketing . . . is itself a crime against the mind."[91] Although the faculty at the University of Chicago, with its long history of shared governance, was able to resist the imposition of thoroughgoing changes to the core curriculum, the incident is emblematic of the way fiscally minded administrators across the country have been trying, often successfully, to gain greater control over the curriculum.

Another way market forces are threatening faculty control of the curriculum, as well as over the appointment of new faculty members, stems from the growing number of cases in which corporate or philanthropic donors have offered funds to support the development of curricular programs reflecting their own ideological agendas. In a period of tight budgets for colleges and universities, administrators (and some faculty members) have found it hard to turn down such funds. Such initiatives normally have not gone through a full review by standing faculty governance bodies, so, in effect, faculty oversight of the curriculum has been undermined. External corporate and philanthropic funding for both private and public institutions of higher learning was certainly not a new phenomenon, but not since the early decades of the twentieth century had such funding posed as serious a threat both to the practices of shared governance and to academic freedom.

For example, in recent years the Charles G. Koch Charitable Foundation has made substantial contributions to many schools in an effort to foster new undergraduate programs that would promote the study of free enterprise. Under the terms of one such grant, to Florida State University in 2007, the Koch Foundation was able to appoint an advisory board to review job applicants for new faculty positions connected to the program and to establish guidelines for new courses to be offered. At almost the same time, the BB&T Charitable Foundation, which like the Koch Foundation supports conservative causes, complemented the Koch donation by giving FSU a substantial sum of money to finance the creation of a new course on morals and ethics in economic systems, with free-market icon Ayn Rand as required reading.[92] BB&T made several similar grants to other institutions, including one to Guilford College that required the school to create, and then offer once a year for ten years, an upper-level course titled "The Moral Foundations of Capitalism." Not only was Ayn Rand's *Atlas Shrugged* required reading for the course, but Guilford also had to agree to provide a copy of the book to every student majoring in business or economics.[93]

The most dramatic example of the application of market models to higher education has been the rapid development of a large for-profit sector. With more than two million students enrolled, the for-profit sector now employs more than one hundred thousand faculty members.[94] Although that figure still represents less than one-tenth of all instructional faculty members in the country, the experience of those teaching in the for-profit sector represents what may well be the logical culmination of many of the trends occurring in the rest of higher education, most notably the idea that colleges and universities ought to regard their students as customers and the resulting challenge to the principle that faculty should exercise primary responsibility for the development of the curriculum and for other aspects of educational policy.

Institutions in the for-profit sector, which offer courses primarily through distance education, are taking the lead in the "unbundling" of faculty work. Rather than expecting faculty members to fulfill a broadly defined role as professionals engaging in teaching, research, and service (including governance work), for-profit institutions hire faculty, usually on a part-time basis, for the sole purpose of teaching an administratively determined curriculum, with no expectation of research or service. As William Tierney and Guilbert Hentschke have argued, academic freedom, tenure, and shared governance, which evolved in order to safeguard the faculty's unfettered pursuit and dissemination of knowledge, are almost totally absent from for- profit schools, which have a very different institutional mission from that of traditional colleges and universities. Schools such as the University of Phoenix, which with more than three hundred thousand students in 2010 had by far the largest enrollment of any single degree-granting institution in the country, are corporate organizations designed primarily to generate profits by narrowly catering to student demands for job-related instruction. They are not designed to create new knowledge or to serve a larger civic purpose. The for-profit schools thus not only lack traditional mechanisms of faculty governance; they are also taking the lead in the broader process of deprofessionalization of the faculty that is occurring throughout American higher education.[95]

The Growing Trend toward the Deprofessionalization of the Faculty

At least until the 1970s, one of the crucial long-term trends in the history of American higher education had been the increasing professionalization of the faculty. This process of professionalization was an essential factor in the development of the principles and practices of shared governance. Over the last several decades, however, the growing tendency of public officials, governing board members, and administrators to treat higher education as an industry that should be subject to market forces like all other industries has led to the implementation of a variety of policies that have contributed to the growing deprofessionalization of the faculty. These policies include the increasing displacement of full-time, tenured or tenure-track faculty by instructors holding contingent, especially part-time, appointments (i.e., not eligible for tenure); direct and indirect attacks on the institution of tenure; and the setting of salaries in ways that undermine the common identity and common interests of professors regardless of their academic discipline. The greater reliance on contingent instructors and the rise of ever-greater salary differentials within the professoriate clearly mimic developments affecting labor throughout the entire economy.

In the for-profit sector, the use of non-tenure-track faculty, especially those employed on only a part-time basis, has been the norm from the industry's beginning, but the use of faculty members on contingent appointments over the last three decades has also become a strategy utilized by most nonprofit schools as a response to growing market pressures and as a means of enhancing managerial authority. As noted previously, approximately half of all faculty members in the United States in 2011 were employed on a part-time basis. If one also includes graduate-student employees engaged in instruction and research, the figure increases to 60 percent. While the use of part-time instructors has mushroomed throughout American higher education, the trend has been especially evident in two-year institutions, where before the end of the 1990s part-timers already clearly outnumbered full-time faculty. There has also been a marked gender dimension to the increasing employment of part-timers, as women have been substantially overrepresented among those in part-time positions.[96] Although the system of shared governance that developed in the twentieth century was largely based on the assumption that the faculty involved in institutional decision making would be career professionals working within a tenure system, by 2011 less than one-quarter of all instructional faculty members were in tenure-eligible positions.

The increasing use of part-time and non-tenure-track faculty has undermined the practices of shared governance in several ways.[97] The development of shared governance in the twentieth century was premised on the emergence of a professionalized faculty with the expertise required to make informed academic judgments and with a career-long commitment to advancing academic values that served the public interest. Most faculty members on contingent appointments, however, have little prospect of developing full-time careers at a college or university, and they are typically appointed without an expectation that they will engage in the full panoply of professorial activities, but rather with an expectation that their only job responsibility will be teaching. Research and service, including participation in institutional governance, are not usually part of their job descriptions. This unbundling of faculty work, together with the low pay and often poor working conditions, such as lack of office space and other forms of institutional support for contingent faculty, amounts to a denial of professional status to what has now become a majority of those engaged in teaching and research on college campuses. It is also hardly coincidental that this development has taken place simultaneously with the employment of greater numbers of women in academia, since historically the influx of women into an occupation has often been associated with a decline in the status of that profession.[98]

One of the hallmarks of the professionalization of faculty and the concomitant development of shared governance has been the centrality of peer review in the appointment and evaluation process. Yet in the case of part-time faculty appointments, Rhoades found that in the more than two hundred union contracts he examined, the overwhelming majority provided for no constraints on managerial discretion in the appointment, nonreappointment, or dismissal of individuals employed on a part-time basis.[99] In other words, although tenure-track faculty over the course of the twentieth century had been able throughout much of higher education to establish their primary responsibility for the appointment and evaluation of fellow tenure-track faculty, this authority has generally not been extended to making decisions about part-time instructors, who now constitute the majority of all faculty members. To the extent that faculty unions in the 1990s tried to address the growing presence of part-time and contingent faculty members, Rhoades found that such attempts sought to limit the numbers of faculty on contingent appointments as a means of upholding professional standards—an attempt that has been largely unsuccessful. More recently, however, with the growing presence of contingent, especially part-time, instructors in faculty unions, either in stand-alone bargaining units or together with their tenured and tenure-track colleagues, unions have put greater emphasis on also trying to win greater due-process rights for faculty on contingent appointments.[100]

Thus, in a variety of ways, the process of deprofessionalization fundamentally undermines the foundation for shared governance. Moreover, as a practical matter, the increasing percentage of faculty members on contingent appointments means that on most campuses the pool of individuals available to fill the various committee and senate positions required for a fully functioning system of shared governance has become ever more limited. This development puts greater demands on tenure-track faculty at the same time that expectations for greater research productivity create a negative incentive for those faculty members to devote time to governance.

The growing presence of instructors on contingent appointments has prompted debates among traditional advocates of shared governance about how to respond to this development. Many tenured professors voice concerns about trying to involve contingent faculty members in governance. These concerns arise out of a fear that job insecurity and lack of tenure protections for their academic freedom make contingent faculty members potentially subject to undue pressure and influence from administrators. In addition, for some critics, the fact that many—though by no means all—contingent faculty members have only a temporary and peripheral connection to their employing institution raises questions about the appropriateness of their involvement in decisions that could affect an institution's long-term interests.[101]

On the other hand, confronted with the reality of ever-growing numbers of faculty on contingent appointments, many of whom share similar academic backgrounds with their tenure-track colleagues, and recognizing the need to resist the trend toward the unbundling of faculty responsibilities in order to defend the professional identity of the entire faculty, the AAUP in 2012 issued a comprehensive statement declaring its support for the inclusion of faculty on contingent appointments in most aspects of institutional governance.[102] The statement, however, recognized that in order to make such involvement effective, it would be necessary to establish greater protections for the academic freedom and academic due-process rights of contingent faculty members. The AAUP's new policy guidelines thus finally acknowledged the need for greater inclusiveness in governance and thereby continued the halting trend that had begun when the AAUP nearly a century earlier expanded its vision of governance beyond the academic elite holding the rank of full professor to include all full-time faculty.

The role of contingent faculty members in governance was central to a controversy that arose at Rensselaer Polytechnic Institute, which in 2011 led to an AAUP sanction of RPI for violations of the norms of shared governance.[103] Founded in 1824, RPI is the country's oldest school of science and engineering. At the time of the dispute, it had approximately 7,500 students and 450 faculty members. Not until 1993 did RPI create a representative faculty senate to serve as the principal vehicle for a collective faculty voice in institutional governance. At that time, those eligible to vote in senate elections included research faculty, librarians, archivists, and retired and emeriti faculty, as well as the active tenured and tenure-track faculty, but not instructors on contingent appointments. When the senate was established, the faculty included very few non-tenure-track instructors, but as throughout academia, the number of such instructors (who at RPI were labeled "clinical faculty") grew significantly in the 1990s and 2000s. In response to this development, as a matter of fairness and also in order to benefit from the views of faculty members who were deeply involved in the educational mission of the institution, the faculty senate in 2006 recommended that voting privileges be extended to the clinical faculty, a position that was subsequently supported by a vote of the entire faculty.

RPI's administration and governing board, however, rejected this recommendation, arguing that only those who either had already gone through the rigorous tenure process, or at least were in line to do so, and who had indicated their commitment "to invest their academic credentials and intellectual energies into the long-term well being of the Institute" deserved the right to vote and thereby to shape educational policy. The administration and governing board also claimed that extending full faculty rights to contingent instructors would detract from RPI's reputation as a "world-class" university, a position for which they offered no evidence. Not only did the board reject the faculty senate recommendation concerning clinical faculty, but it also then directed the senate to change its constitution in order to strip voting rights from librarians, archivists, and emeriti and retired faculty. The board insisted that only tenured or tenure-track faculty with the title of professor, associate professor, or assistant professor should be eligible to vote.

Although a significant number, but not a majority, of faculty members at RPI may have shared the concerns of the administration and governing board regarding the appropriateness of full voting rights for non-tenure-track faculty, widespread resentment arose over the governing board's assertion of its right to tell the faculty who deserved faculty status, a matter that had long been considered the primary responsibility of the faculty itself. In 2007, the senate's refusal to comply with the board's directive to restrict the franchise led President Shirley Jackson to suspend the operations of the faculty senate. This action was the basis for the AAUP's sanction. Although committees with faculty representatives continued to exist at RPI in an "interim" system of governance, the AAUP investigating committee questioned the legitimacy of such bodies so long as the administration refused to recognize the institution-wide elected senate as the primary vehicle for the expression of faculty views.

In the midst of the crisis, the administration initiated a full review of governance at RPI. After four years of deadlock between the faculty and the administration over possible reforms to the institution's system of governance, the faculty and the board finally approved a new senate constitution in 2011. A compromise was reached concerning the role of non-tenure-track faculty in the new governance structure, but questions remained as to whether the "compromise" heralded the reintroduction of an effective system of shared governance or the exhaustion of the faculty after four frustrating years of living under "interim" arrangements. Contingent instructors, now labeled "professors of practice and lecturers," along with librarians, archivists, and retired faculty were not included in the general category of faculty who elected senate officers, but they were allowed to select a limited number of representatives who served in a nonvoting capacity in the reconfigured senate.[104]

The role of contingent, especially part-time, faculty members in institutional decision making is likely to continue to be at the center of coming debates about the meaning of shared governance, especially because the issue generates serious divisions within faculties, as well as between faculties and administrations.

Even the Professional Staff Congress of CUNY—which not only is one of the largest faculty unions in the country, representing more than twenty-five thousand people but also includes more contingent than tenure-track faculty members—has recently experienced difficulty with the issue. In trying to rally opposition against a CUNY governing board initiative to implement a major curricular reform known as Pathways, which had been developed without meaningful faculty involvement, the PSC leadership decided to hold an institution-wide vote of no confidence in the program, but in so doing opted to restrict the vote to full-time faculty members. Although the reasoning behind this decision was a political calculation that such a vote would carry more weight with CUNY's governing board, the controversy highlighted some of the difficult governance questions raised by the increasing percentage of faculty members off the tenure track.[105]

The establishment of tenure in the first half of the twentieth century as a means of safeguarding academic freedom was, to a large extent, a precondition for the development of an effective faculty voice in institutional decision making. At the same time, the creation of a system of faculty governance in which the faculty exercised primary responsibility for the appointment, evaluation, promotion, and dismissal of fellow faculty members became a critical bulwark of the tenure system and the protections of academic freedom that tenure is intended to provide.[106] The rapid recent expansion in the proportion of faculty members appointed outside the tenure system, therefore, not only undermines the practices of shared governance but also represents the greatest threat to the institution of tenure and to academic freedom that has occurred since tenure became a generally accepted professional norm in American colleges and universities.

The increasing use of faculty on contingent appointments, however, is not the only threat to tenure that has surfaced in recent years. There have been some highly publicized direct assaults on the institution of tenure itself, though the overwhelming majority of colleges and universities continue to maintain a tenure system.[107] At three institutions, Lindenwood College, Bennington College, and the University of Minnesota, challenges to tenure were the result of efforts by governing boards and administrators to impose a more businesslike approach to management that had serious implications for faculty governance.[108]

Lindenwood College in Missouri, a small liberal arts school affiliated with the Presbyterian Church, is the second-oldest continuously operating institution of higher education west of the Mississippi River. During the 1980s, Lindenwood suffered a steep decline in enrollment, resulting in its governing board's declaring a state of financial exigency in 1989. Soon thereafter, the board retained the services of Dennis Spellmann, who had already gained a reputation for turning around the fortunes of a number of small schools that had been on the brink of bankruptcy.[109] Key to Spellmann's strategy was the recruitment of students who were eligible for federal financial aid and loans but otherwise seemed unlikely candidates for college admission. Spellman also established a highly centralized system of institutional decision making that would allow the president to eliminate some programs and create new ones with minimal delays in order to attract students quickly. After Spellmann became president, he moved to abolish tenure and eliminate what had been a strong system of faculty governance in order to remove any obstacles to his plans to revive Lindenwood's fortunes. Spellmann may have been successful in dramatically increasing enrollment and improving Lindenwood's financial condition, but his corporate approach to managing the college and trampling on faculty rights led the AAUP in 1994 to make Lindenwood the first institution ever to be formally sanctioned solely on the basis of egregious violations of the governance norms expressed in the 1966 *Statement on Government*.[110]

Bennington College, a small liberal arts institution in Vermont, was founded in 1932 as a women's college but became coeducational in 1970. In 1994 Bennington gained national attention when it not only terminated the appointments of twenty-six faculty members but also ended presumptive tenure (i.e., the promise that dismissal could be only for cause and with academic due process) for all future appointments. The fired faculty members made up more than one-third of Bennington's entire faculty; the majority of those fired held presumptive tenure, and nine had been at the school for more than twenty years.[111] At the same time, Bennington suspended all existing faculty governance bodies and procedures in order to institute a comprehensive plan secretly developed by the governing board to reorganize the college and eliminate several majors. Bennington's governing board claimed that it was acting in response to a condition of financial exigency brought on by a drop in enrollments, but the board made no effort to involve the faculty in determining whether a condition of financial exigency actually existed or in deciding how to respond to the financial difficulties the institution was facing. This was despite Bennington's long-established system of strong faculty governance. In fact, some Bennington faculty members believed that part of the reason for the board's actions was a desire to redress what board members had long seen as excessive faculty power, as evidenced by a successful effort by the faculty some years earlier to block a board-initiated reorganization plan. The ending of tenure thus went hand in hand with an attack on shared governance and an undermining of academic freedom, since most of those who were dismissed had been vocal critics of the administration and governing board.[112]

A major controversy over the institution of tenure that developed in 1996–97 at the University of Minnesota, one of the nation's largest research universities, gained substantial national attention, even though it did not represent as direct an assault on the institution of tenure as the attacks that had occurred at Lindenwood and Bennington. The battle over tenure between the faculty and the board of regents was directly tied to legislative pressures concerning the need to address financial problems in the university's academic health center. The state legislature made a special $8.6 million appropriation for the health center contingent on the adoption of changes in the university's tenure code that would make it easier to terminate the appointments of tenured faculty, but it soon became clear that the governing board itself regarded existing tenure regulations as an impediment to a more efficient operation of the entire university. Although the board never discussed eliminating tenure completely at the university, it put forth several proposals that, in the view of most faculty members, would have seriously undermined tenure as a protection of academic freedom. These included shifting the locus of tenure from the university as a whole to a particular department or program, so that if a department or even possibly a program were eliminated, a professor's services could be more easily terminated; allowing reductions in base salaries for tenured faculty members even if no condition of financial exigency existed; and permitting possible dismissal of a tenured faculty member who did not maintain "a proper attitude of industry and cooperation with others within and without the university community."[113]

The uproar from faculty members in response to these proposals led to a union organizing drive by the AAUP that quickly won enough support for the state's labor agency to order a delay in the administration's instituting any changes in working conditions until a union certification election could be held. The faculty vote in early 1997 nearly succeeded in making Minnesota one of the few major research universities to adopt collective bargaining, but the vote to establish a faculty union lost by the narrow margin of 692 to 666. Nevertheless, in response to the national furor and the threat of unionization that the controversy provoked, the board of regents ultimately backed away from most of its earlier proposals and finally adopted revisions to the tenure code that also won the approval of the faculty senate. Among the changes that were approved was the establishment of a system of post-tenure review (regularized periodic evaluations that were more comprehensive than traditional annual reviews), which was intended primarily for developmental, not punitive, purposes and which, in the case of a termination proceeding, did not threaten faculty rights to due process.[114]

While very few colleges or universities sought to eliminate tenure altogether, Minnesota's adoption of a system of post-tenure review was part of what has become a widespread movement to implement similar revisions to the tenure system. In a 2001 survey of nearly one thousand schools, Gabriel Kaplan reported that almost two-thirds (and three-fourths of public institutions) had adopted some form of post-tenure review. The AAUP, whose position had long been that post-tenure review was not only unnecessary but also a threat to tenure and to academic freedom, responded in 1999 to the increasing frequency of legislatively or administratively mandated post-tenure review systems by developing a policy statement that offered guidelines for institutions that did implement post-tenure review. While highlighting the potential threat to academic freedom entailed in the introduction of post-tenure review, the statement emphasized that, if an institution went forward with developing such a system, it was important that the faculty play the central role in its development.[115]

Since the mid-1970s, another development reflecting the growing power of a market model of management, especially that model's reliance on the laws of supply and demand to determine the allocation of resources and rewards, has been the increasing disparity in faculty salaries depending on academic discipline. By weakening the sense of common interest among faculty members, this development has contributed to the reshaping of the context in which institutional governance takes place. When research universities first emerged in American higher education in the late nineteenth century, salary differentials among faculty members had virtually no correlation to academic field but were based strictly on rank. Even as late as the early 1970s, Jack Schuster and Martin Finkelstein observe that, with the possible exception of medicine and law, "disparities in the salaries of faculty in different fields were small and had remained quite stable over time." By the early years of the twenty-first century, however, a beginning professor in business management could expect to receive a starting salary twice that of a beginning professor in English. Not coincidentally, fields such as education and foreign languages, where women made up a higher percentage of the faculty, were typically the lowest-paying disciplines.[116]

Faculty unions have made some efforts to develop policies, such as provisions for across-the-board salary increases, that would place limited restraints on the growth of greater disparities. Salary dispersion is, in fact, less prevalent in two-year institutions, where unions are strongest. However, Rhoades observes that collective bargaining agreements generally have had to work within and build on the wage stratification structures that have developed since the 1970s. He concludes that the growth of salary disparities based on discipline, institution, and gender have undermined "another dimension of professionalism—collegial governance—that critics believed would be imperiled by unionization. Expanding dispersion and steeper stratification not only contribute to tension and resentment within the collegium, but they make it more difficult and unlikely for faculty to form common cause and to act in a collective faculty interest."[117] Unions, on the other hand, according to Rhoades, "may strengthen faculty's position as *one* profession," even though they have thus far had only limited success in reversing the trend toward ever-greater disparities in salaries.

A final product of the increasingly corporate form of governance in American colleges and universities has been the growth in the number of administrators and a widening gap between administrative and faculty salaries. Between 1975 and 2005, the number of administrators rose by 85 percent, while the number of full-time faculty increased by only 50 percent. Even more strikingly, the number of "other professionals," a category that includes, for example, instructional technology specialists, development officers, and human-resources staffers, increased by 240 percent. At least part of this increase is attributable to the demands for institutional "assessment" being imposed by the states and the federal government.[118]

Of particular importance has been the solidification of academic administration as a career track distinct from the traditional faculty career focused on teaching and research. Whereas half a century ago many academic administrators occupied their positions as a temporary interlude during a professorial career, it has become increasingly common for those entering academic administration to leave behind active careers in teaching and scholarship permanently in the hope of moving up the administrative ladder, often while moving from institution to institution. As a consequence, many academic administrators have less of a sense of loyalty to their institution and are also more likely to adopt a managerial perspective that places less emphasis on academic expertise in institutional decision making and more on administrative efficiency and responsiveness to market forces.[119]

In addition, the almost universal use of private search firms in the hiring of senior administrators and a dramatic increase in presidential and other administrative salaries have also contributed to the solidification of a more corporate environment in American colleges and universities. Presidents have increasingly come to be referred to as "CEOs" and to receive compensation to match the new designation. Thus, for example, Gordon Gee, then president of Ohio State University, in 2007–8 became the first university CEO to earn more than $1 million a year, but by 2010 forty presidents—thirty-six of whom worked at private institutions—earned that much. The high level of administrative compensation at the California State University system and the University of California—even during a time of financial cutbacks—recently became a major issue of public debate, receiving sharp criticism from Governor Jerry Brown and from members of the state legislature, as well as from students and faculty members.[120]

The AGB's Retreat from the 1966 *Statement on Government*
Already by the mid-1980s clear signs had appeared of a breakdown in the general consensus over shared governance that had developed in American higher

education by the 1950s and 1960s. However, nothing more clearly demonstrated the extent of this breakdown than the issuance by the Association of Governing Boards in the late 1990s of two highly publicized statements on governance that represented a distinct backtracking from the AGB's earlier commendation to its members of the 1966 *Statement on Government of Colleges and Universities* that the AGB had jointly formulated with the AAUP and the American Council on Education. The AGB never subsequently fully repudiated the principles of shared governance, continuing to acknowledge in general terms that "faculty views almost always will be decisive on academic issues." However, whereas the AAUP in the decades after 1966 unilaterally issued a number of policy statements intended to elaborate on the need for faculty involvement in a variety of decision-making areas, the AGB's call in the late 1990s to give greater authority to academic presidents ("chief executive officers") and its assertion that the tradition of shared governance urgently needed to be "reshaped" though "not scrapped" reflected the growing strength of a more corporate-influenced approach to management. The AGB argued that such a reshaping was necessary so that when presidents tried to adapt their institutions to the new realities facing American higher education, they would be able to "resist academia's insatiable appetite for the kind of excessive consultation that can bring the institution to a standstill."[121]

The AGB's establishment of a special twenty-two member Commission on the Academic Presidency, chaired by former Virginia governor Gerald L. Baliles and composed of former college and university presidents, board members, and elected officials led first to the publication of a substantial report on the academic presidency in 1996 and then to the adoption of a somewhat briefer *AGB Statement on Institutional Governance* in 1998. Not surprisingly, given that these statements were intended to represent the AGB's particular perspective on these matters, no one representing a specifically faculty point of view was included on the commission. Many people in higher education viewed the 1998 report as a reassessment of, and an alternative to, the 1966 *Statement on Government*.[122] Both AGB reports were premised on the assumption that developments over the last several decades—including the failure of revenues to keep pace with the costs of instruction, public demands for greater accountability, the increasing need of colleges and universities to respond quickly to changes in student interests and to the demands of the job market, the revolution in instructional technology, new competition from for-profit institutions, the rapid expansion of community colleges, and the growing proportion of faculty on contingent appointments—required stronger executive leadership and governance reforms that would enable colleges and universities to be more "nimble" in responding to the rapidly changing environment.

The 1998 AGB statement duly noted the existence of differences between institutions of higher learning and business enterprises, recognizing that non-profit colleges and universities do not "operate with a profit motive" and that their "bottom lines . . . are far more difficult to measure."[123] However, as Neil Hamilton's analysis of the AGB statement points out, even though the AGB made reference to the "special mission" of colleges and universities, the statement made no effort to explain, even in general terms, what that mission was.[124] In contrast to the 1966 *Statement on Government,* which was jointly formulated by the AAUP, the American Council on Education, and the AGB and was suffused with an understanding that the mission of institutions of higher learning was the creation and dissemination of knowledge and that academic freedom, peer review, and shared governance were necessary for the accomplishment of that end, the 1998 AGB statement put far greater emphasis on the need for speed in decision making and the importance of executive authority. This new emphasis was grounded in the belief that, like corporate organizations in the business world, colleges and universities had to be governed in such a way as to be able quickly to respond to market forces and that speedy and decisive action required presidents enjoying greater authority.

Other aspects of the AGB's statement on governance also reflected an increasingly corporate perspective. Whereas the 1966 statement had regarded the governing board, the president, and the full-time faculty as the three principal partners in institutional governance, the AGB's 1998 statement regarded the tenured and tenure-track faculty as one "stakeholder" among many with a claim to being heard in the decision-making process, thereby downplaying the faculty's primary responsibility for carrying out the essential academic mission of institutions of higher education. The AGB bemoaned the publicity attendant upon many presidential searches, arguing that the publicity made the hiring of qualified candidates more difficult. The AGB, therefore, supported confidentiality in the selection process, thus making the process more akin to the way CEOs were chosen in the business world.

Although in the 1990s the AGB was clearly moving toward a more corporate-influenced approach to governance, it still recognized that there ought to be limits to trustee involvement in purely academic decision making. The more overtly conservative American Council of Trustees and Alumni (ACTA), which was founded in the mid-1990s by former head of the National Endowment for the Humanities Lynne Cheney, and which developed in some ways as a rival organization to the older and more established AGB, adopted an even more outspoken position in favor of a top-down approach to institutional decision making. ACTA also proclaimed the need for a more activist role for trustees in guarding against what it regarded as the dangers of "political correctness" on American campuses.[125] In contrast to ACTA, the AGB, after a change in leadership in 2006, once again began to adopt a more conciliatory approach to faculty. AGB's two most recent statements on governance issues in 2010 and 2011, while falling short of an endorsement of the 1966 *Statement on Governance*, do include stronger acknowledgments of the faculty role in academic decision making than do the organization's own 1998 statement or anything put out by ACTA.[126]

Early Twenty-First-Century Governance Surveys: A Critical Analysis

Three broad surveys of four-year institutions carried out between 2001 and 2007 included questions about the faculty role in governance. The most comprehensive in terms of questions asked and the number of schools involved was conducted by Gabriel Kaplan in 2001 with the cooperation of the AAUP and the American Council of Academic Deans and included responses by more than 1,500 administrators, senate leaders, and AAUP representatives from approximately 900 four-year institutions. William Tierney and James Minor's 2003 survey included responses by approximately 2,000 senate chairs, department chairs, and senior academic administrators from approximately 500 four-year institutions. William Cummings and Martin Finkelstein's 2007 survey of more than 1,000 randomly selected faculty members at 78 colleges and universities chosen to represent the broad spectrum of American four-year institutions of higher learning was part of a larger project, the 2007 Changing Academic Profession (CAP) International Survey, which was conducted in nineteen different countries.[127]

Although none of these recently published surveys includes information on the state of governance at individual institutions, both the Kaplan and CAP surveys included specific questions designed to track changes that might have occurred in governance attitudes and practices across American colleges and universities over the previous two or three decades. In his lengthy questionnaire, Kaplan included fifteen questions that had previously been used in the 1970 AAUP governance survey and then made systematic comparisons between the responses he received to these questions and the responses from the earlier AAUP survey. Kaplan made an adjustment for the difference between his sample and the institutions included in the 1970 survey by including in his published results comparisons of only those institutions appearing in both his survey and the earlier AAUP survey. The CAP survey replicated a 1992 international survey sponsored by the Carnegie Foundation for the Advancement of Teaching, thus allowing Cummings and Finkelstein to make observations about changes in attitudes over the previous fifteen years.

The Findings

All three surveys indicated that a majority of respondents believed that faculty typically exercised primary influence in what had become the traditional areas of faculty responsibility: most aspects of the curriculum, the appointment of new faculty colleagues, and promotion and tenure decisions. Moreover, both the CAP and Kaplan surveys indicated that faculty authority in these areas had actually increased in recent decades. The 2007 CAP survey thus showed the proportion of respondents reporting substantial faculty influence in promotion and tenure decisions rising from 37 percent in 1992 to 51 percent in 2007. The results in Kaplan's survey show even more dramatically an apparent growth in faculty authority between 1970 and 2001. The percentage of respondents reporting either faculty determination or joint control with administrators in the appointment of new full-time faculty members rose from 31 to 73; the percentage reporting substantial faculty control over tenure and promotion decisions rose from 36 to 71. Respondents reported less change in faculty responsibility for the curriculum and degree requirements, but only because even in the earlier survey more than 80 percent of respondents believed the faculty exercised substantial control in these areas as compared to slightly above 90 percent in 2001.[128]

Since the academic department had become the principal focus of faculty life, the faculty role in the selection of department chairs or heads had long been a key issue in faculty governance. Of the three surveys discussed here, only Kaplan included a question singling out the faculty role in the selection of chairs or heads, but he found that 54 percent of respondents reported that faculty at their institution had either determinative or joint authority in such decisions, an increase over the 22 percent claiming the existence of such a role in 1970. Conversely, whereas 24 percent of respondents in 1970 said the faculty played no role at all in the selection of department executives, that number had fallen to only 4 percent in 2001.

While these surveys suggest that faculty influence over primarily department-based academic decisions—the area that had long been the main focus of the faculty's governance activity—was considerable in the early twenty-first century, faculty authority in decisions that were made beyond the department level remained significantly weaker and in some key areas remained minimal. Kaplan's survey, for example, found that only 32 percent of those responding reported a substantial role for faculty in the appointment of academic deans. It should be noted, however, that this figure marked an increase from 14 percent in 1970. Only 5 percent, as compared to 29 percent in 1970, said the faculty played no role.

The CAP and Tierney and Minor surveys included questions about the faculty role in the selection of senior administrators (whom Tierney and Minor defined as academic vice presidents) and presidents). Cummings and Finkelstein found that only 8 percent of respondents reported substantial faculty influence in this area of decision making, though this actually represented an increase from the 5 percent who made a similar assertion in 1992. Tierney and Minor reported that the majority of respondents stated that their authority in the selection of senior administrators was only "informal."

In the critical areas of budget making and setting strategic priorities, all three surveys indicated that the faculty role also generally continued to be minimal. In the CAP survey, only 2 percent of respondents believed that the faculty played a substantial role in determining budgetary priorities, which represented a slight decline from the 4 percent recorded in 1992. The numbers in the Tierney and Minor survey were somewhat higher but still low, ranging from a high of 16 percent in baccalaureate institutions to 12 and 13 percent in master's and doctoral institutions.[129] Kaplan's survey produced the most positive response regarding the faculty role in short-range budgetary planning, with 18 percent of respondents reporting that faculty played a substantial role, an increase from the 4 percent who made a similar claim in 1970. However, these numbers still demonstrated the continuing limits on faculty authority in this critical area of institutional decision making.

Critical Analysis of Findings

All three surveys arrived at the rather surprising finding that the faculty role in governance in the first decade of the twenty-first century seemed relatively strong and was, in most respects, probably greater than it had been in the previous generation. Tierney and Minor, for example, found that more than 90 percent of the institutions they surveyed had some form of senate, the large majority of which were chaired by an elected faculty member, and that, at least in the abstract, "overwhelming support for shared governance" existed among both faculty and administrators at all types of four-year institutions (i.e., from liberal arts colleges to research-intensive universities), even if there was no agreement on exactly what the concept of shared governance entailed. Definitions ranged from "fully collaborative decision making" to simple consultation and "information sharing."[130]

Remarkably, in comparing the responses to all fifteen of the questions concerning different areas of institutional decision making that Kaplan repeated from the 1970 AAUP survey, he found that the percentage of respondents indicating substantial faculty control (which he defined as either faculty determination or joint action with the administration, as opposed to simple consultation or discussion) had actually increased. Kaplan also asked the 2001 respondents about their own perceptions of whether the power of the various participants in governance had increased, stayed the same, or declined over the past two decades. Overall, this question produced the implausible response from survey respondents that *every* party to institutional decision making had gained more power than it had lost during the last twenty years. Deans and other division heads were seen as having made the greatest gains in power, though faculty governance bodies were ranked a close second, with state coordinating boards, governing boards, presidents, and department chairs all reported as also gaining in power, but to a lesser degree.

How, then, to make sense of these survey results in light of the contention made throughout this chapter that the last several decades have actually seen both an undermining of an earlier consensus about the meaning of shared governance and serious challenges to the role of faculty in institutional decision making?

One factor to consider is that Kaplan's results consistently reflect the respondents' more favorable perception of the extent and importance of the faculty role in institutional decision making than do the responses of those participating in the other two surveys. In order to assess the results of Kaplan's survey, and especially his comparison of results from matched institutions also included in the 1970 AAUP survey, it is instructive to look at the positions held by those responding to his questions. Kaplan sent questionnaires to campus presidents and to AAUP chapter leaders where campus chapters existed. In addition to asking for a response from the AAUP chapter representative and the institutional president (or a senior administrator designated by the president), Kaplan also requested that each president identify a senior faculty member to complete the survey. In the overwhelming majority of cases, institutional responses did include feedback from both at least one faculty member identified by the president and an administrator. However, in the matched sample of nearly five hundred schools appearing in both the 1970 AAUP survey and Kaplan's 2001 survey, AAUP members participated in answering questions in more than 80 percent of the institutions involved in the 1970 study but in only 15 percent of the schools involved in Kaplan's survey.[131] This dramatic difference in the extent of AAUP participation in these two surveys was largely a reflection of the substantial decline between 1970 and 2001 in the number of campuses with active AAUP chapters.

It is reasonable to conclude that the substantial drop in AAUP member participation may well have affected the extent of the change Kaplan's study seemed to show in faculty power between 1970 and 2001. In all three recent governance surveys, as well as in the 1970 AAUP survey, administrators tended to have a rosier view of the level of faculty influence than did faculty members themselves, and, as Kaplan notes, AAUP members, who often were in a more adversarial position in relation to administrators than were senate leaders, had a still less positive view than did the faculty representatives identified by presidents. While not necessarily invalidating Kaplan's findings, the composition of his survey population does help to explain why his 2001 survey showed such a dramatic increase in positive perceptions of faculty authority since 1970.

An additional factor that must be taken into consideration in evaluating the results from all three recent surveys is that they almost certainly do not represent the views of faculty on contingent appointments, who would likely have a far more pessimistic view of faculty influence on decision making. The faculty members involved in the Tierney and Minor survey were all department chairs or senate leaders and thus more than likely were full-time tenured professors. Kaplan's respondents also likely came from the same strata of the faculty. The CAP survey was sent to a random sample of faculty members drawn from faculty lists provided by the institutions involved. This would have allowed for a broader representation of faculty members, but since most universities do not typically include part-time or even, in some cases, full-time but temporary faculty members on their lists of faculty, non-tenure-track faculty were undoubtedly not proportionally represented in the sample. Of course, the same argument could be made about all previous governance surveys cited here. However, because part-time and contingent faculty made up a much smaller proportion of the professoriate in 1970 than in the first decade of the twenty-first century, the distortion resulting from their exclusion would be significantly greater in the more recent surveys.

Another factor to consider in evaluating the significance of the results of the three recent governance surveys is the extent to which critical aspects of academic decision making had moved, over the past thirty years, outside the academic department, that is, outside the area of most faculty members' primary governance focus and role. At a time of expanding budgets and widespread public support for higher education, faculty control at the departmental level over the curriculum and the appointment and promotion of tenure-track colleagues was of crucial importance to institutional governance. However, when more and more faculty were being hired off the tenure track and more decisions about the addition of new academic programs (as opposed to the establishment of degree requirements) were being made by higher-level administrators on the basis of financial considerations, faculty control over the traditional areas of faculty responsibility has become less meaningful, even though full-time tenure-track faculty continued to perceive their role in areas of traditional faculty governance as quite strong.

This departmental focus might help to explain Tierney and Minor's finding that although respondents to their survey believed faculty exercised strong influence in certain areas of traditional faculty responsibility, respondents also expressed what Tierney and Minor describe as "widespread dissatisfaction with faculty senates" operating on an institution-wide basis. Among all respondents,

43 percent stated that "involvement in the Senate was not highly valued." At doctoral universities in their sample, "only 19 percent of respondents agreed that faculty had high levels of interest in Senate activities," though the figures were higher at baccalaureate (54 percent) and master's (39 percent) institutions, where senates may have been a more recent development. Overall, 53 percent of respondents reported a "low level of interest in Senate activities."[132]

A final factor that helps to account for the surprising results of the three recent governance surveys is a narrowing in the gap between governance practices at non-research-oriented colleges and universities and practices at more research-intensive institutions and highly selective liberal arts colleges. These latter institutions pioneered in the development of shared governance, where the extent of faculty authority probably did not peak until some years after the 1970 AAUP governance survey took place. In the early 1970s, faculty members at research universities and highly selective liberal arts colleges exercised significantly more influence in institutional decision making than did faculty members at other four-year colleges and universities. Two-year institutions lagged still further behind in developing shared-governance practices. Even after the mid-1970s, when a variety of factors may have been undermining the practices of shared governance at research universities, such practices may have been spreading to more non-research-oriented institutions, such as former teachers colleges, which had only recently come to employ more fully professionalized faculties. Cummings and Finkelstein conclude that by 2007,

> the CAP findings suggest that differences in faculty influence . . . attributable to institutional type are barely discernible. In part, that may represent from an institutional perspective, the increasing penetration of the research university model throughout the American system. This in effect minimizes interinstitutional differences by way of bolstering the fortunes and influence of faculty at nonresearch institutions. While that phenomenon may certainly be at work here, the data seem to suggest an actual decline in faculty influence at the research universities between 1992 and 2007. When this decline is combined with the bolstering of faculty at the nonresearch university sector, we see a muting of historic interinstitutional differences in faculty power and authority.[133]

As a result of the development by the mid-1970s of what amounted to a glut of new PhDs, colleges and universities of all types appointed increasing numbers of faculty members with doctorates. Once these new faculty members obtained tenure-track positions, they were more likely than less professionalized faculty members to develop greater expectations about the role they would play in institutional decision making. For all levels of American higher education, the percentage of full-time faculty members holding the doctorate increased after 1969, but the increase at comprehensive and liberal arts institutions was especially noteworthy, rising from 52 percent in 1969 to 69 percent in 1998. Even at two-year institutions, the proportion of faculty with doctorates approximately doubled between 1969 and 1998, reaching nearly 20 percent by the end of the last century. By 2007, the CAP survey found that 85 percent of all full-time faculty members at four-year colleges and universities held the doctorate.[134] At non-research-oriented institutions, the increased presence of faculty with greater professional credentials and expectations, together with the competitive pressures on four-year institutions to improve their academic reputations, may well have contributed to the rise in the overall numbers of faculty and administrators reporting an enhanced role for faculty in institutional governance.

It is also significant that none of the three recent governance surveys included two-year institutions in its sample. In contrast, the 1970 AAUP survey included responses from 177 two-year and technical schools, which undoubtedly resulted in a lower overall assessment of the faculty role in governance at that time, since in 1970 many two-year institutions were still closely associated with the practices of K–12 education.

In spite of their limitations, the recent governance surveys discussed here still indicate that the ideal and practices of shared governance are not yet altogether dead. Faculty today still do exercise considerably more influence over academic decision making than they did early in the twentieth century. However, the trends that have developed in American higher education since the mid-1970s, particularly the deprofessionalization of the faculty, are seriously undermining the foundation upon which the practices of shared governance arose. This development should be of concern not just to faculty members. As discussed in the conclusion, the continuation of present trends would result in seriously compromising the quality of American colleges and universities and in dangerously narrowing the broad democratic purposes of American higher education. These trends, in other words, pose a threat to the very health of American democracy.

Shared Governance and the Future of Liberal Education

The future of shared governance, and of American higher education more generally, will be determined in large part by the extent to which an unfettered corporate-based market model continues to predominate in Americans' thinking about virtually every aspect of society. In spite of such corporate scandals as the Enron debacle and the abuses that led in 2008 to the worst economic crisis since the Great Depression, obeisance to an unalloyed market model is still widespread in American society. What has been happening on American college campuses is only one aspect of a larger and continuing conservative movement challenging the notion that there are viable alternatives to a socioeconomic system in which all incentives are defined solely by the pursuit of self-interest and the laws of supply and demand.

Recent attempts to "reform" American higher education, including its system of governance, have clear echoes in conservative efforts to challenge the legitimacy of other potential obstacles to the untrammeled operation of market forces, such as government regulation and labor unions. Conservative efforts to "reform" American colleges and universities also have clear parallels to the bureaucratization and commercialization being imposed on other professions such as medicine. These "reform" efforts are part of a broader movement that seeks to question the validity of the ideal of professionalism—an ideal premised on the possibility of individuals using their expertise in a disinterested way to advance the common good. The attacks on the principles and practices of shared governance are also directly related to assaults on the idea of "liberal education"—that is, on the notion that higher education should be designed as more than direct preparation for entry into the job market—and to assaults on the view that access to a college education constitutes a public and not just a private good.

Writing in defense of the professional ideal, Louis Menand has acknowledged that there is good reason for "skepticism" about the disinterestedness of professionals. He recognizes that many Americans have come to view professionals' efforts to enjoy certain privileges—such as tenure and a significant degree of autonomy for college professors—as more or less a "racket." Professionals, including professors, lawyers, and doctors, can indeed act in ways that reflect their own self-interested motivations. Many professors have come to focus so narrowly on their own disciplines and on their own advancement that they have failed to identify with the broader purposes of higher education and the obligations and responsibilities of their profession. Menand argues, however, that whatever their shortcomings, professions remain a necessary component of a largely market-based economy, because in "a system designed to be driven by efficiency and self-interest, professions set standards for performance that value quality over dollars."[1]

In the case of higher education, a professional professoriate acting through the mechanisms of shared governance is potentially the last-line defender against the triumph of a narrowly utilitarian definition of the purposes of higher education that views students as customers and sees job training as the sole function of colleges and universities. Sociologist Robert Bellah has pointed out that it is "the teacher, not the student, who knows what the student needs to learn." He argues that a purely market model is fundamentally flawed when applied to higher education because that model is predicated on the existence of a "fixed preference in the mind of the consumer, who simply shops for the best way to fulfill that preference. In the teacher-student relationship, which is not intrinsically an economic one, there can be no fixed preference in advance." Bellah goes on to contend that higher education must have a broader mission than helping students "get good jobs," though that goal is one of the purposes of a college education. More broadly, higher education in a democratic society should "contribute to the self-understanding of society, so that both individually and collectively we can make sense of our world, can orient our action, and can make better decisions in many spheres—family, community, nation, and, to be sure, economy as well."[2]

The successful fulfillment of these broad goals of higher education is not subject to easy measurement and quantification. The current drive for accountability and assessment and for performance-based standards to justify funding for institutions of higher education that is being pushed by many politicians, corporate leaders, and governing board members may be understandable in light of the increasing cost of a college education. However, this movement as currently constituted, with its reliance on corporate-based assumptions about the possibility of establishing readily quantifiable bottom-line "outcomes," is likely to result in colleges and universities placing an ever-greater emphasis on fulfilling those aspects of their mission that are most easily measured (such as narrowly defined job competencies) than on carrying out their broader democratic mission.[3] Ironically, just as such a bottom-line approach as applied to K–12 education through George W. Bush's No Child Left Behind program has become increasingly discredited, the Obama administration is now contemplating applying the same bottom-line approach to higher education.[4]

I have written elsewhere on the connection between the survival of a liberal conception of the purpose of higher education and the fate of shared governance:

> The principle of shared governance may be historically grounded in notions of expertise and professionalism, rather than in the concept of democracy. Yet in the context of today's misguided efforts to apply what is already a discredited corporate model of management to higher education, shared governance is taking on new importance as a means of trying to preserve the ideals of liberal education that are necessary for the continued vitality of our democratic society. For a democratic society to flourish, its citizens must be able to think critically, be independent minded, and have a sense of history and an understanding of the world in which they live. These have long been the goals of a liberal education.
>
> But liberal education is today coming under increasing attack. It is no coincidence that many of those who seek to reduce higher education to a form of narrowly conceived job training are also in the forefront of efforts to replace shared governance with a corporate model of management. Advocates of a top-down management style who want to transform faculty from professionals into "employees" and students into "consumers" tend to see liberal education as a waste of time and resources, because they fail to see the immediate "payoff" of the liberal and fine arts and because they are willing to allow the "market" to determine what should and should not be taught.[5]

In coming years, if current trends continue, the global preeminence of American colleges and universities is at risk. This is true not only because of the cutbacks in government funding for higher education at both the state and federal levels that have occurred in recent years. It is true also because the narrowing of the mission of American colleges and universities and the subsequent downgrading of the critical role of the humanities and liberal arts will lead to the elimination of what has been one of the unique characteristics of the American academic tradition: namely, the assumption that a college education should seek to foster the growth of the whole individual. As Ellen Schrecker has pointed out, American higher education has been one of the few systems in the world that exposes all of its students to the humanities, rather than offering early in a student's career specifically vocational tracks with a narrow curricular focus. American higher education, consequently, has become noted for cultivating creativity and independent thinking in its students, traits that have long enabled American colleges and universities to attract top students from around the world. Universities in other countries are now beginning to emulate this approach, leading Schrecker to observe that it "would be ironic, indeed, if just at the moment when other societies embrace a more humanities-oriented higher education, the United States abandons it."[6]

A reestablishment of the faculty's primary responsibility for academic decision making is no guarantee that American higher education will in the future successfully resist the commercialization and narrowing of purpose that has recently taken hold on American college campuses. After all, faculty members themselves must bear some of the responsibility for the retreat from higher education's democratic purposes that has already occurred in American colleges and universities. Not all faculty members are committed to a broad view of the purposes of higher education. A small segment of the professoriate has clearly benefited economically from the greater opportunities for entrepreneurial activity provided by the contemporary university, including the chance to compete for external funding for research that can produce "profitable" results. These faculty members may, therefore, tend to shun involvement in institutional governance because it takes away from the time they could use to try to reap potentially significant personal gains from the system of academic capitalism that has emerged over the last several decades. They have also been too ready to accept, and even support, the expansion of contingent appointments among the faculty as a means of relieving their own teaching "burden," even though that expansion is resulting in the deprofessionalization of the professoriate as a whole.

Even many faculty members who appreciate the value of preserving liberal education as an essential element of the mission of our colleges and universities and have little prospect of reaping great personal rewards in the new entrepreneurial university may feel that as a matter of personal survival they are unable to devote time and energy to governance work to defend a broad vision of higher education's purpose. The lack of institutional recognition and reward for such work and the pressures on faculty members to focus on disciplinary activity rather than on service to their home institution if they hope to gain promotion and salary increases (which in recent years have not kept up with inflation) help to explain the widespread lack of interest in governance activities among faculty members surveyed by Tierney and Minor.[7] For those on part-time appointments, the lack of institutional support and the frequent need to divide their time among multiple institutions make it even harder for them to take on a fully active role in governance.

But if any group is to take the lead in standing up for academic values and the importance of a liberal education and trying to prevent the further degradation of the quality and narrowing of purpose of our colleges and universities, it must be the faculty, who must reassert their commitment to a broad conception of their professional rights and responsibilities. Current graduate training too often fails to teach future faculty members about the importance of academic traditions such as shared governance and academic freedom, as well as about the professional responsibilities that are entailed in being a faculty member. Yet no group is more likely to be able to appreciate the dangers of reducing higher education to just another "industry" than faculty members who are willing to devote many years of their lives in preparation for entry into a profession whose attraction is typically intellectual, not simply economic.

Faculty must make the case to the American public that current trends, including the deprofessionalization of the faculty and the retreat from the practices of shared governance, pose a danger to the future well-being of American society.[8] Even as the market model and a top-down approach to management have gained predominance in most aspects of American life, some voices outside academe have long recognized that in a "knowledge-based society" management ignores professional expertise at its peril. Management guru Peter Drucker thus argued as early as 1980 that the increasing importance of expertise and professional groups in modern "postindustrial" society would require "new, and fairly radical, organizational concepts." He predicted that the "hospital or the university will be a better model than the traditional military" as organizations become "concentric, overlapping, coordinated rings, rather than pyramids." Drucker concluded that there needed to be a recognition "that within given fields the professionals should set the standards and determine what their contribution should be."[9] Rather than being an obstacle to "progress" and greater "efficiencies," a "collegial" form of shared governance represents a model that, in many respects, has made possible the success of many cutting-edge high-tech firms and companies in other areas of the economy that are especially dependent on the expertise and creativity of their knowledge workers.

During the twentieth century, the growth of a major role in institutional governance for an increasingly professionalized faculty was instrumental in the development of more rigorous academic standards and in the rise of American higher education to a position of global preeminence. The practices of shared governance that developed in American colleges and universities were thus not simply a privilege and perquisite of the professoriate; they were a necessary condition for the development of a system of higher education that became the envy of the rest of the world. Reinvigorating the practices of shared governance on American college and university campuses will be critical if the United States is to maintain its position of global leadership in higher education.

1924 AAUP Governance Survey Results

Institution	Franchise	Select admin.	Select pres.	Select fac.	Budget
U Akron	1	0	0	0	0
U Alabama	2	0	0	0	2
Albright C	3	0	0	0	0
Alfred U	1	1	1	0	0
Alma C	1	1	0	0	0
Amherst C	1	1	0	2	0
Antioch C	2	0	0	2	0
Baker U	1	0	0	2	0
Baylor U	1	0	0	0	0
Beaver C	1	0	0	1	0
Berea C	1	0	0	0	1
Bowdoin C	1	0	0	1	2
Bradley Institute	1	0	0	0	0
Bucknell U	2	0	0	0	0
Butler C	1	0	0	0	0
UC Berkeley	1	0	0	1	1
Carleton C	1	0	0	2	2
Carroll C	1	0	0	0	1
Case School of Applied Science	2	0	0	0	0
Catholic U	3	1	0	1	0
Cedarville C	3	0	0	0	0
Central Wesleyan C	1	0	0	1	1
U Cincinnati	1	0	0	0	0
Citadel	1	0	0	0	0
Clark U	1	1	0	1	0
Clarkson C of Technology	2	0	0	0	1
Colgate U	2	0	0	0	0
U Colorado	2	1	1	0	0
Connecticut C	2	1	0	0	0
Cornell C	1	0	0	0	0
Cornell U	2	0	0	2	0
Cotner C	3	0	0	0	0

(continued)

1 = all
2 = no instructors and/or asst prof.
3 = full profs
4 = no clear response.

Institution	Franchise	Select admin.	Select pres.	Select fac.	Budget
Dartmouth C	1	0	0	0	0
U Delaware	2	0	0	0	0
DePauw U	1	0	0	0	0
Dickinson C	2	0	1	0	0
Doane C	1	0	0	0	0
Earlham C	1	0	0	0	0
Emporia C	1	0	0	0	0
Eureka C	1	1	0	0	0
U Florida	2	0	0	0	0
Friends U	1	0	0	2	0
Geneva C	0	0	0	0	0
George Peabody C for Teachers	1	0	0	2	0
Georgia Tech	2	0	0	0	0
Grove City C	1	0	0	2	0
Guilford C	1	1	0	1	0
Gustavus Adolphus C	1	1	0	0	0
Hamilton C	1	0	0	0	2
Hampden Sidney C	2	0	0	0	0
Harvard U	0	0	0	0	0
Haverford C	1	0	0	2	0
Hiram C	3	0	0	0	0
Hope C	1	1	0	0	0
C of Idaho	1	1	0	0	0
U Idaho	2	0	0	0	0
Illinois C	1	0	0	0	1
Illinois Wesleyan U	1	0	0	0	0
Illinois Women's C	0	0	0	0	0
Indiana U	1	0	0	0	1
Intermountain Union C	1	0	1	0	1
Iowa Wesleyan C	1	0	0	0	0
James Millikin U	3	1	0	0	0
Johns Hopkins U	2	1	0	0	1
Juniata C	1	0	0	0	0
U Kansas	2	1	1	0	0
U Kentucky	2	0	1	0	0
Knox C	1	0	0	1	0
Lafayette C	1	0	0	0	1
Lawrence C	1	0	0	1	1
Lehigh U	2	0	1	0	0
Lombard C	1	0	0	0	0
Louisiana C	1	0	0	0	0
Marietta C	1	0	0	1	1
Maryville C	3	1	0	1	1
McPherson C	1	0	0	1	0
MIT	1	0	0	0	0
Miami U (OH)	2	0	0	1	0
U Michigan	2	0	0	0	1
Middlebury C	1	0	0	0	0
Mills C	1	1	0	0	0
Millsaps C	2	0	0	0	0

Institution	Franchise	Select admin.	Select pres.	Select fac.	Budget
Milton C	1	0	0	0	0
Milwaukee-Downer C	1	0	0	0	0
U Minnesota	1	0	0	1	0
U Missouri	2	0	0	0	1
Missouri Valley C	1	0	0	0	0
U Montana	1	1	0	0	1
Morningside C	3	0	0	0	0
Mount Union C	2	0	0	1	0
Muhlenberg C	1	0	0	0	0
Muskingum C	3	1	1	1	0
U Nebraska	2	1	0	0	0
Nebraska Wesleyan U	3	0	0	0	0
NY State C for Teachers, Albany	2	0	0	1	2
CCNY	1	0	0	1	0
NYU	2	0	0	0	1
U North Dakota	2	0	1	0	0
Northern Illinois State Teachers C	1	0	0	0	2
Northwestern C	1	0	0	0	0
Northwestern U	1	0	0	0	1
U Notre Dame	2	0	0	0	0
Oberlin C	1	1	0	1	1
Ohio Wesleyan U	1	0	1	1	0
U Oklahoma	0	0	0	0	0
U Oregon	2	0	0	0	1
Ottawa U	1	0	0	0	0
Otterbein C	2	1	0	0	0
C of the Pacific	1	0	0	0	0
Park C	1	0	1	0	0
Pennsylvania State C	0	0	0	0	0
U Pennsylvania	2	0	0	0	0
Phillips U	0	0	0	0	0
Presbyterian C of South Carolina	3	1	0	0	0
Princeton U	2	0	0	1	0
U Puerto Rico	1	0	0	0	0
Radcliffe C	0	0	0	0	0
Randolph-Macon Woman's C	3	0	0	0	0
Reed C	1	1	1	1	1
Rhode Island C of Education	1	0	0	2	2
Rhode Island State C	2	0	0	0	0
Roanoke C	1	0	0	1	0
U Rochester	1	1	0	0	0
Rockford C	2	0	0	0	0
Rutgers C and U of New Jersey	2	0	0	0	0
St. John's C	1	0	0	1	1

(*continued*)

Institution	Franchise	Select admin.	Select pres.	Select fac.	Budget
Simmons C	1	0	0	0	0
Smith C	1	0	0	1	0
U South Carolina	2	0	0	0	0
U South Dakota	2	0	0	0	0
Stanford U	2	0	0	1	0
Sterling C	3	0	0	0	1
Swarthmore C	2	1	1	2	0
Sweet Briar C	3	0	0	0	0
Syracuse U	2	1	0	2	0
Temple U	0	0	0	2	0
U Texas	2	0	0	1	2
Thiel C	2	1	0	0	0
Transylvania C	3	0	0	0	0
Trinity C (CT)	2	0	0	1	0
Trinity C (NC)	1	0	0	0	0
Trinity U (TX)	3	0	0	0	0
Tufts C	1	1	0	0	0
Tulane U	0	0	0	0	0
Union C	2	0	0	0	0
Vanderbilt U	2	1	0	2	2
Vassar C	1	1	0	1	1
VMI	0	0	0	0	0
U Virginia	2	0	0	1	0
U Washington	1	0	1	0	0
Washington U (St. Louis)	2	0	0	0	0
Washington & Jefferson C	3	0	0	2	2
Washington & Lee U	2	0	1	1	0
Wellesley C	0	0	0	0	2
Wells C	2	0	0	0	0
Wesleyan U (CT)	1	1	0	1	0
Western Reserve U	1	1	1	1	1
Wheaton C	0	0	0	0	0
William & Mary C	2	0	0	0	0
William Jewell C	1	0	0	0	0
Williams C	2	0	0	1	0
Wilson C	2	1	0	0	0
Wittenberg C	2	0	0	0	1
C Wooster	1	1	1	1	1
Wyoming U	2	0	0	1	0
Yale U	1	1	0	1	0
Yankton C	3	0	0	1	0

Sources: Data derived from survey results reported in AAUP, "Report of Committee T: Data Concerning the Actual Status of Faculties in University Government in a Number of Institutions." *Bulletin of the AAUP* 10 (May 1924): 43–104. Questions as they appeared in the original survey. Coding system developed by author.

Questions and coding system:

Franchise: To what ranks is the franchise restricted in your Faculty or Faculties?
 1 = All
 2 = No instructors and/or asst profs
 3 = Full profs.
 0 = No clear response

Select admin.: Does the Faculty participate in the selection of its own administrative officers other than the President? If so, how does it work?

   1 = Formal involvement
   2 = Significant involvement
   0 = No involvement or no clear reply

Select pres.: Does the Faculty have any voice in the selection of the President?

   1 = Yes
   0 = No

Select fac.: To what extent and how do the Faculty members participate in the selection of members of the teaching staff?

   1 = Formal involvement
   2 = Significant involvement
   0 = No involvement or no clear reply

Budget: Has the Faculty any voice in the making of the budget or in determining the salary scale? If so, how?

   1 = Formal involvement
   2 = Significant consultation
   0 = No involvement or no clear reply

Note: One question from the original six-question survey has been omitted from the coded results: How does the Faculty participate in the determination of educational policies? Is there provision for regular conferences in these matters between the Trustees and the Faculty? If so, how does it work?

1939 AAUP Governance Survey Results

Institution	Board	Pres.	Appts.	Deans	Budget	Com.	Dept. ex.	Total
U Akron	0	4	1	0	2	0	0	7
Alabama Polytechnic Institute	0	0	1	0	2	0	0	3
U Alabama	0	0	0	0	0	0	0	0
Allegheny C	0	4	1	0	1	2	0	8
Amherst C	4	0	3	2	1	4	4	18
Antioch C	4	4	3	2	4	2	2	21
U Arizona	0	0	1	0	2	0	0	3
U Arkansas	0	0	2	1	2		0	5
U Arkansas School of Medicine	0	0	1		2	0	0	3
Ashland C	4	0	3	0	4	4	0	15
Atlanta U	0	0	1	0	1	2	0	4
Augustana C	0	0	1	0	0	4	0	5
Baldwin-Wallace C	0	4	1	0	1	1	0	7
Ball State Teachers C	0	0	1	0	2	0	0	3
Baylor U	0	0	1	0	0	2	0	3
Berea C	4	4	0	0	2	0	0	10
Boston U	4	4	1	0	2	0	0	11
Bowling Green State U	0	0	1	0	2	2	0	5
Bradley Polytechnic Institute	0	0	1	0	2	2	0	5
Brooklyn C	4	4	4	0	4	4	4	24

(continued)

Institution	Board	Pres.	Appts.	Deans	Budget	Com.	Dept. ex.	Total
Brown U	4	4	2	0	2	2	0	14
Bryn Mawr C	4	4	4	2	0	4	0	18
Bucknell U	0	4	1	1	2	2	4	14
U Buffalo	0	0	4	2	2	2	0	10
Caltech	4	0	2	2	4	2	0	14
UCLA	0	4	4	2	4	4	0	18
Carnegie Tech	0	0	3	0	2	2	0	7
Case School of Applied Science	0	4	0	0	0	2	0	6
Catholic U	0	0	0	2	0		2	4
Centenary C of Louisiana	0	0	0	0	0	0	0	0
Central YMCA	0	0	1	0	2	2	0	5
U Chicago	0	4	1	1	2	2	1	11
U Cincinnati	0	4	3	1	2	2	0	12
CCNY (Commerce Center)	4	4	3	2	3	4	4	24
CCNY	4	4	4	0	4	2	4	22
Coe C	0	0	1	1	1	0	0	3
Colgate U	0	0	1	0	2	0	0	3
Colorado State C of Agriculture & Mechanical Arts	0	0	0	0	0	2	0	2
U Colorado	4	4	3	2	4	2	4	23
Columbia U	0	0	1	0	3	2	2	8
Concord State Teachers C	0	0	0	0	1	0	0	1
Conn C for Women	0	0	1	4	2	4	0	11
U Connecticut	0	0	2	1	2	2	0	7
Cornell C	4	4	3	0	0	4	0	15
Cornell U	4	4	2	2	4	4	0	20
Creighton U	0	0	3	0	0	0	0	3
Culver-Stockton C	0	0	0	0	1	2	0	3
Dalhousie U	4	0	1	0	1	4	0	10
Dartmouth C	4	0	4	0	2	4	0	14
U Delaware	0	0	1	2	2	0	0	5
Denison U	0	0	1	0	4	4	0	9
U Denver	4	4	3	0	4	4	0	19
DePauw U	0	4	4	0	0	2	2	12
Drake U	0	0	0	0	0	2	0	2
Drew U	4	0	0	0	4	0	0	8
Duke U	0	0	1	1	2	0	0	4
Emory U	0	4	0	1	0	2	0	7
Fairmount State Teachers C	0	0	0	0	0	0	0	0
Findlay C	0	0	0	0	0	0	0	0
Florida State C for Women	0	0	0	0	0	0	0	0
U Florida	0	0	1	0	2	0	0	3
Fordham U	0	0	3	0	0	0	0	3
Franklin & Marshall C	0	0	1	0	0	0	0	1

Institution	Board	Pres.	Appts.	Deans	Budget	Com.	Dept. ex.	Total
Franklin C	0	0	1	0	2	0	0	3
Fresno State C	0	0	2	0	4	2	0	8
Furman U	0	0	0	0	0	2	0	2
George Washington U	0	4	3	0	2	2	0	11
Georgia State C for Women	0	0	1	0	2	0	0	3
U Georgia	0	0	1	2	4	4	2	13
Gettysburg C	0	0	1	0	0	0	0	1
Goucher C	0	4	3	0	2	2	2	13
Grinnell C	4	4	1	4	4	2	4	23
Harris Teachers C	0	0	0	0	0	0	0	0
Harvard U	0	0	4	0	3	2	0	9
Hastings C	4	0	1	0	0	2	0	7
Heidelberg C	0	4	1	0	0	0	0	5
Hobart C (William Smith)	4	0	1	0	2	2	2	11
Hood C	0	0	1	1	2	2	0	6
Howard U	4	0	1	0	2	2	0	9
Hunter C	4		4	0	4	4	4	20
Illinois State Normal U (Normal)	0	0	1	0	2	0	0	3
Illinois State Normal U (Southern)	0	0	1	1	4	2	0	8
Illinois State Teachers C (DeKalb)	0	0	1	0	0	0	0	1
Illinois State Teachers C (Macomb)	0	0	1	0	0	0	0	1
U Illinois	4	4	4	2	4	4	4	24
Indiana State Teachers C	0	0	1	1	2	2	4	10
Indiana U	4	0	1	1	2	0	0	8
Iowa State C	0	0	3	0	2	2	0	7
Iowa State Teachers C	0	0	1	0	0	0	0	1
Iowa State U	0	0	1	0	2	2	1	6
Johns Hopkins U	0	4	4	2	4	0	4	18
U Kansas City	0	0	1	1	1	2	0	5
Kansas State C of Agriculture & Applied Science	0	0	1	0	2	0	0	3
Kansas State Teachers C (Emporia)	0	0	1	0	0	0	0	1
Kansas State Teachers C (Pittsburg)	0	0	1	0	0	0	0	1
U Kansas	0	0	2	0	2	2	2	8
Kent State U	0	0	1	1	2	2	0	6
Kenyon C	0	0	1	0	0	2	0	3
Keuka C	0	0	1	0	2	0	0	3
Knox C	0	0	1	2	2	2	0	7
Lafayette C	0	4	3	0	2	0	0	9
Lake Forest C	0	0	1	0	0	0	0	1

(*continued*)

Institution	Board	Pres.	Appts.	Deans	Budget	Com.	Dept. ex.	Total
Lawrence C	0	0	0	1	1	0	0	2
Lincoln U	0	0	0	0	0	0	0	0
Linfield C	0	0	0	0	0	0	0	0
Louisiana State Normal C	0	0	1	0	0	0	0	1
Louisiana State U	0	0	0	0	2	0	0	2
U Louisville	0	0	1	1	2	0	1	5
Lynchburg C	0	0	1	1	0	0	0	2
Macalester C	4	0	3	2	4	4	0	17
U Maine	4	0	2	1	2	2	2	13
Marshall C	0	0	0	0	2	0	0	2
U Maryland	0	0	1	0	1	0	0	2
MIT	0	0	2	0	2	2	0	6
Michigan State Normal C	0	0	1	0	1	0	0	2
Mills C	4	0	1	0	1	2	0	8
U Minnesota	0	0	1	1	1	0	0	3
Northwest Missouri State Teachers C	0	0	0	0	2	0	0	2
Southeast Missouri State Teachers C	0	0	0	0	0	0	0	0
U Missouri	0	4	0	1	2	0	0	7
Montana State C	0	0	0	0	2	2	0	4
Montana State U	0	0	1	0	3	2	0	6
Morehouse C	0	0	1	0	1	2	0	4
Morningside C	0	4	0	0	0	0	0	4
Mount Holyoke C	4	4	4	2	2	4	0	20
Mount Union C	0	4	1	0	0	0	0	5
Muhlenberg C	4	0	1	0	2	2	0	9
Nebraska State Teachers C (Kearney)	0	0	0	0	2	0	0	2
Nebraska State Teachers C (Wayne)	0	0	0	0	2	0	0	2
U Nebraska	0	0	0	0	2	0	0	2
U Nevada	0	0	1	0	2	0	0	3
U New Hampshire	0	0	1	0	2	0	0	3
New Jersey State Teachers C (Montclair)	0	0	1	0	1	0	0	2
New Mexico C of Agriculture & Mechanic Arts	4	0	1	0	2	2	0	9
New Mexico Normal U	0	0	1	0	0	2	0	3
U New Mexico	0	0	3	0	4	2	2	11
New York State C for Teachers	0	0	1	0	1	0	0	2
NYU	0	0	2	2	2	2	1	9
North Carolina State C of Agriculture & Engineering	0	4	3	0	2	2	0	11
U North Carolina	4	4	3	1	4	2	2	20
U North Carolina Women's C	0	0	3	1	2	2	2	10

Institution	Board	Pres.	Appts.	Deans	Budget	Com.	Dept. ex.	Total
U North Dakota	0	4	1	0	2	2	0	9
Northwestern U	0	4	1	1	2	0	0	8
Oberlin C	4	4	4	4	4	4	2	26
Occidental C	4	0	2	0	2	4	2	14
Ohio U	0	0	1	0	2	2	4	9
Ohio State U	0	4	1	0	3	4	0	12
Ohio Wesleyan U	0	4	3	0	4	2	0	13
Oklahoma A&M	0	0	2	0	2	0	0	4
Northwestern Oklahoma State Teachers C	0	0	0	0	3	0	0	3
U Oklahoma	0	0	1	0	2	0	0	3
Oregon C of Education	0	0	0	0	1	0	0	1
Oregon State C	0	4	1	0	2	0	0	7
U Oregon	0	4	3	0	4	2	0	13
Pennsylvania State C	0	0	1	0	2	0	0	3
Pomona C	4	4	3	2	2	0	2	17
Reed C	4	4	4	2	4	2	4	24
Rhode Island State C	0	0	1	0	2	0	0	3
Rice Institute	0	0	1	0	2	0	0	3
U Rochester	0	0	2	1	2	4	0	9
Rockford C	0	0	3	0	1	2	0	6
Rose Polytechnic Institute	4	0	1	0	2	0	0	7
St. Lawrence U	0	0	1	0	2	2	2	7
St. Mary-of-the-Woods C	0	0	0	0	0	0	0	0
San Diego State C	0	0	3	0	2	2	0	7
San Francisco State C	0	0	1	0	0	0	4	5
Scripps C	4	0	3	0	0	2	4	13
Shepherd State Teachers C	0	0	0	0	0	0	0	0
Shurtleff C	0	0	0	0	0	0	0	0
Simmons C	4	4	0	1	2	2	0	13
Skidmore C	4	0	3	0	4	2	2	15
Smith C	0	0	2	0	2	2	4	10
Northern State Teachers C (SD)	0	0	1	0	2	0	0	3
U South Dakota	0	0	1	0	2	0	0	3
U Southern California	0	4	1	0	1	0	0	6
SMU	0	4	1	0	2	0	0	7
U South	0	0	1	0	0	2	0	3
Spelman C	0	0	0	0	1	0	0	1
Springfield C	0	4	0	0	2	0	0	6
Stanford U	0	0	3	0	2	0	0	5
Swarthmore C	0	4	0	1	2	2	0	9
Syracuse U	0	4	1	1	1	2	0	9
Temple U	4	0	0	0	1	4	0	9
U Tennessee	0	0	1	1	2	2	0	6
Texas A&M C	0	0	1	0	2	0	0	3
Texas Tech C	0	4	1	0	2	0	0	7
U Texas	0	4	2	0	2	0	0	8
U Toledo	4	0	2	1	0	2	0	9

(*continued*)

Institution	Board	Pres.	Appts.	Deans	Budget	Com.	Dept. ex.	Total
Trinity C	4	0	3	1	1	4	0	13
Tufts C	0	4	1	0	0	0	0	5
Tulane U	0	0	1	0	2	0	0	3
U Tulsa	0	4	0	0	2	0	0	6
U Utah	4	0	3	1	2	2	0	12
Vanderbilt U	0	4	1	1	2	0	0	8
Vassar C	4	0	3	4	4	4	4	23
U Vermont	0	0	1	0	2	2	2	7
Medical C of Virginia	0	0	1	0	2	0	0	3
Virginia Polytechnic Institute	0	0	1	1	2	0	0	4
Virginia State Teachers C	0	0	0	0	1	0	0	1
U Virginia	0	0	1	0	2	2	0	5
Washburn C	0	0	3	2	2	2	0	9
Washington U	0	0	1	0	2	0	0	3
U Washington	4	4	2	1	4	4	0	19
Washington State C	0	0	1	0	2	2	0	5
Washington & Jefferson C	0	0	1	0	0	0	0	1
Washington & Lee U	4	4	3	0	0	2	0	13
Washington C of Education (Western)	0	0	0	0	2	0	0	2
Wayne U	0	0	1	0	2	0	0	3
Wellesley C	4	4	3	2	2	4	4	23
Wells C	0	0	3	0	2	2	0	7
Wesleyan U	4	0	4	4	2	2	4	20
Westminster C (MO)	0	0	1	0	2	2	0	5
Westminster C (PA)	0	0	1	0	2	0	0	3
West Virginia U	0	0	0	0	0	0	0	0
Wheaton C (MA)	0	0	1	0	0	2	0	3
U Wichita	0	0	1	0	2	0	0	3
Willamette U	0	0	0	2	0	0	0	2
C of William & Mary	0	0	1	0	0	2	0	3
C of William & Mary (Norfolk)	0	0	3	0	0	0	0	3
Williams C	0	0	2	0	2	2	0	6
Winthrop C	0	0	1	0	0	0	0	1
U Wisconsin	4	4	2	1	3	4	4	22
Wisconsin State Teachers C	0	0	0	0	1	2	0	3
Wittenberg C	4	0	3	0	4	2	0	13
C of Wooster	0	0	4	2	1	2	0	9
U Wyoming	0	0	3	1	2	2	0	8
Xavier U of New Orleans	0	0	1	0	1	0	4	6

Sources: Data derived from individual institutional survey responses found in AAUP Archives, Committee T on College and University Government, Special Collections, Research Center, Gelman Library, George Washington University, Washington, DC, box 19. Summary results were published in AAUP, "Report of Committee T on Place and Function of Faculties in College and University Government," *Bulletin of the AAUP* 27 (April 1941): 155–73.

Questions and scoring system created by Committee T:

Board: Definite plan for exchange of opinion with trustees?
  0 = No
  4 = Yes

Pres.: Is faculty consulted in choice of new president?
  0 = No
  4 = Yes

Appts.: Is faculty consulted in appointments, promotions, dismissals? How?
  0 = None at all
  1 = Depts. through head only
  2 = By dept'al com
  3 = By fac. com.
  4 = By both fac. and dept.

Deans: How are your deans selected?
  0 = App'd by Pres. & Bd. without consult.
  1 = After inform. consult.
  2 = After panel or formal consult
  4 = Elect.

Budget: Faculty consulted in Making budget? How?
  0 = Not at all
  1 = Dept. re supplies and equipment
  2 = Dept. re all needs incl. per. thru head only
  3 = Thru fac. com. re dept. needs
  4 = Thru fac. com. re dept. budgets and gen. budget

Com.: Faculty Control over Committees?
  0 = None elect. by fac.
  2 = Fac. elect. some (at least one)
  4 = Fac. elects all or elects appointing officer(s)

Dept. ex.: Departmental executives?
  0 = App'd
  2 = App'd from panel or after formal consult.
  4 = Elect.
Total: Overall score out of possible 28

1953 AAUP Governance Survey Results

This table was created by the author using the "Institutional Procedure Check Sheets" found in the Committee T archives, but not all institutions responding to the survey returned a check sheet. Some returned only a longer-form questionnaire that provided the basis for Committee T's assigning a self-government index score based on a 28-point scale. For institutions providing both a check sheet and a more complete long-form survey in which responses may have differed, an average was calculated by Committee T. Consequently, there are slight discrepancies in the index scores that might be calculated from this table and the final scores reported in the table that follows, comparing the 1939 and 1953 survey results. In that table, all institutions responding to the survey are included. See below for an explanation of the coding system used for this table and how these numbers were used to determine an institution's self-government index score.

Institution	Board	Pres.	Appts.	Deans	Budget	Com.	Dept. ex.	Self-govt. index score
Adams State C	1	0	2	1	1	0	0	3
Adelphi C	1	4	2	1	1	2	1	14
Alabama C (Montevallo)	2	0	2	1	2	2	1	8
Alabama Polytechnic Institute	1	0	2	1	2	2	0	4
Alabama State Teachers C (Jacksonville)	1	0	2	1	0	0	0	1
Alabama State Teachers C (Troy)	0	0	0	0	0	0	0	0
U Alabama	2	4	2	1	2	0	2	9
U Alaska	1	0	0	1	1	0	0	2
Albion C	2	4	2	1	1	2	1	8
Allegheny C	1	4	2	1	5	4	0	13
American International C	6	0	0	0	0	3	0	6
Appalachian State Teachers C	0	0	0	0	0	0	0	0
Arizona State C	1	0	2	1	2	2	1	6
U Arizona	0		2	1	0		0	3
U Arkansas	1	4	2	2	2	0	4	12
U Arkansas School of Medicine	1	0	2	2	2	0	1	8
Army Language School		0	2	0	0	0	0	1
Augustana C	2	0	2	0	0	4	0	5
Ball State Teachers C	1	2	1	3	2	4	2	12
Bard C	1	4	4		5	3	3	18
Bates C	1	3	2	0	0	2	0	4
Beloit C	1	4	0	1	1	0	0	7
Berea C	2	4	2	3	2	4	2	17
Blackburn C	1	3	2	0	0	0	0	4
Bluefield State C	2	0	4	1			0	8
Boston U	5	4	2	1	2	3	2	13

Institution	Board	Pres.	Appts.	Deans	Budget	Com.	Dept. ex.	Self-govt. index score
Bowdoin C	2	1	2	1	1	2	1	11
Bowling Green State U	1	5	1	0	1	3	1	9
Brandeis U	1		2	1	2	2		7
U Bridgeport	2		2	1	1	1		4
Brooklyn C		4	3	1	2	4	4	18
Brown U	6	1	2	0	2	3	0	12
Bryn Mawr C	7	4		3		3	4	15
Bucknell U	7	0	2	0	1	2	4	12
U Buffalo	2	3	2	3	2	2	1	11
Butler U	0	0	2	2	2	0	0	5
Caltech	1	3	2	2	2	4	1	9
UC Berkeley	0		4	3	3	2	2	12
UCLA	0		3	3	3	3	2	19
Capital U	5	3	2	2	5	2	2	14
Carnegie Institute of Technology	1	1	3	1	2	3	1	10
Case Institute of Technology	1	3	2	1	2	4	1	10
Catholic U	0	0	2	5	0		4	11
Central C (IA)	1	0	2	0	0	0	0	2
Centre C of Kentucky	1	0	3	3	0	0	2	7
Champlain C	0	0	2	0	2	3	0	4
Chicago City Junior C	1	0	2		1	4	2	5
Chico State C	0	2	2	1	2	3	1	8
U Cincinnati	1	3	2	1	0	0	2	2
Colby C	1	0	2	0	2	2	0	6
Colgate U	5	2	2	1	2	3	2	13
Colorado C	6	3	2	3	2	4	0	15
Colorado School of Mines	1	0	2	0	1	0	0	2
U Colorado	2	3	3	4	5	4	4	17
Columbia U	2	4	2	2	2	0	4	13
Connecticut C	1	4	2	1	1	4	0	12
Cooper Union	1	0	2	2	2	0	0	4
Cornell C	1	3	2	2	0	4	0	6
Dartmouth C	1	0	3	0	0	3	0	14
U Delaware	0	1	2	0	2	0	0	6
Denison U	2	5	2	2	2	3	3	12
U Denver	4	5	2	2	3	3	2	18
DePaul U	2	0	3	1	2	2	1	9
DePauw U	5	2	4	2	2	4	1	16
Dickinson C	0	0	0	0	0	2	0	2
Drake U	1	2	2	0	1	0	0	2
Drew U	0	4	1	1	1	0	4	13
Duke U	2	2	2	1	0	2	2	6

(*continued*)

Institution	Board	Pres.	Appts.	Deans	Budget	Com.	Dept. ex.	Self-govt. index score
Duquesne U	1	0	0	0	0	0	1	1
Earlham C	2	4	2	1	0	4	1	11
Elmhurst C	0	0	1	0	0		0	2
Elmira C	0	5	2	1	1	3	0	11
Emory U	1	0	2	0	2	2	1	4
Fenn C	1	4	2	0	2	2	0	9
Fisk U	1	0	2	0	1	3	0	4
Florida A&M	0	0	1	0	1	0	1	3
Florida State U	1	0	2	1	2	2	2	6
U Florida	1	3	2	0	2	0	0	4
Fordham U	0	0	2	0	1	0	0	2
Franklin & Marshall C	5	0	4	1	2	2	2	14
Fresno State C	1	2	2	0	1	0	2	4
Furman U	1	0	2	0	1	0	2	8
George Peabody C for Teachers	1	1	2	1	2	2	2	10
George Pepperdine C	1	0	4	0	1	0	1	8
George Washington U	1		2	1	2	0	0	7
Georgia Tech	0	0	2	0	2	3	2	8
U Georgia	0	0	2	1	2	4	2	8
Goucher C	1	4	4	3	2	4	0	15
Grinnell C	2	4	2		3	4	2	16
Hamilton C	1	0	2	0	0	3	0	5
Hamline U	2	3	2	2	2	4	0	9
Harpur C	1		2	1	2	4	4	12
U Hawaii	0	0	2	0	2	0	4	5
Hobart & William Smith Colleges	6	3	3	0	1	4	0	14
Hofstra C	0	3	2	2	1	2	1	7
Hood C	1	4	2	4	1	2	2	10
Hunter C	1	3	4	3	2	4	4	21
Idaho State C	0	2	2	0	1	1	0	4
U Idaho	1	0	2	1	2	0	1	3
Eastern Illinois State C	1	0	3	3	2	4	1	15
Illinois State Normal U	3	0	3	0	3	4	4	16
Southern Illinois U	3	2	1		3	3	2	14
U Illinois	1	4	4	4	3	2	4	19
U Illinois Navy Pier	1	0	2	0	2	0	2	4
Indiana U	1	0	2	1	1	0	2	7
Iowa State C of Agricultural and Mechanic Arts	1	2	2	2	2	0	1	5
Iowa State Teachers C	2	3	2	3	2	4	2	13
Iowa Wesleyan C	2	3	1	1	1	0	0	6

Institution	Board	Pres.	Appts.	Deans	Budget	Com.	Dept. ex.	Self-govt. index score
Jacksonville Junior C	1	0	0	0	1	4		3
James Millikin U	2	4	2	1	1	3	0	10
Jersey City Junior C	1	0	0	0	1	1	0	1
John Carroll U	2	0	2	0	2	2	0	6
Joplin Junior C	2	0	0	0	1	1		1
Kansas State C of Agriculture and Applied Science	1	2	1	1	0	3	1	8
Kansas State Teachers C (Emporia)	1	0	2	0	0	4	0	4
Kansas State Teachers C (Pittsburg)	1	0	2	0	2	2	0	6
U Kansas	1	3	2	1	2	2	2	11
U Kansas City	1	2	4	0	0	0	0	5
Kent State U	1	0	2	3	0	1	1	4
Eastern Kentucky State C	1	0	2	0	1	0	0	1
U Kentucky	3	3	2	1	2	0	2	8
Keuka C	2	5	2	1	1	0	0	7
Lafayette C	5	4	3	1	2	2	1	13
Lake Erie C	1	0	2	1	2	0	1	9
Lake Forest C	1	0	2	1	0	4	1	7
Lewis & Clark C	6	0	2	0	0	0	0	9
Los Angeles City C	2	0		1	0	0	2	6
Los Angeles State C	1	0	2	1	1	2	1	6
U Louisville	1	3	2	2	2	3	2	12
Lycoming C	1		2	1	1	2	1	4
Lynchburg C	5	4	2	1	2	1	0	10
Macalester C	1	2	2	0	2	3	2	9
U Maine	0	3	2	1	2	0	2	8
Marquette U	0	0	0	0	0	0	0	0
Western Maryland C	1	3	2	5	1	2	2	11
MIT	0	0	2	1	2	3	1	7
Mass State Teachers C (Framingham)	1	0	1	1	2	1		3
Mass State Teachers C (Lowell)	1	0	0	1	1	1	0	2
Memphis State C	1	0	2	0	0	2		3
Mercer U	1	3	2	1	1	0	0	3
Michigan State C	0	0	2	1	2	2	0	5
Michigan State Normal C	0	0	4	1	0	4	4	13
U Michigan	1	1	4	4	5	4	3	18
Middlebury C	2	1	2	0	1	0	0	3
Mills C	1	4	0	1	1	3	3	11

(continued)

Institution	Board	Pres.	Appts.	Deans	Budget	Com.	Dept. ex.	Self-govt. index score
Millsaps C	7	3	2	2	2	4	2	13
Milwaukee-Downer C	1	3	2	2	1	2	2	9
Minnesota State Teachers C (St. Cloud)	2	4	2	1	2	3	2	14
U Minnesota		4	3	3	2	3		13
U Minnesota Duluth	1	0	2	2	2	0	4	4
Mississippi Southern C	1	0	2	1	1	0	1	4
Mississippi State C for Women	1	0	2	0	1	0	0	2
U Mississippi	2	0	2	1	2	4	2	11
Southeast Missouri State C	1	0	2	1	2	0	1	4
Southwest Missouri State C	0	0	2	0	1	0	0	2
U Missouri	0	0	2	1	2	0	2	7
Eastern Montana C of Education	1	0	2	2	3	3	2	10
Montana State C	1	0	2	1	2	0	1	5
Montana State U	1		2	1	2	2	2	9
Moorehead State C	1	0	0	0	1	3	0	2
Morgan State C	1	0	2	0	1	2	0	6
Mount Holyoke C	2	3	2	2	2	4	2	15
Muhlenberg C	6	2	2	0	1	4	0	9
Muskingum C	1	3	1	2	0	1	2	5
Nebraska State Teachers C (Kearney)	1	0	2	0	1	0	0	0
U Nebraska	1	4	4	3	5	3	3	19
U New Hampshire	2	3	2	2	2	3	4	13
New Jersey State Teachers C (Newark)	1	0	2	0	1	0	0	1
New Mexico C of Agriculture and Mechanic Arts	1	0	2	0	2	3	1	5
New Mexico Highlands U	2	4	4	4	2	1	2	15
New Mexico Institute of Mining & Technology	1	0	2	0	1	0	0	1
New Mexico Western C	1	0	2	0	2	0	0	6
SUNY C of Agriculture & Technology	1	0	2	1	5	0	0	6

Institution	Board	Pres.	Appts.	Deans	Budget	Com.	Dept. ex.	Self-govt. index score
New York State C for Teachers (Albany)	1	0	2	1	1	0	2	5
New York State Teachers C (Fredonia)	1	2	2	0	2	1	2	6
New York State Teachers C (New Paltz)	1	0	3	2	2	0	0	5
U North Carolina	2	1	3	3	2	4	3	16
U North Carolina Woman's C	2	3	2	0	2	2	2	13
North Dakota State Teachers C (Minot)	0	0	2	0	0	2	0	4
Norwich U	3	2	2	1	1	0	0	3
U Notre Dame	1	0	2	0	0	0	0	2
Oberlin C	6	4	3	4	0	3	2	18
Occidental C	1	0	2	1	1	0	0	3
Ohio U	2	3	2	2	2	2	2	13
Ohio Wesleyan U	5	4	4	3	4	3	1	18
Oklahoma A&M	0	0	2	0	2	2	1	3
Northwestern Oklahoma State Teachers C	1	0	0	0	0	0	0	0
U Oklahoma	2	4	3	4	4	3	2	18
Olympic C	1	0	0	0	0	2	0	1
U Omaha	1	2	2	1	2	0	2	8
Oregon C of Education	1	4	0	1	1	0	1	6
Eastern Oregon C of Education	2	3	4	2	1	4	2	14
Southern Oregon C of Education	1	4	2		2	0	2	7
Oregon State C	3	1	2	2	2	0	2	8
Portland State C	2	0	2	0	3	4	0	9
Pace C	4	0	2	0	0	3	0	6
Pasadena C	1	3	2	1	2	4	2	11
Penn State Teachers C (East Stroudsburg)	0	0	0	0	0	0	0	0
Penn State Teachers C (Indiana)	1	0	2	1	2	0	2	6
Penn State Teachers C (Kutztown)	1	0	2	0	1	0	0	2
Penn State Teachers C (Millersville)	1	0	2	0	1	0	0	2

(*continued*)

Institution	Board	Pres.	Appts.	Deans	Budget	Com.	Dept. ex.	Self-govt. index score
Penn State Teachers C (Shippensburg)	1	0	0	0	0	0	0	0
U Pittsburgh	5		3		3	4	2	11
C of Puget Sound	1	3	0	1	0	1	0	3
Purdue U	1	0	2	1	2	3	0	6
Queens C (NC)	2	3	2	1	1	0	1	6
Queens C (NY)	6	3	4	1	4	3	4	22
Randolph-Macon Woman's C	2	5	2	1	0	0	1	8
Rensselaer Polytechnic Institute	2	3	2	1	2	0	1	5
U Rhode Island	1	0	2	0	2	2	0	5
Rice Institute	1	0	2	0	2	0	0	3
Ripon C	1	0	0	0	1	2	0	2
Roosevelt C	7		4	2	5	3	3	17
St. John's U (NY)	1	0	0	0	0	0	0	0
St. Mary's C (CA)	6	3	2	1	1	2	1	11
St. Olaf C	1	0	2	4	2	3	1	10
Simpson C	2	2	2	1	2	0	0	4
Skidmore C	6		2	1	1	3	2	13
Smith C	6	2	2	3	2	4	4	21
U of the South	1	1	1	0	1	2	0	8
South Dakota State C of Agricultural and Mechanical Arts	1	0	2	2	2	3	0	8
U South Dakota	2		2	1	2	2	1	7
U Southern California	0	1	2	0	1	1	0	4
Southern State C	1	3	2	2	2	2	2	7
Stanford U	1	4	2	1	1	3	1	11
Stephens C	1	3	2	2	2	3	1	9
Stout Institute	1	0	2	1	1	0	0	3
Stowe Teachers C	0	0	0	0	0	0	0	0
Sweetbriar C	6	1	2	4	2	3	0	14
Temple U	5	3	4	3	1	0	2	12
U Tennessee	2	4	2	2	2	4	2	12
Texas C of Arts & Industries	1	0	2	0	2	0	0	3
North Texas State C	0	4	2	2	2	0	1	8
Texas Tech C	0	0	2	0	1	2	0	5
U Texas	2	4	3	1	3	3	1	14
U Toledo	1	0	2	1	2	2	0	7
Trinity C (CT)	5	1	2	2	0	4	1	11
Trinity U (TX)	0	0	0	0	0	0	0	0
Tufts C	1	0	2	0	0	2	1	3
Tulane U	1	0	2	2	2	0	2	6
Upsala C	5	0	2	0	1	2	0	7
Ursinius C	7	0	2	1	1	2	1	7

Institution	Board	Pres.	Appts.	Deans	Budget	Com.	Dept. ex.	Self-govt. index score
U Utah	1	4	4	2	1	3	2	11
Vanderbilt U	1	0	2	1	2	0	1	4
Vassar C	6	4	2	4	3	3	4	24
Villanova C	1	0	0	0	0	0	0	0
Mary Washington C (U Virginia)	1	0	2	1	1	2	0	6
Medical C of Virginia	0	0	2	3	2	0	2	8
Wabash C	7	5	2	5	2	2	2	19
Wake Forest C	5	2	2	1	2	0	1	9
Washburn Municipal U of Topeka	0	0	2	0	1	2	0	3
Washington C (MD)	1	1	3	0	1	0	0	7
Central Washington C of Education	1		2	0	2	0	0	4
Eastern Washington C of Education	2	2	4	0	2	0	2	10
Western Washington C of Education	1	0	2	1	2	0	2	5
Washington State C	7	4	2	1	2	2	3	15
Washington U	1	3	2	2	2	2	1	7
U Washington	1	2	3	3	2	3	3	14
Wayne U	2	4	4	2	2	3	2	16
Wellesley C	2	4	4	2	2	4	4	20
Wells C	1	5	2	0	1	3	2	14
Wesleyan U	6	3	2	5	1	4	4	20
West Virginia U	0	0	2	1	2	4	2	8
West Virginia Wesleyan C	3	3	3	2	0	0	0	7
Western C for Women (OH)	6	3	2	1	4	4	1	18
U Western Ontario	5	0	2	0	1	3	0	6
Western Reserve U	1	3	4	3	2	2	3	15
Westminster C (PA)	1	0	2	1	2	0	0	4
Wheaton C (MA)	6	3	2	0	0	3	0	10
Whitman C	0	0	2	0	1	3	4	9
Whittier C	6	0	2	0	0	0	0	8
U Wichita	1	1	2	2	2	2	2	7
Willamette U	0	0	0	0	0	0	0	0
C of William & Mary	6	0	2		2		1	13
William & Mary Norfolk	0	0	2	0	0	1	1	1

(*continued*)

Institution	Board	Pres.	Appts.	Deans	Budget	Com.	Dept. ex.	Self-govt. index score
William & Mary Richmond	0	0	0	1	1	0	0	2
Williams C	1		3	1	1	2	1	7
Winthrop C	0	0	2	0	1	3	0	5
Wisconsin State C Eau Claire	1	0	2	1	1	2	4	10
Wisconsin State C Milwaukee	7	0	2		1	4	0	8
Wisconsin State C River Falls	7	2	2	1	2	2	1	12
Wisconsin State C Whitewater	2	0		1	1	3	1	7
U Wisconsin	6	4	3	4	5	3	3	22
Wittenberg C	1	0	2	0	0	2	0	5
C of Wooster	6	4	4	5	0	4	2	21
U Wyoming	0	4	2	1	2	3	2	11
Yakima Junior C	1	0	2		1	4	0	4
Yale U	1	1	4	2	2	0	2	16
Yankton C	1	4	0	0	0	0	0	5

Sources: Data derived from individual institutional survey responses and AAUP, "Confidential Report to the Officers and Members of the Council," February 1, 1955, both in AAUP Archives, Committee T on College and University Government, Special Collections, Research Center, Gelman Library, George Washington University, Washington, DC, box 13. Summary results were published in AAUP, "Report of Committee T on Place and Function of Faculties in College and University Government: Final Report on the 1953 Study," *Bulletin of the AAUP* 41 (Spring 1955): 62–81.

Questions and scoring system: The questions closely parallel those used in the 1939 AAUP survey, but the "Institutional Procedure Check Sheet" provided for a greater range of responses to each question. The coding used in this table, therefore, does not directly translate into the self-government index score. The points awarded for each response to calculate this score are indicated in brackets.

Board: Is there exchange of opinion between trustees (regents) and faculty?
  0 = No contact with trustees and are not supposed to consult with them [0]
  1 = Only social and accidental contact [0]
  2 = Can go to trustees on own initiative at any time [1]
  3 = If president differs with faculty, he is obligated by board rules to present both positions to trustees [1]
  4 = Have trustees regularly sitting in our faculty senate [2]
  5 = Have standing committees with trustee and faculty members [3]
  6 = Conference committee of trustees and faculty that meets regularly [4]
  7 = Elect faculty representatives to board [4]

Pres.: Is the faculty consulted in the selection of a new president?
  0 = Not consulted [0]
  1 = Asked to submit names by mail to trustees or selection committee [1]
  2 = Asked to formulate criteria to guide selection by the trustees [1]
  3 = Individual faculty members selected by trustees to advise selection committee [1]
  4 = Asked to elect faculty members to a joint committee to advise trustees [3]
  5 = Asked to elect faculty members to sit with trustees on selection committee [4]

Appts.: Is there consultation between faculty and administration concerning appointments, promotions, and dismissals?
  0 = Not consulted [0]
  1 = Not consulted concerning appointments but are consulted concerning promotions (or vice versa) [1]
  2 = Departmental chairmen are consulted [1]

3 = Departmental committees are consulted [2]
4 = Departmental committees report to a faculty (or divisional) committee and consult with them in making decisions [4]

Deans: Are faculty members consulted concerning the selection deans (or division heads)?
  0 = Deans appointed without consultation [0]
  1 = Some senior colleagues are consulted informally [1]
  2 = All departmental chairmen are informally consulted [1]
  3 = Committee including faculty members is appointed by president to make selection [2]
  4 = Faculty committee is elected by panel to make the appointment [3]
  5 = Dean elected by faculty vote [4]

Budget: Is the faculty consulted in the making of the institution's budget?
  0 = Not consulted [0]
  1 = Departmental chairmen consulted concerning budgeting of supplies and equipment [1]
  2 = Departmental chairmen consulted concerning all needs including personnel [2]
  3 = Faculty committee handles all budgetary matters for all departments [3]
  4 = Faculty committee handles departmental budgets and the institution's general budget [4]
  5 = Departmental committees handle departmental budgets and general faculty committee handles general institutional budget [4]

Com.: How are faculty committees appointed and their assignments determined?
  0 = All faculty committees appointed by the administration [0]
  1 = Faculty members may volunteer and thereby get appointed [0]
  2 = Faculty elect one committee and the rest are appointed [2]
  3 = All important committees are elected; others are appointed [3]
  4 = All faculty committee are elected by faculty (or appointed by elected committees) [4]

Dept. ex.: How are departmental chairmen (or heads) selected at your institution?
  0 = Appointed without faculty consultation [0]
  1 = Senior faculty members are informally consulted [1]
  2 = Departmental members and others are informally consulted [2]
  3 = Appointments made after a panel is drawn up or after other formal consultation involving a ballot [2]
  4 = Elected by a formal vote of the department [4]

Comparison of Institutional Governance Scores: 1939 and 1953 AAUP Surveys

Institution	1939	1953
Adams State C		3
Adelphi C		14
U Akron	7	8
Alabama C		8
Alabama Polytechnic Institute	3	4
Alabama State Teachers C (Jacksonville)		1
Alabama State Teachers C (Troy)		0
U Alabama	0	9
U Alaska		2
Albion C		8
Alfred U		3
Allegheny C	8	13
American International C		6
Amherst C	18	22
Antioch C	21	
Appalachian State Teachers C		0

(continued)

Institution	1939	1953
Arizona State C (Tempe)		6
U Arizona	3	3
U Arkansas	5	12
U Arkansas School of Medicine	3	8
Army Language School		1
Ashland C	15	
Atlanta U	4	
Augustana C	5	5
Baldwin-Wallace C	7	
Ball State Teachers C	3	12
Bard C		18
Bates C		4
Baylor U	3	8
Beloit C		7
Berea C	10	17
Blackburn C		4
Bluefield State C		8
Boston U	11	13
Bowdoin C		11
Bowling Green State U	5	9
Bradley U	5	
Brandeis U		7
U Bridgeport		4
Brooklyn C	24	18
Brown U	14	12
Bryn Mawr C	18	15
Bucknell U	14	12
U Buffalo	10	11
Butler U		5
U California		12
UCLA	18	19
U California Santa Barbara		10
Caltech	14	9
Capital U		14
Carnegie Institute of Technology	7	10
Carthage C		7
Case Institute of Technology	6	10
Catholic U of America	4	11
Centenary C of Louisiana	0	
Central C (Iowa)		2
Central State C (Ohio)		6
Centre C of Kentucky		7
Champlain C		4
Chicago City Junior C (Wilson Branch)		5
U Chicago	11	19
Chico State C		8
U Cincinnati	12	2
CCNY	22	20
CCNY (Commerce Center)	24	
Clark U		13
Coe C	3	3

Institution	1939	1953
Colby C		6
Colgate U	3	13
Colorado A&M C	2	13
Colorado C		15
Colorado School of Mines		2
Western State C of Colorado		3
U Colorado	23	17
Columbia U	8	13
Concord C	1	
Connecticut C	11	12
U Connecticut	7	9
Cornell C	15	6
Cornell U	20	22
Creighton U	3	
Culver-Stockton C	3	
Dalhousie U	10	
Dartmouth C	14	14
Davidson C		14
U Delaware	5	6
Denison U	9	12
U Denver	19	18
DePaul U		9
DePauw U	12	16
Dickinson C		2
Drake U	2	2
Drew U	8	13
Duke U	4	6
Duquesne U		1
Earlham C		11
Elmhurst C		2
Elmira C		11
Emory U	7	4
Evansville C		4
Fairmont State C	0	
Fenn C		9
Findlay C	0	
Fisk U		4
Florida A&M C		3
Florida State U	0	6
U Florida	3	4
Fordham U (Manhattan)	3	2
Franklin C (IN)	3	6
Franklin & Marshall C	1	14
Fresno State C	8	4
Furman U	2	8
Geneva C		3
George Peabody C for Teachers		10
George Pepperdine C		8
George Washington U	11	7

(*continued*)

Institution	1939	1953
Georgia Tech		8
Georgia State C for Women	3	
U Georgia	13	8
Gettysburg C	1	5
Goucher C	13	15
Grinnell C	23	16
Hamilton C		5
Hamline U		9
Harpur C		12
Harris Teachers C	0	
Harvard U	9	
Hastings C	7	
Haverford C		19
U Hawaii		5
Heidelberg C	5	
Hobart & William Smith Colleges	11	14
Hofstra C		7
Hood C	6	10
Howard U	9	6
Hunter C	20	21
North Idaho Junior C		7
Idaho State C		4
U Idaho		3
Eastern Illinois State C		15
Western Illinois State C	1	18
Illinois State Normal U	3	16
Northern Illinois State Teachers C	1	
Southern Illinois U	8	14
U Illinois	24	19
U Illinois (Navy Pier)		4
Indiana State Teachers C	10	13
Indiana U	8	7
Iowa State C of A&M Arts	7	5
Iowa State Teachers C	1	13
Iowa State U	6	
Iowa Wesleyan C		6
Jacksonville Junior C		3
Jersey City Junior C		1
John Carroll U		6
Johns Hopkins U	18	21
Johnson C. Smith U		0
Joplin Junior C		1
Kalamazoo C		7
Kansas State C of Agriculture	3	8
Kansas State Teachers C (Emporia)	1	4
Kansas State Teachers C (Pittsburg)	1	6
U Kansas	8	11
U Kansas City	5	5
Kent State U	6	4
Eastern Kentucky State C		1
Western Kentucky State C		0

Institution	1939	1953
U Kentucky		8
Kenyon C	3	6
Keuka C	3	7
Knox C	7	
Lafayette C	9	13
Lake Erie C		9
Lake Forest C	1	7
Lawrence C	2	
Lewis & Clark C		9
Lincoln U (MO)	0	
Lindenwood C		3
Linfield C	0	
Longwood C	1	8
Los Angeles City C		6
Los Angeles State C		6
Northwestern State C of Louisiana	1	
Louisiana State U	2	13
U Louisville	5	12
Lowell Technological Institute		2
Lycoming C		4
Lynchburg C	2	10
Macalester C	17	9
U Maine	13	8
Marietta C		21
Marquette U		0
Marshall C	2	6
Western Maryland C		11
U Maryland	2	
MIT	6	7
Massachusetts State Teachers C (Fitchburg)		5
Massachusetts State Teachers C (Framingham)		3
Massachusetts State Teachers C (Lowell)		2
Memphis State C		3
Mercer U		3
Northern Michigan C of Education		3
Michigan State C		5
Michigan State Normal C	2	13
U Michigan	13	18
Middlebury C		3
Millikin U		10
Mills C	8	11
Millsaps C		13
Milwaukee-Downer C		9
Minnesota State Teachers C (St. Cloud)		14
U Minnesota	3	13
U Minnesota (Duluth)		4
Mississippi Southern C		4
Mississippi State C		3
Mississippi State C for Women		2

(*continued*)

Institution	1939	1953
U Mississippi		11
Northwest Missouri State C	2	2
Southeast Missouri State C	0	4
Southwest Missouri State C		2
U Missouri	7	7
Eastern Montana C of Education		10
Montana State C	4	5
Montana State U	6	9
Morehead State C		2
Morgan State C		6
Morningside C	4	
Mount Holyoke C	20	15
Mount Union C	5	9
Muhlenberg C	9	9
Muskingum C		5
Nebraska State Teachers C (Kearney)	2	0
Nebraska State Teachers C (Wayne)	2	
U Nebraska	2	19
U Nevada	3	3
U New Hampshire	3	13
New Jersey State Teachers C (Montclair)	2	
New Jersey State Teachers C (Newark)		1
New Mexico C of Agriculture and Mechanic Arts	9	5
New Mexico Highlands U	3	15
New Mexico Institute of Mining		1
U New Mexico	11	
New Mexico Western C		6
New York State Teachers C (Albany)	2	5
New York State Teachers C (Buffalo)		16
New York State Teachers C (Brockport)		7
New York State Teachers C (Cortland)		11
New York State Teachers C (Fredonia)		6
New York State Teachers C (New Paltz)		5
New York U	9	8
New York State Agricultural & Technical Institute		6
North Carolina State C of Agriculture & Engineering	11	
U North Carolina	20	16
U North Carolina Woman's C	12	13
North Dakota State Teachers C (Minot)		4
U North Dakota	9	6
Northern State Teachers C	3	
Northwestern State C (OK)	3	0
Northwestern U (IL)	8	
Norwich U		3
U Notre Dame		2
Oberlin C	26	18
Occidental C	14	3
Ohio State U	12	18
Ohio U	9	13
Ohio Wesleyan U	13	18
Oklahoma A&M C	4	3

Institution	1939	1953
U Oklahoma	3	18
Olympic C		1
U Omaha		8
Oregon C of Education	1	6
Eastern Oregon C of Education		14
Southern Oregon C of Education		7
Oregon State C	7	8
Oregon State System of Higher Education, General		9
U Oregon	13	
Pace C		6
C of the Pacific		10
Pacific U		17
Pasadena C		11
Pennsylvania C for Women		5
Pennsylvania State C	3	
Pennsylvania State Teachers C (East Stroudsburg)		0
Pennsylvania State Teachers C (Indiana)		6
Pennsylvania State Teachers C (Kutztown)		2
Pennsylvania State Teachers C (Millersville)		1
Pennsylvania State Teachers C (Shippensburg)		0
U Pittsburgh		11
Pomona C	17	
U Portland		0
C of Puget Sound		3
Purdue U		6
Queen's C (NY)		22
Queen's C (NC)		6
Randolph-Macon Women's C		8
U Redlands		11
Reed C	24	21
Rensselaer Polytechnic Institute		5
U Rhode Island	3	5
Rice Institute	3	3
Ripon C		2
U Rochester	9	
Rockford C	6	14
Roosevelt U		17
Rose Polytechnic Institute	7	
Sacramento State C		2
St. John's U (NY)		0
St. Lawrence U	7	4
St. Mary's C (CA)		11
St. Mary-of-the-Woods C	0	
St. Michael's C		2
St. Olaf C		10
San Diego State C	7	12
San Francisco State C	5	
San Jose State C		17
Scripps C	13	10

(continued)

Institution	1939	1953
Shepherd C	0	
Shurtleff C	0	
Simmons C	13	
Simpson C		4
Skidmore C	15	13
Smith C	10	21
U of the South	3	8
U South Carolina		0
South Dakota State C of Agricultural & Mechanical Arts		8
U South Dakota	3	7
U Southern California	6	4
SMU	7	
Southern State C		7
Spelman C	1	
Springfield C	6	
Stanford U	5	11
Stephens C		9
Stout Institute		3
Stowe Teachers C		0
Swarthmore C	9	
Sweet Briar C		14
Syracuse U	9	10
Syracuse U (Utica C)		5
Temple U	9	12
Middle Tennessee State C		5
U Tennessee	6	12
Texas A&M C	3	
Texas C of Arts & Industry		3
North Texas State C		8
Texas State C for Women		7
Texas Tech C	7	5
U Texas	8	14
U Toledo	9	7
Trinity C (CT)	13	11
Trinity U		0
Tufts C	5	3
Tulane U	3	6
U Tulsa	6	3
Upsala C		7
Ursinus C		7
Utah State Agricultural C		12
U Utah	12	11
Vanderbilt U	8	4
Vassar C	23	24
U Vermont	7	
Villanova C		0
Medical C of Virginia	3	8
Virginia Polytechnic Institute	4	2
U Virginia	5	
U Virginia (Mary Washington C)		6

Institution	1939	1953
Wabash C		19
Wake Forest C		9
Washburn Municipal U of Topeka	9	3
Washington C		7
Central Washington C of Education		4
Eastern Washington C of Education		10
Western Washington C of Education	2	5
State C of Washington	5	15
Washington U	3	7
U Washington	19	14
Washington & Jefferson C	1	2
Washington & Lee U	13	
Wayne U	3	16
Wellesley C	23	20
Wells C	7	14
Wesleyan U	20	20
West Virginia State C		14
West Virginia U	0	8
West Virginia Wesleyan C		7
Western C for Women		18
U Western Ontario		6
Western Reserve U		15
Westminster C (MO)	5	
Westminster C (PA)	3	4
Wheaton C (MA)	3	10
Whitman C		9
Whittier C		8
Municipal U of Wichita	3	7
Willamette U	2	0
C of William & Mary	2	13
C of William & Mary Norfolk	3	1
C of William & Mary Richmond		2
Williams C	6	7
Winthrop C	1	5
Wisconsin State C Eau Claire		10
Wisconsin State C LaCrosse	3	16
Wisconsin State C Milwaukee		8
Wisconsin State C River Falls		12
Wisconsin State C Whitewater		7
U Wisconsin	22	22
Wittenberg C	13	5
C of Wooster	9	21
U Wyoming	8	11
Xavier U (LA)	6	
Yakima Valley Junior C		4
Yale U		16
Yankton C		5

Source: Reproduced from table in AAUP, "Confidential Report to the Officers and Members of the Council," February 1, 1955, in AAUP Archives, Committee T on College and University Government, Special Collections, Research Center, Gelman Library, George Washington University, Washington, DC, box 13.

Introduction

1. See, for example, M. Taylor, *Crisis on Campus*; Hacker and Dreifus, *Higher Education?*; Fogel and Malson-Huddle, *Precipice or Crossroads*; Newfield, *Unmaking of the Public University*; Christensen and Horn, "Colleges in Crisis"; Deresiewicz, "Faulty Towers"; Fischer, "Crisis of Confidence Threatens Colleges."

2. Thelin, *History of American Higher Education*, ix.

3. Tierney, *Competing Conceptions of Academic Governance*.

4. These calls for the corporatization of American higher education have drawn spirited responses from a number of scholars who defend the continuing importance of shared governance. See, for example, Burgan, *What Ever Happened to the Faculty?*; Ginsberg, *Fall of the Faculty*; Nelson, *No University Is an Island*; Schrecker, *Lost Soul of Higher Education*.

5. In Germany, powerful individual faculty chairs dominated institutional decision making, whereas in England, residential undergraduate colleges rather than discipline-based departments exercised greater authority. Abbott, *Chaos of Disciplines*, 122–26.

6. Women in the United States began to earn doctorates as early as 1877, and by 1910 20 percent of all faculty were women. Most, however, were employed at women's or teachers colleges. Until after World War Two, women were largely excluded from the faculties of most research-intensive universities. Harvard, for example, did not appoint its first female faculty member until 1956. Solomon, *In the Company of Educated Women*, 133–36; Graham, "Expansion and Exclusion," 767.

7. AAUP, "Inclusion in Governance."

8. See, for example, M. Taylor, *Crisis on Campus*; Hacker and Dreifus, *Higher Education?*

Chapter 1 · College Governance before 1876

1. The other eight colleges were William and Mary (1693), Collegiate School at New Haven (Yale) (1701), College of Philadelphia (University of Pennsylvania) (1740); College of New Jersey (Princeton) (1746); King's College (Columbia) (1754); College of Rhode Island (Brown) (1764); Queen's College (Rutgers) (1766); and Dartmouth College (1769). Lucas, *American Higher Education*, 105.

2. For background on the development of the medieval university as it relates to subsequent developments in colonial North America, see Cowley, *Presidents, Professors, and Trustees*; Duryea, *Academic Corporation*; Herbst, *From Crisis to Crisis*; Hofstadter, *Academic*

Freedom in the Age of the College; and Lucas, *American Higher Education*. See also Ridder-Symoens, *History of the University in Europe*, vol. 1, *Universities in the Middle Ages*, and vol. 2, *Universities in Early Modern Europe*; and Brockliss, "European University in the Age of Revolution."

3. Thelin, *History of American Higher Education*, 21; Ridder-Symoens, *A History of the University in Europe*, 2:302–11; Brockliss, "European University in the Age of Revolution," 121.

4. Herbst, *From Crisis to Crisis*, 94.

5. Carrell, "American College Professors, 1750–1800," 290.

6. Finkelstein, "From Tutor to Professor," 101; Smith, "Teacher in Puritan Culture," 401. See also Finkelstein, *American Academic Profession*, 8–9.

7. Hofstadter, *Academic Freedom*, 114–16; Thelin, *History of American Higher Education*, 31–32.

8. Herbst, *From Crisis to Crisis*, 48–49.

9. Tutors at Harvard in the 1720s and the teaching masters at William and Mary in the 1750s tried to win the power of self-government, but they failed in what Herbst describes as "the triumph of external government." Ibid., 48–61, 94.

10. Thelin, *History of American Higher Education*, 12; Herbst, *From Crisis to Crisis*, 5–61; Cowley, *Presidents, Professors, and Trustees*, 37–48.

11. For a comprehensive list of all colleges chartered by 1820, see Herbst, *From Crisis to Crisis*, 244–53.

12. Whitehead, *Separation of College and State*, 20–27, 43–44.

13. Herbst, *From Crisis to Crisis*, 232–43; Thelin, *History of American Higher Education*, 70–73; Whitehead, *Separation of College and State*, 76–80.

14. Brockliss, "European University in the Age of Revolution," 121–22.

15. Kelley, *Yale*, 142–43.

16. Stand-alone medical colleges of dubious quality did begin to proliferate throughout the new nation in the early decades of the nineteenth century, but many of these were devised as for-profit entrepreneurial endeavors that at the time had little impact on the shape of American higher education. The relatively small number of medical schools attached to traditional liberal arts colleges had only a loose connection and did not require a baccalaureate degree for admission. Thelin, *History of American Higher Education*, 53–55.

17. McCaughey, "Transformation of American Academic Life," 25–55. In his study of the lives of the approximately two hundred individuals who served as professors in American colleges between 1750 and 1800, William D. Carrell found that very few had made a lifelong career as academics. "American College Professors, 1750–1800." Kennedy, "Changing Academic Characteristics," 355–401.

18. B. Kimball, *True Professional Ideal*.

19. Finkelstein, *American Academic Profession*, 9–10.

20. Ibid., 18. See also Tobias, *Old Dartmouth on Trial*.

21. According to George P. Schmidt, nine out of ten pre–Civil War presidents were ministers. *Old Time College President*, 184.

22. Metzger, *Academic Freedom*, 29–30.

23. Kirkpatrick, *American College and Its Rulers*, 23.

24. Hofstadter, *Academic Freedom*, 235.

25. Kelley, *Yale*, 141.

26. Wertenbaker, *Princeton*, 121.

27. For a complete listing of the colleges founded in this period, see Tewksbury, *Founding of American Colleges and Universities*; Geiger, "Era of Multipurpose Colleges," 133; Burke, *American Collegiate Populations*, 54, 216.

28. Wertenbaker, *Princeton*, 180; Thelin, *History of American Higher Education*, 63.

29. Finkelstein, *American Academic Profession*, 18–24.

30. Richard Hofstadter has argued that the proliferation of colleges retarded the development of higher-quality institutions, in part because of the close correlation between the size of a college and the extent of academic freedom and self-government enjoyed by the faculty. *Academic Freedom*, 222–23.

31. Cowley, *Presidents, Professors, and Trustees*, 72–73; Story, *Forging of an Aristocracy*, 75; Morison, *Three Centuries of Harvard*, 231–34.

32. W. Clark, *Academic Charisma*; Thwing, *The German and the American University*.

33. Geiger, "Introduction." in *American College in the Nineteenth Century*. See also McCaughey, "Transformation of American Academic Life," regarding the growing professionalism of faculty at Harvard.

34. Wagoner, *Jefferson and Education*, 113–46; Kirkpatrick, *American College*, 55–57; Thelin, *History of American Higher Education*, 51–52.

35. Kelley, *Yale*, 182–87, 257; Beach, "Professors, Presidents and Trustees," 42; Hawkins, *Between Harvard and America*, 23.

36. Creutz, "From College Teacher to University Scholar," 41–56; Beach, "Professors, Presidents and Trustees," 85–86.

37. Sagendorph, *Michigan*, 71, 88.

38. Turner and Bernard, "German Model."

39. Creutz, "From College Teacher to University Scholar," 241–42, 337.

40. Perry, *Henry Philip Tappan*, 317; Steneck, "Faculty Governance at the University of Michigan."

41. Metzger, *Academic Freedom*, 35; "Barnard Argues for Enlarged Faculty Powers," 391.

42. Fletcher, *History of Oberlin College*, 1:178; Kirkpatrick, *American College*, 54–55.

43. Fletcher, *History of Oberlin College*, 2:667–68.

44. Adams was John Quincy Adams's cousin.

45. Easterby, *History of the College of Charleston*, 74–89, 121–31.

46. Michael, "The American Institute of Instruction," *History of Education Journal* 3 (Autumn 1951): 27–32.

47. "Jasper Adams on the Relation between Trustees and Faculty," 318–21. See also Hofstadter, *Academic Freedom*, 236–37.

48. "Jasper Adams on the Relation between Trustees and Faculty," 325–26.

49. Ibid., 325–27.

50. This is a central theme in many of the essays in Geiger, *American College in the Nineteenth Century*.

51. Johnson, "Misconceptions about the Early Land-Grant Colleges," 52 (July–August 1981): 333–51.

52. Morison, *Development of Harvard University*, xxxiv, xc; Hawkins, *Between Harvard and America*. McCaughey offers the most detailed account of the increasing professionalism of the Harvard faculty, citing the more extensive graduate training and greater

commitment to a long-term career in academia of the faculty of 1869 compared to Harvard faculty members earlier in the nineteenth century. "Transformation of American Academic Life," 271.

53. Metzger, *Academic Freedom*, 104; Geiger, "Era of Multipurpose Colleges," 133.

54. Kennedy, "Changing Academic Characteristics."

55. Metzger, *Academic Freedom*, 23.

56. Larson, *Rise of Professionalism*, x; Wilson, *Academic Man*, 113–14.

57. Veysey, *Emergence of the American University*, 174.

58. *New York Times*, August 7, 1874.

Chapter 2 · The Emergence of a Professional Faculty, 1870–1920

1. Brubacher and Rudy, *Higher Education in Transition*, 178–82; Veysey, *Emergence of the American University*; Metzger, *Academic Freedom*, 46–92. On the changing nature of traditional liberal arts colleges in this period, see Leslie, *Gentlemen and Scholars*; and G. Peterson, *New England College*.

2. Geiger, *To Advance Knowledge*.

3. Ross, *Origins of American Social Science*.

4. Barrow, *Universities and the Capitalist State*.

5. "The Colleges and the Professors."

6. US Bureau of the Census, *Historical Statistics*, 210–11.

7. Columbia, with 6,232 students, had the largest enrollment. The other institutions with more than five thousand students were Harvard, Chicago, Michigan, Pennsylvania, and Cornell. Columbia, Harvard, and Yale had more than five hundred instructional staff. Slosson, *Great American Universities*, x, 475.

8. Stameshkin, *The Town's College*, 255.

9. In the 1890s, for example, at the rapidly growing University of Wisconsin, deans were appointed for the first time for each of the separate faculties, and committees "multiplied like leaves on the trees in the first warm days of spring." Curti and Carstensen, *University of Wisconsin*, 610.

10. B. Clark, "Faculty Organization and Authority"; Veysey, *Emergence of the American University*, 320–22; Geiger, *To Advance Knowledge*, 20–37. A sociological study conducted in the 1960s by Walter F. Boland found statistical evidence that the increased size of a college or university was positively correlated with the development of more powerful faculty senates or other faculty governance bodies, as well with "the greater autonomy of subject-matter departments over matters of particular concern to them." "Size, Organization, and Environmental Mediation," 60.

11. W. Clark, *Academic Charisma*.

12. Thwing, *The German and the American University*, 40–77; Metzger, *Academic Freedom*, 111–12; Cowley, *Presidents, Professors, and Trustees*, 22–28.

13. Turner and Bernard, "The German Model and the Graduate School."

14. James, "The Ph.D. Octopus," 333, 338.

15. These organizations remained open to nonacademics, but they still fostered a new sense of professionalism among their members. Wiebe, *Search for Order*, 121; Furner, *Advocacy and Objectivity*.

16. The Supreme Court case of *Dent v. West Virginia* (1888) was a milestone in the growth of professional prerogatives, since the court held that only "an authority competent

to judge" could determine whether an individual had the appropriate qualifications to practice a profession. According to historian Samuel Haber, "That authority turned out to be the profession itself." *Authority and Honor*, 201–2. See also B. Kimball, *True Professional Ideal*.

17. Sociologist Burton R. Clark makes this argument in "Faculty Authority."

18. Bishop, *History of Cornell*, 74.

19. Ibid., 76.

20. Ibid., 155–56.

21. White, *Autobiography*, 436.

22. Bishop, *History of Cornell*, 76.

23. White, *Autobiography*, 390; Beach, "Professors, Presidents and Trustees," 162–79; Altschuler, *Andrew D. White*, 83–84; Bishop, *History of Cornell*, 263.

24. Anthony quoted in Altschuler, *Andrew D. White*, 136.

25. Bishop, *History of Cornell*, 219.

26. Hewett, "University Administration," 510, 515.

27. Bishop, *History of Cornell*, 263–68, 354–55; Beach, "Professors, Presidents and Trustees," 199–209. See also Schurman's annual report to the Cornell board of trustees, "Faculty Participation in University Government"; and D. Kimball, "Faculty Aspects of University Administration."

28. Eliot, "New Education," March 1869, 366.

29. Eliot, "New Education," February 1869, 215.

30. Quoted in Hawkins, *Between Harvard and America*, 56.

31. McCaughey, "Transformation of American Academic Life," 278–314.

32. Hawkins, *Between Harvard and America*, 67–68.

33. Morison, *Development of Harvard University*, xxxii–xxxiii.

34. Such developments were becoming more widespread at this time at other institutions that were also growing into modern universities. Veysey, *Emergence of the American University*, 312.

35. Hawkins, *Between Harvard and America*, 62, 272–73.

36. McCaughey, *Stand, Columbia*, 178–80, 192–93.

37. Hawkins, *Pioneer*, 3–4.

38. Ibid., 122, 240.

39. Flexner, *Daniel Coit Gilman*.

40. Hawkins, *Pioneer*, 57, 81–90; Flexner, *Daniel Coit Gilman*, 96.

41. Hawkins, *Pioneer*, 74, 80–82.

42. Flexner, *Daniel Coit Gilman*, 73.

43. Hawkins, *Pioneer*, 91, 213–14; Beach, "Professors, Presidents and Trustees," 227–33.

44. Gilman, *Launching of a University*, 43.

45. Hawkins, *Pioneer*, 213–14; Beach, "Professors, Presidents and Trustees," 233–36.

46. Hawkins, *Pioneer*, 130–31.

47. Storr, *Harper's University*, 76, 109–10; Slosson, *Great American Universities*, 475.

48. Storr, *Harper's University*, 18–19.

49. Ibid., 62.

50. Ibid., 90–95.

51. Ibid., 336–40.

52. Ibid., 83–85, 96–98; Metzger, *Academic Freedom*, 153–61.

53. G. Peterson, *New England College*; B. Kimball, *True Professional Ideal*.

54. Quoted in G. Peterson, *New England College*, 120.

55. Leslie, *Gentlemen and Scholars*, 214.

56. Ibid.

57. Tobias, *Old Dartmouth on Trial*, 33–37. The figures cited in the text do not include the medical college faculty, which operated separately from the "Academical" and other departments.

58. Tobias, *Old Dartmouth on Trial*, 31–33.

59. G. Peterson, *New England College*, 100–108.

60. The colleges are Amherst, Bowdoin, Dartmouth, Union, Wesleyan, and Williams. G. Peterson, *New England College*.

61. Le Duc, *Piety and Intellect at Amherst College*, 50.

62. G. Peterson, *New England College*, 133–34.

63. Le Duc, *Piety and Intellect at Amherst College*, 150–51; Fuess, *Amherst*, 269.

64. Axtell, *Making of Princeton University*, 51.

65. Ibid., 76–77.

66. Metzger, *Academic Freedom*, 146–47; Furner, *Advocacy and Objectivity*.

67. Metzger, *Academic Freedom*, 113.

68. Van Alstyne, "Specific Theory of Academic Freedom."

69. Quoted in Furner, *Advocacy and Objectivity*, 114. See also Metzger, *Academic Freedom*, 152–53.

70. Metzger, *Academic Freedom*, 168–71, 201–2.

71. Barrow, *Universities and the Capitalist State*.

72. Cooke, *Academic and Industrial Efficiency*, 17.

73. Ibid., 12–15, 22. Cooke was also a forceful advocate of what would later be called "assessment," proposing that each college or university establish a bureau of inspection to determine how well each administrative unit was carrying out its role. He also helped pioneer the development of the student credit hour as a standardized measure that would allow for comparisons across departments. The Carnegie Foundation was able to use its financial support for a faculty pension system at elite institutions as a means of offering an incentive to those colleges and universities that adopted some of the reforms advocated by Cooke. Barrow, *Universities and the Capitalist State*, 64–88.

74. Veblen, *Higher Learning in America*, 169. Veblen left the University of Chicago in 1906 because of a scandal caused by his philandering to take up a position at Stanford. Dorfman, *Thorstein Veblen and His America*, 252–57, 269–71.

75. McCaughey, *Stand, Columbia*, 234–37, 242–45; Rosenthal, *Nicholas Miraculous*, 226–35.

76. Cattell's plan was originally published in 1906 in *Science* but was reprinted in 1913 with additional material in Cattell, *University Control*, 17–21, 44. Ironically, Cattell, who was an outspoken critic of the bureaucratization of academic administration, gained great prominence as an experimental psychologist by pioneering in forms of mental testing that would subsequently be used in ways that reinforced bureaucratic approaches to management. Butler, *Across the Busy Years*, 162; "James McKeen Cattell."

77. Of the 299 respondents, more than one-third came from seven institutions: Harvard, Yale, Columbia, Pennsylvania, Johns Hopkins, Chicago, and Cornell. Six were university presidents, and a handful of others had scientific appointments outside of academia.

Cattell also included in *University Control* previously published essays by nine men who supported reform in higher education governance. These included prominent psychologists Joseph Jastrow and George Stratton, as well as Cornell University president Jacob Gould Schurman.

78. Stratton, "Externalism in American Universities," 426.

79. Creighton, "Government of American Universities," 395–96.

80. "A National Association of University Professors," 458–59; Metzger, *Academic Freedom*, 200–203.

81. In the AAUP's first years, membership was by nomination and was open only to those with a reputation for scholarship who had ten years of college or university service. Consequently, in 1920 the ten largest chapters were all at leading research universities. In order of size of membership, these were: Wisconsin, Chicago, Yale, California, Columbia, Princeton, Harvard, Pennsylvania, Michigan, and Stanford. AAUP, "Members of the Association." As early as 1919, however, membership was opened to those with only three years of experience. Hutcheson, *Professional Professoriate*, 11–13.

82. Lovejoy, "Annual Message of the President," 26. The issue of whether the AAUP was to be strictly a "professional association" or might also function as a trade union is explored more fully in subsequent chapters. For a work that examines this issue primarily in the period after World War Two, see Hutcheson, *Professional Professoriate*.

83. AAUP, "1915 Declaration of Principles," 291.

84. AAUP, "Report of the Committee of Inquiry on Nearing," 5–57.

85. Ibid.

86. AAUP, "1915 Declaration of Principles," 291–301. The AAUP adopted what was at one and the same time both a broader and narrower conception of academic freedom than the German concept of *Lehrfreiheit*. The "Declaration of Principles" also included "freedom of extramural utterance and action"—a freedom not guaranteed to German professors, who were civil servants. On the other hand, the AAUP statement put more emphasis on the obligation of American professors to be objective and to refrain from one-sided advocacy, which contrasted with the German defense of a professor's freedom, at least in the classroom and in published research, to advance a particular point of view. Novick, *That Noble Dream*, 64–68.

87. AAUP, "1915 Declaration of Principles," 294–95.

88. Ibid., 298–300.

89. Arthur O. Lovejoy played a critical role both in deciding to launch this first formal investigation and in drafting the committee report. See Metzger, "First Investigation."

90. AAUP, "Report of Conditions at the University of Utah."

91. AAUP, "Report of Committee T on Place and Function" (March 1920), 22.

92. Ibid., 24–25.

93. Ibid., 27.

94. The sixty-eight institutions whose responses were recorded included all the leading research universities in the country, a wide range of state universities, and many private liberal arts colleges such as Oberlin, Grinnell, Williams, and Reed.

95. Lovejoy, "Organization of the American Association of University Professors," 154. On the elite status of the founders of the AAUP, see Hutcheson, *Professional Professoriate*, 11–12.

96. AAUP, "Report of President Meiklejohn."

97. AAUP, "Report of Committee T on Place and Function" (March 1920), 32–34.

98. AAUP, "Annual Meeting."

99. AAUP, "Report of Committee T on Place and Function" (March 1920), 38–45.

100. Ibid., 23.

101. AAUP, "Annual Meeting."

Chapter 3 · *The Development of Faculty Governance, 1920–1940*

1. Cole, *Great American University*, 85. See also Geiger, *To Advance Knowledge*.

2. The arrival after 1933 of a significant number of leading scholars fleeing persecution in Europe who were attracted to the freedoms of American colleges and universities also contributed to the later rise of American institutions of higher education to a preeminent position in the world.

3. Ruml and Tickton, *Teaching Salaries Then and Now*.

4. Counts, "Social Status of Occupations."

5. Peter Novick has argued that at least in the case of historians, the gradual opening of the professoriate in this period to native and foreign-born Jews and Catholics, as well as to others from less privileged backgrounds, undercut the prestige of an academic career. He also cites a narrowing of the gap in salaries between academics and ordinary wage laborers as an indication that the process of professionalization "stalled" during the interwar years. *That Noble Dream*, 169–74. This view is countered by Wilson, *Academic Man*, 16; and by B. Kimball, *True Professional Ideal*, 283.

6. Nielson, "MLA Presidential Address."

7. Metzger, *Academic Freedom*, 211–15. For background on the AAC (which later became the Association of American Colleges and Universities), see Hawkins, *Banding Together*.

8. Geiger, *To Advance Knowledge*.

9. In 1920, 8 percent of Americans eighteen to twenty-one years old were enrolled as college students; in 1940, 16 percent were. The number of faculty increased from 48,600 to 146,000, while the number of PhDs granted increased from 600 to 3,300 between 1920 and 1940. US Bureau of the Census, *Historical Statistics*, 210–11.

10. The eight universities with more than one thousand instructional staff were the University of California, Columbia, Cornell, Harvard, the University of Illinois, New York University, Ohio State, and the University of Pennsylvania. Irvine, *World Almanac 1940*, 575–83; Slosson, *Great American Universities*, x, 475.

11. Kirkpatrick, *American College*. For a compilation of many of his articles, see Kirkpatrick, *Academic Organization and Control*. Cain and Gump, "John Ervin Kirkpatrick."

12. AAUP, "Report of the Committee of Inquiry on Washburn College," 66–137.

13. Ibid. Kirkpatrick never regained his position at Washburn but did go on to teach for several years at Harvard, the University of Michigan, and Olivet College, before being dismissed from Olivet for continuing to express views on college administration that were unacceptable to the college's governing board. Cain and Gump, "John Ervin Kirkpatrick." Nearly a century later, the issue of academic freedom as it relates to speech concerning institutional governance would be highlighted by the Supreme Court's ruling in *Garcetti v. Ceballos*. AAUP, "Protecting an Independent Faculty Voice."

14. Veysey, *Emergence of the American University*, 165–71.

15. AAUP, "Report of Committee of Inquiry Concerning Clark University," 65.

16. Ibid., 58.

17. Stadtman, *University of California*, 33, 52–53.

18. For accounts of these events, see ibid., 239–49; and A. Taylor, *Academic Senate.*

19. A. Taylor, *Academic Senate*, 3–4; Stadtman, *University of California*, 248; Louderback, "Faculty-Administration Cooperation."

20. Lyman, *World Almanac 1930*, 458–64.

21. What follows is based on Oldfather, "The Executive Committee System."

22. The same term was used to describe quite similar governance reforms that were adopted in the early 1930s at the University of Michigan. Thorpe, "Executive Committee System."

23. Oldfather, "Executive Committee System," 202. The AAUP's Committee T used the results of a governance survey of existing campus chapters that was completed in 1940 to develop a 28-point scale for determining the extent of faculty participation in institutional governance. Although such scores represented the perceptions of the AAUP leaders doing the rating rather than some objective reality, they do give a rough measure of the relative state of faculty governance at different institutions. No institution received a perfect score, but Illinois, with a score of 24, was exceeded only by Oberlin, which had a score of 26. In publishing its results, Committee T did not reveal the scores for individual institutions, but a document with these scores can be found in the papers of the committee in the AAUP archives. Both a list of the institutions that responded to the survey and the questions used for creating the Faculty Self-Government Index can be found in the appendix to this volume. "Institutional Scores on Twenty-Eight Point Scale," prepared by Committee T for the confidential use of the national officers of the American Association of University Professors, revised to January 12, 1941, in AAUP Archives, Committee T on College and University Government (hereafter AAUP Committee T Archives), box 19.

24. Gates, *First Century*, 138.

25. The granting to faculty of the right to choose the members of its own committees was becoming increasingly common at this time. The AAUP governance survey completed in 1940 referred to above revealed that in more than 50 percent of the institutions reporting, the faculty elected at least some of its committees either directly or indirectly.

26. Gates, *First Century*, 188–92; Padelford, "Administrative Code."

27. Neckers, "College Faculty Senate"; Blewett, "A New Type of Faculty Organization"; AAUP, "Temple University Chapter"; Larrabee, "Adventure in College Government."

28. Almost 90 percent of the institutions that responded to the AAUP survey reported still having some form of body including all members of the general faculty. Although the AAUP survey was limited to institutions that had local membership chapters, respondents included a wide variety of colleges and universities from all across the country, ranging from virtually all of the nation's most prestigious research universities to teachers colleges and small church-controlled schools. AAUP, "Report of Committee T on Place and Function" (April 1941) (hereafter "1941 Committee T Report").

29. Oldfather, "Executive Committee System," 200; B. Clark, *The Distinctive College*, 121.

30. Sabrosky, "Development of a Divisional Faculty Plan."

31. AAUP, "Report of Committee T: Data." Institutions responding to this survey are listed in the appendix to this volume.

32. Among the institutions that responded to the AAUP survey, twenty-seven reported having no general faculty body. "1941 Committee T Report." The expansion of voting rights to a greater range of faculty members was also reflected in the AAUP's own membership requirements. When the organization was established in 1915, membership was open only to full professors with ten years of academic experience and an established scholarly reputation. Although membership requirements were eased soon thereafter, the requirement of some period of service was not entirely eliminated until 1939. In that same year, membership was also opened to faculty members at junior colleges. Hutcheson, *A Professional Professoriate*, 13.

33. Millikan, *Autobiography*, 223.

34. Ibid., 226–28; Gilbert, "Executive Council Plan." When Lee DuBridge replaced Millikan as president of Caltech in 1946, he abolished the executive council and adopted a more traditional form of governance. DuBridge, interview by Finn Aaserud.

35. Geiger, *To Advance Knowledge*, 188.

36. Lyman, *World Almanac 1930*, 458.

37. B. Clark, *The Distinctive College*, 13–41; Henderson, "Faculty Participation."

38. B. Clark, *The Distinctive College*, 54.

39. Antioch's emphasis on student engagement also resulted in three students being elected to the Ad Cil by the entire campus, which also voted on the selection of two of the five faculty members on the council. B. Clark, *The Distinctive College*, 54; Henderson, "Faculty Participation," 178–88.

40. On Committee T's 28-point scale for determining the extent of faculty participation in institutional governance, Antioch, with a score of 21, was among the highest-scoring schools in the country. "Institutional Scores on Twenty-Eight Point Scale," AAUP Committee T Archives, box 19. Ironically, Antioch, which had one of the most robust forms of faculty governance of any institution in the country in 1940, would have its administration sanctioned by the AAUP for violations of the association's governance standards seventy years later. . See AAUP, "College and University Government: Antioch."

41. Foster quoted in B. Clark, *The Distinctive College*, 96.

42. Ibid., 104–5, 122–23.

43. In 1940, out of a total faculty of thirty-seven, eighteen were full professors. B. Clark, *The Distinctive College*, 121–23.

44. Clark's assessment of the strength of faculty governance at Reed is confirmed by the AAUP survey results cited above. Reed received a score of 24 on the 28-point scale, which tied it for second among all institutions reporting.

45. Rudy, *College of the City of New York*; Irvine, *World Almanac 1940*; Edel, *Struggle for Academic Democracy*.

46. Edel, *Struggle for Academic Democracy*, 4.

47. Yellowitz, "Academic Governance," 8.

48. In appendixes to *Struggle for Academic Democracy*, Edel, who chaired the union's educational policies committee that first drafted the reform proposals, has conveniently supplied a thorough summary of the changes instituted by the new bylaws, as well as copies of the proposals generated by his committee. One year after the adoption of CCNY's new governance bylaws, longtime CCNY faculty member Joseph Allen wrote to Paul Ward, the chair of the AAUP's Committee T, assessing the impact of the new rules. Thirty years earlier, Allen had participated in a successful effort to extend voting rights to assis-

tant professors. Ironically, he now wrote: "Our own experience of one year under the new Bylaws suggest [*sic*] the dangers of too much democratization in university government." He complained in particular about the granting of tenure to instructors after "too short" a period (three years) and the requirement that instructors be represented on every faculty council and every departmental committee on appointment. Joseph Allen to Paul W. Ward, November 27, 1939, AAUP Committee T Archives, box 6; Rudy, *College of the City of New York*, 235, 286.

49. Edel, *Struggle for Academic Democracy*, 67–82; Tead, "Place and Function," 168. In the AAUP's rankings of the degree of faculty involvement in governance, Brooklyn College was tied for second (with Reed, Illinois, and the Commerce Center of City College) out of more than two hundred schools surveyed. CCNY and Hunter College were also very close to the top of the rankings.

50. AAUP, "Report of Committee T on Place and Function" (April 1940), 173, 181; "1941 Committee T Report," 155–73.

51. In addition to the statistical summary of the survey results published in "1941 Committee T Report," 156, see also Temple University AAUP Chapter report, "Faculty Representation on Boards of Trustees," enclosed in James W. Woodard to Paul W. Ward, December 2, 1940, AAUP Committee T Archives, box 19.

52. AAUP, "Report of Committee T: Data." This report is the source for further comparisons discussed below. The 167 institutions that responded to this survey are listed in the appendix to this volume. Although there is significant overlap between the institutions included in the 1924 and 1941 survey reports, about half of the schools reporting in 1924 are not included in the later survey.

53. Bretz, "Selecting a President," 150.

54. AAUP, "Local and Chapter Notes" (October 1925), 308; Peckham, *Making of the University of Michigan*, 177–90. The same year that Michigan used a joint faculty-trustee search committee in selecting a new president, the University of Chicago adopted a similar procedure, with faculty enjoying equal representation on the committee that chose Max Mason as the first person from outside the university to follow in the footsteps of William Rainey Harper. AAUP, "Local and Chapter Notes" (December 1925), 426.

55. Akers, "Allegheny College."

56. At Yale, deans were elected by the full professors of each college. Kelley, *Yale*, 325, 364.

57. In addition to the colleges of the city of New York, other schools with elected chairs were Antioch, Bucknell, the University of Colorado, Grinnell, the University of Illinois, Indiana State, Johns Hopkins, Ohio University, Reed, San Francisco State, Scripps, Smith, Vassar, Wellesley, Wesleyan, the University of Wisconsin, and Xavier of New Orleans. Survey responses from individual institutions were not published by the AAUP's Committee T, but they can be found in the AAUP Committee T Archives, box 19.

58. In addition to the sources previously cited, see also Paul T. Ward to Robert E. Matthews (Ohio State University), January 8, 1942, in AAUP Committee T Archives, box 19.

59. The questions relating to this subject on the two surveys are not identical, and the format for recording responses is quite different, but I have coded the responses to the 1924 survey that were published by Committee T to make these comparisons as effective as possible. On the issue of faculty participating in appointments, in 1924 in addition to the 38

out of 167 institutions reporting a formal mechanism for registering faculty opinion, another 15 referred to a significant degree of informal consultation.

60. Geiger, *To Advance Knowledge*, 36–37.

61. Willey, *Depression, Recovery and Higher Education*, 468.

62. Paul Ward, the chair of Committee T, also observed that in general the entire sample in the AAUP governance survey probably represented "institutions of a generally superior grade" because only accredited institutions were included, that being a requirement for the formation of an AAUP chapter. He noted that of the 1,699 institutions of higher education listed by the US Office of Education in 1940, only about half at that time had some sort of accredited status granted by one of the regional or national accrediting associations. "1941 Committee T Report," 165–67.

63. McConaughy, "Report of the Commission." McConaughy, who was then president of Wesleyan University, would go on to become not only president of the AAC but also governor of Connecticut.

64. "1941 Committee T Report," 168–69.

Chapter 4 · *The Developing Consensus on Shared Governance, 1940–1975*

1. On the rise of American universities to a position of global preeminence, see Cole, *Great American University*; Graham and Diamond, *Rise of American Research Universities*; and Geiger, *Research and Relevant Knowledge*.

2. Figures are compiled from statistics appearing annually in the *Bulletin of the AAUP*.

3. The idea that institutions with widely differing histories and initial missions were all engaged in a growing competition for status after World War Two that resulted in a converging emphasis on research and graduate education and greater faculty power is the central thesis of Freeland, *Academia's Golden Age*. These developments are also highlighted in Jencks and Riesman's pathbreaking study of American higher education, *The Academic Revolution*.

4. National Center for Education Statistics, *120 Years of American Education*, 75–89; National Center for Education Statistics, *Digest of Education Statistics: 2011*, table 263. Even accounting for inflation, which according to the consumer price index was 384 percent between 1940 and 1975, the increase in spending on higher education is impressive. The rate of increase in real dollar expenditures, however, did slow in the 1970s because of the rapid increase in the price level in that decade. For inflation calculators, see "Measuring Worth."

5. Carnegie Commission on Higher Education, *Governance of Higher Education*, 75.

6. Between 1972 and 1977, the use of part-time faculty rose by 50 percent, while the increase in full-time staff was only 9 percent. AAUP, "Status of Part-Time Faculty," 73.

7. Whereas in 1940 two-year schools represented only 21 percent of all institutions of higher education in the United States, in 1975 that figure had risen to 31 percent; the percentage of students attending two-year schools increased at an even greater rate, going from 10 percent in 1940 to 35 percent in 1975. National Center for Education Statistics, *120 Years of American Education*, 77, 80.

8. Carnegie Commission, *Governance of Higher Education*, 13. For example, one sociological study from this period that utilized a statistical approach showed a clear correlation between the quality of a college or university and the degree of faculty influence in institutional governance. Lazarsfeld and Thielens, *The Academic Mind*, 168–72. Lazarsfeld and

Thielens used published data on the size of the institution's library, the percentage of faculty holding PhDs, expenditures per student, and the number of students obtaining scholarships or other honors after graduation to determine the quality of the schools in their study.

9. B. Clark, "Faculty Authority," 299–300.

10. The number of students enrolled in American colleges and universities fell from 1.5 million in 1940 to 1.2 million in 1944. US Bureau of the Census, *Historical Statistics*, 210.

11. Cole, *Great American University*, 85–108; Geiger, *Research and Relevant Knowledge*, 3–29.

12. Thelin, *History of American Higher Education*, 262–67.

13. AAUP, "Place and Function of Faculties" (Spring 1955).

14. Although scores for individual institutions were not included in the published report of the committee, they can be found in "Confidential Report to the Officers and Members of the Council," dated February 1, 1955, in AAUP Committee T Archives, box 13. The eighteen institutions with increases of ten points or more were Colorado Agricultural and Mechanical, Franklin & Marshall, Illinois State Normal, Illinois State Western, Iowa State Teachers, Louisiana State, Minnesota, Nebraska, New Hampshire, New Mexico Highlands, Oklahoma, Smith, Washington State, Wayne, William and Mary, Wisconsin–La Crosse, and Wooster.

15. Lottinville was responsible for building the University of Oklahoma Press into a major scholarly publisher. Cross, *University of Oklahoma and World War II*, xiv, 107. For a biographical sketch of Lottinville, see Oklahoma Historical Society, "Lottinville, Savoie (1906–1997)."

16. "Confidential Report," February 1, 1955, AAUP Committee T Archives.

17. Cross, *University of Oklahoma and World War II*, xiv.

18. Ibid., 11–16, 47, 252.

19. Ibid., 62, 66. Cross had also inherited a controversy involving charges of unfair treatment by an untenured professor, which had elicited an expression of concern from the national office of the AAUP. Taking the initiative to head off a possible AAUP investigation, Cross visited the national office on his own initiative to assure the AAUP staff that Oklahoma fully upheld the principles of academic freedom and tenure. Ibid., 132.

20. Irvine, *World Almanac 1940*, 579.

21. Knoll, *Prairie University*, 103–8.

22. The highest-rated institution was Vassar (24), followed by Amherst, Cornell, Queens, Wisconsin (all 22); Hunter, Johns Hopkins, Marietta, Reed, Smith, Wooster (all 21); and CCNY, Wellesley, and Wesleyan (all 20).

23. Freed, *Educating Illinois*, 233.

24. Ibid., 255. Illinois State's sister institution, Southern Illinois State Normal University (later Southern Illinois University), was already at this time beginning its own transition into a university with a system of shared governance, establishing an elected faculty senate and a greatly strengthened curriculum committee in 1937. Neckers, "College Faculty Senate." Not coincidentally, AAUP membership at Southern Illinois skyrocketed from 9 in 1935 to 156 in 1950.

25. Freed, *Educating Illinois*, 256.

26. S. Griffith, *Liberalizing the Mind*; Irvine, *World Almanac 1940*, 577.

27. S. Griffith, *Liberalizing the Mind*, 195–96.

28. Ibid., 222–27.

29. The University of Pennsylvania did not participate in either the 1939 or 1953 AAUP governance surveys, so it is not possible to "score" the change that took place, but Morrow's account makes it clear that the change was substantial. Morrow, "University of Pennsylvania."

30. Godson et al., *College of William & Mary.*

31. Baldridge, "Environmental Pressure." For an overview of the development of two-year colleges, see Brint and Karabel, *The Diverted Dream.*

32. Under various titles, Schlaefer had been the chief administrator at Monmouth since its founding in 1933. AAUP, "Faculty-Administration Relationships," 5–6.

33. Ibid., 9–10, 20.

34. AAUP, "Faculty Participation in the Governance of Junior and Community Colleges," 175.

35. Changes in the AAUP's own membership requirements in this period also reflected a continued trend toward greater inclusiveness. In 1958, the organization finally eliminated the requirement that new members be admitted only through a process of nomination. Hutcheson, *Professional Professoriate,* 40.

36. Lehmberg and Plaum, *University of Minnesota,* 66–67; Eckert, "Share of the Teaching Faculty," 346–51.

37. AAUP, "On the Relationship."

38. Schrecker, *No Ivory Tower.*

39. AAUP, "Place and Function of Faculties" (Spring 1955), 77.

40. The possibility was raised at a conference sponsored by the ACE's Commission on Instruction and Evaluation, held in New York in May 1957. The meeting was funded in part by the Carnegie Corporation. In addition to representatives of the ACE and the Carnegie Corporation, AAUP general secretary Ralph F. Fuchs and a vice president of the AGB attended. Fuchs, "American Council on Education Conference, May 7–9, 1957," memorandum to Committee T file, June 13, 1957, in AAUP Committee T Archives, box 17.

41. AAUP, "Place and Function of Faculties" (February 1938).

42. AAUP, "Faculty Participation in College and University Government."

43. Millett, *Academic Community,* 27. On the creation of the National Association of State Universities and Land-Grant Colleges, see StateUniversity.com, "NASULGC."

44. Millett, *Academic Community,* 62.

45. Ibid., 94–96, 226, 252.

46. Louis Joughin, "Review of ACE-AAUP possible joint drafting effort," September 22, 1964, in AAUP Committee T Archives, box 8.

47. Wilson, *Academic Man.* Wilson also served as president of the University of Texas during the 1950s. Louis Joughin, "Second report on ACE-AAUP possible joint statement," January 6, 1965, AAUP Committee T Archives, box 8. The chief drafters of the statement were Louis Joughin of the AAUP and Edward L. Katzenbach Jr. of the ACE. Katzenbach had been assistant secretary of defense in the Kennedy administration, having previously been a faculty member at Princeton, Columbia, Harvard, and Brandeis. John Millett and Ralph S. Brown Jr., professor of law at Yale and chair of Committee T, were also members of the drafting committee.

48. The files of Committee T contain copies of unsigned responses by members of the ACE Commission on Administrative Affairs to the June 8, 1965, draft of the statement,

most of which express skepticism about much of the statement as it was then formulated. AAUP Committee T Archives, box 8, folder "Tripartite Statement, 3/30–12/31/65."

49. AAUP, *Statement on Government.*

50. Although the language on the faculty role in budgeting differed from the wording initially put forward by the AAUP, Committee T chair Ralph Brown explained to the AAUP's 1966 annual meeting that the significance of the change in final language was "not entirely clear," and that "one reason for chronic difficulty in drafting this part is that . . . faculty participation in the budgeting process has been minimal." Brown concluded that, since "we have little practice to go by . . . anything that the statement puts forward about faculty participation in the budgeting process, even if it is not crystal clear, represents an advance." AAUP, "Report of Committee T, 1966–67," 214.

51. Ralph S. Brown Jr., Memorandum to Members of Committee T, March 17, 1966, AAUP Committee T Archives, box 8.

52. AAUP, "Draft Statement on Student Participation."

53. Hodgkinson, *The Campus Senate*; Millett, *New Structures of Campus Power*, 41–48, 55–63.

54. Schuster et al., *Strategic Governance*, 33–35.

55. Ibid., 66–67.

56. Carnegie Commission, *Governance of Higher Education*, 53, 55–58.

57. Mortimer and McConnell, *Sharing Authority Effectively*, 95–96.

58. Millett, *New Structures of Campus Power*, 50.

59. See, for example, Dill, *Case Studies in University Governance*; Dykes, *Faculty Participation in Academic Decision Making*; McConnell and Mortimer, *The Faculty in University Governance*; Weber et al., *Faculty Participation in Academic Governance*; Hodgkinson and Meeth, *Power and Authority*; Mason, *College and University Government*; and Carnegie Commission, *Governance of Higher Education*.

60. Carnegie Commission, *Governance of Higher Education*, 41.

61. AAUP, "Report of Committee T, 1968–69," 178. The full text of the resolution adopted by the California State Colleges trustees appears in AAUP, "California State College Trustees," 404.

62. The survey authors noted that there was statistical evidence that administrators tended to take a more optimistic view of the extent of faculty authority than did faculty members. AAUP, "Report of the Survey Subcommittee."

63. In contrast to the two previous surveys, however, results for each individual institution reporting were published in the lengthy committee report that appeared in the *AAUP Bulletin*.

64. AAUP, "Report of the Survey Subcommittee," 123.

65. Ibid., 73.

66. Probably the most highly publicized assertion of faculty power in university governance at this time was Jencks and Riesman, *The Academic Revolution*. Riesman later reassessed his claims about the extent of faculty power. Riesman, *On Higher Education*.

67. The study also noted the rapid expansion of state coordinating bodies having some oversight responsibility for either all of the state's higher education or one particular segment (four-year or two-year institutions), observing that the number of such bodies had increased from twenty-five in 1959–60 to forty-seven in 1968–69. However, the authors

observed that such coordinating bodies rarely had legislative authority and thus played less of a role in reshaping campus governance than did the governing authorities in charge of multicampus systems. Lee and Bowen, *Multicampus University*, 4.

68. Ibid., xix, 7.

69. Carnegie Commission, *Governance of Higher Education*, 1.

70. Lee and Bowen, *Multicampus University*, xi–xiii.

71. Ibid., 180–81.

72. Weber et al., *Faculty Participation in Academic Governance*, 42.

73. Lee and Bowen, *Multicampus University*, 179.

74. Freeland, *Academia's Golden Age*. Freeland examined Boston College, Boston University, Brandeis, Harvard, MIT, Northeastern, Tufts, and the University of Massachusetts.

75. Baldridge, *Power and Conflict*. Although Baldridge painted a very positive picture of NYU's transformation in the 1960s into a more prestigious institution with considerably higher academic standards, David L. Kirp, writing three decades later, described NYU as "teetering on the knife edge of bankruptcy" in the early 1970s and dated the institution's rise to prominence as beginning in the 1980s. *Shakespeare, Einstein, and the Bottom Line*, 66.

76. Lee and Bowen, *Multicampus University*, 178–79, 278–79.

77. Ibid., 388.

78. AAUP, "College and University Government: Long Island University." In contrast to the situation with academic freedom and tenure cases, where investigations could lead to a formal censure of an institution's administration, until the early 1990s there was no provision by which AAUP governance investigations could lead to a formal sanctioning of an institution. See also Strong, *Running on Empty*, especially chapter 4.

79. AAUP, "College and University Government: Long Island University," 64.

80. Ibid., 63.

81. AAUP, "College and University Government: Texas El Paso."

82. Logan Wilson had first served as interim chancellor in 1954 and then was appointed to the position in 1960, serving for only a year. University of Texas System, "History of the UT System"; Fenlon, "State-Wide Coordination."

83. As a postscript to the University of Texas story, soon after the publication of the AAUP report, the board of regents summarily fired the president of the Austin campus and then disregarded the wishes of an elected faculty-student advisory committee in naming a new president. Duffey, "Board of Regents."

84. Schuster and Finkelstein, *American Faculty*, 240–43.

85. Carnegie Commission on Higher Education, *Priorities for Action*, 3–4.

86. Cheit, *New Depression*.

87. In constant 2003–4 dollar values, average salaries for full-time instructional faculty fell by more than $10,000 between 1970 and 1980. Schuster and Finkelstein, *American Faculty*, 242.

88. Mortimer and McConnell, *Sharing Authority Effectively*, 118.

89. Danforth, "Management and Accountability," 135. See also Birnbaum, *Management Fads*, 33–52, for a discussion of the initial introduction of new management approaches in the 1960s and early 1970s.

90. Schuster and Finkelstein, *American Faculty*, 41, 233.

91. Lieberman, "Representational Systems in Higher Education." Lieberman was a candidate for the AFT presidency in 1962 but decades later became a critic of education unions. Lieberman, *The Teacher Unions*.

92. Hutcheson, *Professional Professoriate*, 68. In 1962, the AFT had organized the teachers at the Milwaukee Vocational School, but this institution was more an extension of the public school system than a traditional college or university.

93. Kemerer and Baldridge, *Unions on Campus*, 1.

94. Kemerer and Baldridge identified just twelve unionized institutions in 1974, including Rutgers, Temple, CUNY, and SUNY, which could be classified as multiversities. *Unions on Campus*, 56–57.

95. Benjamin and Mauer, *Academic Collective Bargaining*, 23–24, 80.

96. Kemerer and Baldridge, *Unions on Campus*; Ladd and Lipset, *Professors, Unions, and American Higher Education*; Garbarino, *Faculty Bargaining*.

97. Of the three leading contemporary studies of the rise of the faculty unionism cited in the previous note, only Ladd and Lipset question the role played by concerns about governance as a significant cause of faculty interest in collective bargaining.

98. Weber et al., *Faculty Participation in Academic Governance*, 1–12.

99. Kemerer and Baldridge, *Unions on Campus*, 38–69; Garbarino, *Faculty Bargaining*, 69–72.

100. Greenberg, "Monmouth University."

101. Kemerer and Baldridge cite the examples of Pennsylvania State University, CUNY, and Central Michigan University. *Unions on Campus*, 210. See also the discussion to follow of the California State Colleges.

102. Marmion, "Unions in Higher Education," 346. Following the passage of state enabling legislation in 1979, a new vote among faculty in the California State system led to union recognition in 1982. Ehrenberg et al., "Collective Bargaining," 210.

103. AAUP, "California State College Trustees," 403.

104. Ibid., 403–4.

105. Joughin, "Three Problems," 234.

106. Weber et al., *Faculty Participation in Academic Governance*, 21; Northwestern University Archives, "The Presidents of Northwestern."

107. Hutcheson, *Professional Professoriate*, provides an extended discussion of the internal debates within the AAUP over the issue of collective bargaining.

108. In addition to Hutcheson, *Professional Professoriate*, arguments within the AAUP both in opposition to and in favor of collective bargaining are summarized in AAUP, "Council Position on Collective Bargaining" (Spring 1972).

109. AAUP, "Council Position on Collective Bargaining" (Winter 1971), 511. The new policy was subsequently approved by the membership at the 1972 annual meeting.

110. Ibid. Over one-third of council members initially opposed the change in policy and continued to view collective bargaining as basically inconsistent with professional values and the ideal of shared governance. Hutcheson, *Professional Professoriate*, 154. See also Finkin, "Collective Bargaining and University Government."

111. For the St. John's governance investigation, see AAUP, "College and University Government: St. John's University (N.Y.)." See also Scimecca and Damiano, *Crisis at St. John's*, which includes the full text of the Middle States report.

112. Finkin, "Collective Bargaining and University Government," 156–57.

113. Polishook, "Unions and Governance"; Yellowitz, "Academic Governance and Collective Bargaining."

114. Mortimer and McConnell, *Sharing Authority Effectively*, 83–84.

115. Marc Belth, untitled (revision of paper given at Queens faculty meeting, March 21, 1968), AAUP Committee T Archives, box 11, folder "Representation of Economic Interests, 1969."

116. The AAHE-NEA Task Force report in 1967 had also used the word "unstable" to describe the likely relation between senates and unions.

117. Kemerer and Baldridge, *Unions on Campus*, 7.

118. Schuster and Finkelstein, *American Faculty*, 260.

Chapter 5 · Corporatization and the Challenges to Shared Governance, 1975–Present

1. Thelin, *History of American Higher Education*, 321.

2. Tierney and Hentschke, *New Players, Different Game*.

3. National Center for Education Statistics, *Digest of Education Statistics: 2011*, tables 196 and 263.

4. Ibid., tables 213 and 279.

5. As recently as 1970, only 22 percent of all faculty were on part-time appointments. Ibid.

6. AAUP, "Trends in Instructional Staff"; Schuster and Finkelstein, *American Faculty*, 176, 233.

7. National Center for Education Statistics, *Digest of Education Statistics: 2011*, tables 366 and 371.

8. Newfield, *Unmaking the Public University*, 91, 173; Quinterno, *The Great Cost Shift*.

9. Kirshstein and Hulbert, *Revenues*.

10. University of Virginia, "Financing the University 101"; University of Michigan, "Financial Statements."

11. Geiger, *Knowledge and Money*, 45. See, for example, the call for greater accountability by Ronald Reagan's assistant secretary of education, Finn, "Context for Governance."

12. Bowen, *Costs of Higher Education*.

13. Schuster and Finkelstein, *American Faculty*, 242–44.

14. Geiger, *Research and Relevant Knowledge*, 243–46.

15. Ehrenberg, *Tuition Rising*.

16. Kaplan, "How Academic Ships Actually Navigate," 192.

17. Cooke, *Academic and Industrial Efficiency*.

18. Birnbaum, *Management Fads*.

19. Slaughter and Rhoades, *Academic Capitalism and the New Economy*, especially chapter 7; Kirp, *Shakespeare, Einstein, and the Bottom Line*, especially chapter 6, which examines the experiences of the University of Southern California and the University of Michigan with RCB.

20. Keller, *Academic Strategy*; Keller, "Does Higher Education Research Need Revisions?," 278. See Birnbaum, *Management Fads*, 63–75, for a critical overview of the impact of strategic planning.

21. Keller, *Academic Strategy*, 3, 27, 35.

22. Ibid., 36.

23. Ibid., 67.

24. In the AAUP's 1953 governance survey, Wesleyan was tied for the twelfth-highest ranking; although the responses to the AAUP's 1970 survey (which came exclusively from the administration) are not as overwhelmingly positive, they still indicate the continuing existence of a substantial degree of faculty involvement in governance.

25. Wesleyan University, Office of the President, "Wesleyan's Thirteenth President."

26. Wessel, "Wesleyan Faculty Seeking Endowment-Loss Accounting."

27. Press, "Student Trustees at Wesleyan"; Lender, "Faculty Gets Recommendations."

28. Keller, *Academic Strategy*, 48.

29. Ibid., 61.

30. Schuster et al., *Strategic Governance*, 31–48.

31. Ibid., 80–96.

32. Ibid., 64–79.

33. AAUP, "City University of New York," 60–65.

34. Ibid., 71.

35. Ibid., 69–81.

36. AAUP, "Academic Freedom and Tenure: The State University of New York."

37. Ibid., 239.

38. I. Peterson, "State U. Planning a Self-Appraisal."

39. The number of faculty members (professors, associate professors, assistant professors, and instructors) at SUNY stood at 7,774 in 1975–76 and increased to 7,878 in 1976–77. AAUP, "Academic Freedom and Tenure: State University of New York," 257.

40. Ibid., 259.

41. Kemerer and Baldridge, *Unions on Campus*, 1.

42. Benedict and Benedict, "Ohio SB5 and the Attempt to 'Yeshiva' Public University Faculty."

43. Gorman, "AAUP and Collective Bargaining," 2a.

44. Polishook, "Unions and Governance"; Yellowitz, "Academic Governance and Collective Bargaining."

45. The California law declared: "The Legislature recognizes that joint decision-making and consultation between administration and faculty or academic employees is the long-accepted manner of governing institutions of higher learning and is essential to the performance of the educational missions of these institutions, and declares that it is the purpose of this chapter to both preserve and encourage that process. Nothing contained in this chapter shall be construed to restrict, limit, or prohibit the full exercise of the functions of the faculty in any shared governance mechanisms or practices, including the Academic Senate of the University of California and the divisions thereof, the Academic Senates of the California State University, and other faculty councils, with respect to policies on academic and professional matters." The full text of the law appears at California Public Employment Relations Board, "Higher Education Employer-Employee Act (1979)." While the faculties of the Cal State system quickly took advantage of the right to bargain collectively, none of the University of California faculties followed a similar strategy.

46. Polishook, "Unions and Governance," 16.

47. As early as 1950, 250 faculty members belonged to the local AAUP chapter. "Membership," *Bulletin of the AAUP* 36 (Spring 1950).

48. Kilgore, *Transformations*, 350; Zabel, "Boston University Strike."

49. Ringer, "Academic Governance," 42.

50. Freeland, *Academia's Golden Age*, 53.

51. Zabel, "Boston University Strike"; Kilgore, *Transformations*, 350–54, 364–65.

52. As employees of state and local governments, faculty members at public colleges and universities are not covered by the National Labor Relations Act. Before 1970, federal labor law had not applied to private institutions either, because the National Labor Relations Board had not considered them to be involved in interstate commerce, a position the NLRB reversed in the *Cornell University* case. Clarke, "The Yeshiva Case," 453–54.

53. Following the *Yeshiva* ruling, union recognition was also withdrawn at the University of New Haven and Villanova University. Weidhorn, "The Yeshiva Faculty Union," 24.

54. Almost the entire texts of the majority and minority opinions in the case are reproduced in Gorman, "The Yeshiva Decision," 190–97.

55. Weidhorn, "The Yeshiva Faculty Union." Weidhorn was an officer in the Yeshiva Faculty Association.

56. AAUP, "Academic Freedom and Tenure: Yeshiva."

57. Gorman, "The Yeshiva Decision," 197.

58. Ibid., 195–96.

59. AAUP, "Faculty Governance in the 80s," 383; AAUP, "Four Issues in Contemporary Campus Governance."

60. AASCU, *Governance of State Colleges and Universities*. See also AAUP, "AASCU's Statement on Academic Government," 60.

61. Rhoades, *Managed Professionals*, 253.

62. Berry and Savarese, *Directory of U.S. Faculty Contracts*.

63. Rodda, "Collective Bargaining in California."

64. Rubiales, "Collective Bargaining at Community Colleges," 42.

65. Assembly Bill 1725.

66. K. White, "Shared Governance in California."; Collins, "Shared Governance."

67. AAUP, "College and University Government: Miami-Dade."

68. Smallwood, "Union In, Governance Out"; University of Akron, "History"; AAUP, "Chapter Profile: University of Akron."

69. Benedict and Benedict, "Ohio SB5 and the Attempt to 'Yeshiva' Public University Faculty."

70. Jaschik, "Union Certified at Illinois-Chicago"; "2 Faculty Bargaining Units Certified at Illinois-Chicago"; Basu, "Union Win at Oregon." At the University Illinois at Chicago, the bargaining unit initially included both tenure-track and non-tenure-track faculty. However, the administration obtained a court ruling that Illinois law prohibited such a bargaining unit. The union organizers subsequently gained state certification as bargaining agents for two separate units.

71. While current fund expenditures per student for all colleges and universities combined actually declined in constant dollars between 1971 and 1982, such expenditures began a steady upward trend in the two decades after 1983. This trend, however, would be reversed as a result of the Great Recession following the financial collapse of 2007–8. National Center for Education Statistics, *Digest of Education Statistics: 2005*, table 339.

72. Slaughter, "Retrenchment in the 1980s"; Gumport, "Contested Terrain"; AAUP, "Financial Exigency."

73. Kaplan, "How Academic Ships Actually Navigate,"196.

74. For a partial indication of such actions around the country between 2008 and 2011, see AAUP, "Program Closures."

75. Rhoades, *Managed Professionals*, 98.

76. AAUP, *Recommended Institutional Regulations on Academic Freedom and Tenure*, 24.

77. The frequency of such actions, including highly publicized program closures in the aftermath of the Great Recession at the State University of New York at Albany, the University of Northern Iowa, and the University of Nevada, Reno, led the AAUP in 2013 to issue new recommended regulations that include a less restrictive definition of "financial exigency." The new regulations were part of an effort by the AAUP to establish more explicit guidelines for faculty involvement in program closures that resulted from financial stress falling short of a demonstrable threat to the institution's continued existence. AAUP, "Role of Faculty."

78. Miller, "Budget Cuts and Shared Governance: A Faculty Member's Perspective"; R. Griffith, "Budget Cuts and Shared Governance: An Administrator's Perspective"; Woodward et al., "Faculty Exigency, Academic Governance," 109.

79. Slaughter, "Retrenchment in the 1980s," 260.

80. The twenty-eight investigations represented only a partial sample of all such instances of retrenchment during this period. Woodward et al., "Faculty Exigency, Academic Governance," 108.

81. Geiger, *Knowledge and Money*, especially 162–72; Slaughter and Leslie, *Academic Capitalism*, especially 174–77.

82. Mallon, "Disjointed Governance"; Collis, "Paradox of Scope."

83. AAUP, "Summary of Recommendations."

84. Rhoades, *Managed Professionals*, 193.

85. Rivard, "The Fine Print."

86. AAUP, "College and University Governance: University of Virginia."

87. Ironically, just before assuming the presidency of the University of Virginia, Sullivan had written an essay warning about the dangers of the deprofessionalization of the faculty and the erosion of shared governance in American colleges and universities. Sullivan, "Professional Control in the Complex University."

88. Burgan, *What Ever Happened to the Faculty?*, 77, 80–81.

89. Western Governors University website, www.wgu.edu; Neem, "University without Intellectuals."

90. Slaughter and Rhoades, *Academic Capitalism and the New Economy*, 303.

91. Kirp, *Shakespeare, Einstein, and the Bottom Line*, 36.

92. Miller and Bellamy, "Fine Print."

93. Zweigenhaft, "Is This Curriculum for Sale?"; Jones, "Universities, the Major Battleground."

94. National Center for Education Statistics, *Digest of Education Statistics: 2011*, tables 196 and 263.

95. Tierney and Hentschke, *New Players, Different Game*; National Center for Education Statistics, "Fast Facts."

96. Schuster and Finkelstein, *American Faculty*, 43–46.

97. AAUP, "Inclusion in Governance."

98. Carter and Carter, "Women's Recent Progress in the Professions."

99. Rhoades, *Managed Professionals*, 131–71.

100. See for example, AAUP, "Contingent Appointments and the Academic Profession"; and AAUP, "Recommended Institutional Regulations," sect. 13, "Part-Time Faculty Appointments."

101. These arguments are examined more fully in AAUP, "Inclusion in Governance."

102. AAUP, "Inclusion in Governance." The statement, however, acknowledges the appropriateness of excluding faculty on contingent appointments from involvement in the evaluation of their tenured and tenure-track colleagues.

103. The narrative to follow is based on the report of the AAUP's investigating committee, "College and University Governance: Rensselaer Polytechnic Institute"; and Campbell and Koretz, "Demise of Shared Governance." Before the early 1990s, the AAUP expressed formal condemnation ("censure") of an institution's administration only for violations of the AAUP's standards of academic freedom and tenure. In the early 1990s, the AAUP established a separate list of "sanctioned" institutions that had been found to depart substantially from the association's standards of governance. Such a sanction represented only a symbolic black mark against an institution's reputation, since it carried no legal weight or clearly measurable consequences. However, the AAUP's creation of a "sanction" list for governance violations to go alongside its long-standing "censure" list of administrations found violating the AAUP's standards on academic freedom and tenure was one indication of the organization's growing concern about the governance problems occurring in American higher education at this time.

104. Koretz, "Governance vs. Shared Governance"; Rensselaer Faculty Senate, Constitution of the Rensselaer Faculty Senate.

105. Jaschik, "Union Democracy for Some?"; CUNY Contingents Unite, "About."

106. For a full explication of how tenure and shared governance are "inextricably linked," see AAUP, "On the Relationship." See also McPherson and Schapiro, "Tenure Issues in Higher Education," which argues that there are actually economic benefits in terms of efficiency resulting from the "constraints" imposed by tenure "on the discretion of managers (the 'administration') over various aspects of the academic enterprise."

107. A survey conducted in 2001 of nearly one thousand four-year colleges and universities found that over 90 percent (and 98 percent of public institutions) had a tenure system. Kaplan, "How Academic Ships Actually Navigate," 192.

108. For a brief overview of the implications of the events at Bennington and Minnesota, see Burgan, *What Ever Happened to the Faculty?*, 110–13.

109. Mannies, "Cure for Colleges"; Burton, "Some Colleges Survived." One of the institutions that Spellmann had apparently saved, Tarkio College, subsequently had to close its doors after it became the subject of a federal audit concerning its student financial aid practices. DePalma, "College Acts in Desperation."

110. AAUP, "College and University Government: Lindenwood."

111. Before 1994, Bennington had a system of what was the equivalent of post-tenure review for faculty members. After the successful completion of a first five-year contract, faculty members gained "presumptive tenure" in subsequent consideration for new five-year contracts. No faculty member in Bennington's history before 1994 had ever been dis-

missed after having gained presumptive tenure. AAUP, "Academic Freedom and Tenure: Bennington."

112. Some years later, Bennington College agreed to a settlement with seventeen of the dismissed professors that called for payments totaling nearly $2 million and a direct apology for the actions taken. Jacobson, "Bennington Settles."

113. Brauer, "Tenure Crisis at Minnesota"; Magner, "Minnesota Professors Irate."

114. Magner, "Fierce Battle."

115. AAUP, "Post-Tenure Review."

116. Schuster and Finkelstein, *American Faculty*, 258–59.

117. Rhoades, *Managed Professionals*, 79.

118. Ginsberg, *Fall of the Faculty*; Bowen, *Costs of Higher Education*.

119. Ginsberg, *Fall of the Faculty*.

120. Hebel, "On Campuses"; Stripling and Fuller, "Presidential Pay"; Gordon, "UC Regents Approve Pay Hikes."

121. Since 1966 the AAUP has issued policy statements on the appropriate role of faculty in such areas as the selection, evaluation, and retention of administrators; budgetary and salary matters; and the reform of intercollegiate athletics, all of which are contained in AAUP, *Policy Documents and Reports*. Association of Governing Boards, *Renewing the Academic Presidency*, x–xi. For a contemporary response to the AGB statement on the academic presidency, see Gerber, "Reaffirming the Value of Shared Governance."

122. Association of Governing Boards, *AGB Statement on Institutional Governance*. For a detailed comparison of the two statements, see Hamilton, "Comparing AAUP and AGB."

123. Association of Governing Boards, *AGB Statement on Institutional Governance*, 4.

124. Hamilton, "Comparing AAUP and AGB."

125. ACTA began in 1995 as the National Alumni Forum but changed its name in 1998. The organization now offers a variety of training programs and conferences targeting college and university trustees that make it a conservative rival of the AGB. See the ACTA website,www.goacta.org/. Selden, "Who's Paying for the Culture Wars?"

126. Association of Governing Boards, *Board Responsibility for Institutional Governance*; Association of Governing Boards, *AGB Statement on Board Responsibility for the Oversight of Educational Quality*.

127. Kaplan, "How Academic Ships Actually Navigate"; Tierney and Minor, *Challenges for Governance*; Cummings and Finkelstein, *Scholars in the Changing Academy*, chap. 8.

128. Kaplan found that for all fifteen of the questions he repeated from the earlier survey, comparisons of responses from the nearly five hundred institutions that were included in both surveys very closely paralleled the results obtained by comparing the responses from all institutions responding in each survey. Thus, for example, for respondents from matched institutions, 31 percent in 1970 reported faculty control over appointments of full-time faculty, whereas in the 2001 survey, 73 percent reported such faculty control, which is identical to results obtained by comparing all institutions in both surveys. Kaplan generously provided me with some of his raw data so that I could determine not only the number of matched institutions appearing in both surveys but also which particular institutions were in his matched sample and whether the responses he received for each institution came from an administrator, a senate leader, or an AAUP chapter representative—information that does not appear in the published results.

129. The other surveys do not break down responses to these questions by type of institution.

130. Tierney and Minor, *Challenges for Governance*, 5, 9.

131. AAUP members were involved in formulating institutional responses for more than 75 percent of all the schools in the 1970 survey; in Kaplan's survey, AAUP members were involved in formulating responses in only 10 percent of all schools involved.

132. Tierney and Minor, *Challenges for Governance*, 6.

133. Cummings and Finkelstein, *Scholars in the Changing Academy*, 145.

134. Schuster and Finkelstein, *American Faculty*, 165; Cummings and Finkelstein, *Scholars in the Changing Academy*, 68.

Conclusion

1. Menand, "Trashing of Professionalism," 17.

2. Bellah, "Freedom, Coercion, Authority," 19–20.

3. Côté and Allahar have voiced similar concerns regarding Canadian universities in *Lowering Higher Education*.

4. Stripling, "President's Proposal."

5. Gerber, "Inextricably Linked."

6. Schrecker, "Humanities on Life Support," 53.

7. Tierney and Minor, *Challenges for Governance*, 6.

8. Nelson's *No University Is an Island* is one of the most impassioned statements of this argument.

9. Drucker, *Managing in Turbulent Times*, 132–33. Mary Burgan also cites Drucker in her defense of shared governance. Burgan, *What Ever Happened to the Faculty?*, 108–9.

AASCU. *Governance of State Colleges and Universities: Achieving Institutional Mission.* Washington, DC: American Association of State Colleges and Universities, 1985.

AAUP. "AASCU's Statement on Academic Government: A Response from Committee T." *Academe* 71 (May–June 1985): 60.

AAUP. "Academic Freedom and Tenure: Bennington College." *Academe* 81 (March–April 1995): 91–103.

AAUP. "Academic Freedom and Tenure: The State University of New York." *Bulletin of the AAUP* 63 (August 1977): 237–60.

AAUP. "Academic Freedom and Tenure: Yeshiva University." *Academe* 67 (August 1981): 186–95.

AAUP. "Annual Meeting." *Bulletin of the AAUP* 8 (February 1922): 87–88.

AAUP. "California State College Trustees Approve 1966 Statement on Government." *AAUP Bulletin* 53 (Winter 1967): 403–4.

AAUP. "Chapter Profile: University of Akron." *Academe* 96 (July–August 2010): 16–17.

AAUP. "City University of New York: Mass Dismissals under Financial Exigency." *Bulletin of the AAUP* 63 (April 1977): 60–81.

AAUP. "College and University Governance: Rensselaer Polytechnic Institute." *Bulletin of the AAUP* 97 (2011): 51–66.

AAUP. "College and University Governance: The University of Virginia Governing Board's Attempt to Remove the President" (March 2013). www.aaup.org/file/uva-investigation.pdf.

AAUP. "College and University Government: Antioch University and the Closing of Antioch College." *Academe* 95 (November–December 2009): 41–63.

AAUP. "College and University Government: Lindenwood College (Missouri)." *Academe* 80 (May–June 1994): 60–68.

AAUP. "College and University Government: Long Island University." *AAUP Bulletin* 57 (Spring 1971): 58–67.

AAUP. "College and University Government: Miami-Dade Community College (Florida)." *Academe* 86 (May–June 2000): 73–88.

AAUP. "College and University Government: St. John's University (N.Y.)." *AAUP Bulletin* 54 (Autumn 1968): 325–61.

AAUP. "College and University Government: The University of Texas at El Paso." *AAUP Bulletin* 60 (Summer 1974): 126–38.

AAUP. "Contingent Appointments and the Academic Profession." In AAUP, *Policy Documents and Reports*, 98–114.

AAUP. "Council Position on Collective Bargaining." *AAUP Bulletin* 57 (Winter 1971): 511–12.

AAUP. "Council Position on Collective Bargaining." *AAUP Bulletin* 58 (Spring 1972): 46–61.

AAUP. "Draft Statement on Student Participation in College and University Government." *AAUP Bulletin* 56 (Spring 1970): 33–34.

AAUP. "Faculty-Administration Relationships: Monmouth College (New Jersey)." *AAUP Bulletin* 47 (March 1961): 5–23.

AAUP. "Faculty Governance in the 80s: Adverse Conditions, Diverse Responses; A Preliminary Wingspread Report." *Academe* 67 (December 1981): 383–86.

AAUP. "Faculty Participation in College and University Government: Statement of Principles Approved by the Council, October 26, 1962." *AAUP Bulletin* 48 (December 1962): 321–23.

AAUP. "Faculty Participation in the Governance of Junior and Community Colleges." *AAUP Bulletin* 48 (June 1962): 175.

AAUP. "Financial Exigency, Academic Governance, and Related Matters." *Academe* 90 (March–April 2004): 104–12.

AAUP. "Four Issues in Contemporary Campus Governance." *Academe* 68 (January–February 1982): 3A–14A.

AAUP. "The Inclusion in Governance of Faculty Members Holding Contingent Appointments" (January 2013). www.aaup.org/file/contingent-inclusion-in-governance_0.pdf.

AAUP. "Local and Chapter Notes." *Bulletin of the AAUP* 11 (October 1925): 306–15.

AAUP. "Local and Chapter Notes." *Bulletin of the AAUP* 11 (December 1925): 426–37.

AAUP. "Members of the Association." *Bulletin of the AAUP* 6 (January 1920): 8–41.

AAUP. "Membership." *Bulletin of the AAUP* 36 (Winter 1950): 128–58.

AAUP. "1915 Declaration of Principles on Academic Freedom and Tenure." In AAUP, *Policy Documents and Reports*.

AAUP. "On the Relationship of Faculty Governance to Academic Freedom." In AAUP, *Policy Documents and Reports*.

AAUP. "The Place and Function of Faculties in College and University Government: Final Report on the 1953 Study." *Bulletin of the AAUP* 41 (Spring 1955): 62–81.

AAUP. "The Place and Function of Faculties in University and College Government: Report of Committee T." *Bulletin of the AAUP* 24 (February 1938): 141–50.

AAUP. *Policy Documents and Reports*. 10th ed. Washington, DC: AAUP, 2006.

AAUP. "Post-Tenure Review: An AAUP Response." In AAUP, *Policy Documents and Reports*, 60–66.

AAUP. "Program Closures." Accessed January 22, 2013. www.aaup.org/program-closures.

AAUP. "Protecting an Independent Faculty Voice: Academic Freedom after *Garcetti v. Ceballos*." *Academe* 95 (November–December 2009): 64–88.

AAUP. *Recommended Institutional Regulations on Academic Freedom and Tenure*. In AAUP, *Policy Documents and Reports*.

AAUP. "Recommended Institutional Regulations on Academic Freedom and Tenure." Accessed May 25, 2013. www.aaup.org/report/recommended-institutional-regulations -academic-freedom-and-tenure.

AAUP. "Report of Committee of Inquiry Concerning Clark University." *Bulletin of the AAUP* 10 (October 1924): 40–107.

AAUP. "Report of Committee T: Data Concerning the Actual Status of Faculties in University Government in a Number of Institutions." *Bulletin of the AAUP* 10 (May 1924): 43–104.

AAUP. "Report of Committee T, 1966–67." *AAUP Bulletin* 53 (Summer 1967): 214.

AAUP. "Report of Committee T, 1968–69." *AAUP Bulletin* 55 (Summer 1969): 178–80.

AAUP. "Report of Committee T on Place and Function of Faculties in College and University Government." *Bulletin of the AAUP* 26 (April 1940): 171–216.

AAUP. "Report of Committee T on Place and Function of Faculties in College and University Government." *Bulletin of the AAUP* 27 (April 1941): 155–73.

AAUP. "Report of Committee T on Place and Function of Faculties in University Government and Administration." *Bulletin of the AAUP* 6 (March 1920): 17–47.

AAUP. "Report of Conditions at the University of Utah" (December 1915). In *Academic Freedom and Tenure: Published Case Reports, 1915–2006*, 2nd ed. Washington, DC: AAUP, 2007. CD-ROM.

AAUP. "Report of President Meiklejohn to Trustees of Amherst College." *Bulletin of the AAUP* 5 (May 1919): 64–65.

AAUP. "Report of the Committee of Inquiry on Conditions at Washburn College." *Bulletin of the AAUP* 7 (January–February 1921): 66–137.

AAUP. "Report of the Committee of Inquiry on the Case of Professor Scott Nearing of the University of Pennsylvania." *Bulletin of the AAUP* 2 (May 1916): 5–57.

AAUP. "Report of the Survey Subcommittee of Committee T." *AAUP Bulletin* 57 (March 1971): 68–124.

AAUP. "The Role of the Faculty in Conditions of Financial Exigency" (July 2013). www.aaup.org/report/role-faculty-conditions-financial-exigency.

AAUP. *Statement on Government of Colleges and Universities.* In AAUP, *Policy Documents and Reports*, 135–40.

AAUP. "The Status of Part-Time Faculty" (approved for publication in November 1980). In AAUP, *Policy Documents and Reports*.

AAUP. "Summary of Recommendations: 56 Principles to Guide Academy-Industry Engagement." Accessed November 6, 2013. www.aaup.org/sites/default/files/files/Principles-summary.pdf.

AAUP. "Temple University Chapter Assists in Establishing Faculty Senate." *Bulletin of the AAUP* 23 (November 1937): 578–80.

AAUP. "Trends in Instructional Staff Employment Status, 1975–2011" (April 2013). www.aaup.org/sites/default/files/files/AAUP_Report_InstrStaff-75-11_apr2013.pdf.

AAUP Archives. Committee T on College and University Government. Special Collections Research Center, Gelman Library, George Washington University, Washington, DC.

Abbott, Andrew. *Chaos of Disciplines.* Chicago: University of Chicago Press, 2001.

Akers, Oscar P. "Allegheny College, Faculty Participation in Nominating a President." *Bulletin of the AAUP* 17 (May 1931): 402–3.

Altschuler, Glenn C. *Andrew D. White: Educator, Historian, Diplomat.* Ithaca, NY: Cornell University Press, 1979.

Assembly Bill 1725 (September 19, 1988). Faculty Association of California Community Colleges website. www.faccc.org/advocacy/bills/historical/ab1725.PDF.

Association of Governing Boards. *AGB Statement on Board Responsibility for the Oversight of Educational Quality* (March 17, 2011). www.agb.org/sites/agb.org/files/u3/AGBBoardsand EdQuality.pdf.

Association of Governing Boards. *AGB Statement on Institutional Governance, as Adopted by the AGB Board of Directors November 8, 1998*. Washington, DC: Association of Governing Boards, 1999.

Association of Governing Boards. *Board Responsibility for Institutional Governance* (January 22, 2010). www.agb.org/sites/agb.org/files/u3/Statement%20on%20Institutional%20 Governance.pdf.

Association of Governing Boards. *Renewing the Academic Presidency: Stronger Leadership for Tougher Times*. Washington, DC: Association of Governing Boards, 1996.

Axtell, James. *The Making of Princeton University: From Woodrow Wilson to the Present*. Princeton, NJ: Princeton University Press, 2006.

Baldridge, J. Victor., ed. *Academic Governance: Research on Institutional Politics and Decision Making*. Berkeley, CA: McCutchan, 1971.

Baldridge, J. Victor. "Environmental Pressure, Professional Autonomy and Coping Strategies in Academic Organizations." In Baldridge, *Academic Governance*.

Baldridge, J. Victor. *Power and Conflict in the University: Research in the Sociology of Complex Organizations*. New York: John Wiley and Sons, 1971.

"Barnard Argues for Enlarged Faculty Powers." In Hofstadter and Smith, *American Higher Education*.

Barrow, Clyde W. *Universities and the Capitalist State: Corporate Liberalism and the Reconstruction of American Higher Education, 1894–1928*. Madison: University of Wisconsin Press, 1990.

Basu, Kaustuv. "Union Win at Oregon." *Inside Higher Ed*, March 15, 2012. www.insidehighered .com/news/2012/03/15/university-oregon-faculty-takes-step-toward-unionizing.

Beach, Mark Broklebank. "Professors, Presidents and Trustees: A Study of University Governance, 1825–1918." PhD diss., University of Wisconsin, 1966.

Bellah, Robert. "Freedom, Coercion, Authority." *Academe* 85 (January–February 1999): 16–21.

Benedict, Mary Ellen, and Louis M. Benedict. "Ohio SB5 and the Attempt to 'Yeshiva' Public University Faculty." *Journal of Collective Bargaining in the Academy* 4 (February 20, 2013). thekeep.eiu.edu/jcba/vol4/iss1/2.

Benjamin, Ernst, and Michael Mauer, eds. *Academic Collective Bargaining*. Washington, DC: AAUP and Modern Language Association of America, 2006.

Berry, Joe, and Michelle Savarese. *Directory of U.S. Faculty Contracts and Bargaining Agents in Institutions of Higher Education*. New York: National Center for the Study of Collective Bargaining in Higher Education and the Professions, Hunter College (prepublication version), 2012. Accessed May 1, 2013. www.insidehighered.com/sites/default/server _files/files/facdirectory.pdf.

Birnbaum, Robert. *Management Fads in Higher Education: Where They Come From, What They Do, Why They Fail*. San Francisco: Jossey-Bass, 2000.

Bishop, Morris. *A History of Cornell*. Ithaca, NY: Cornell University Press, 1962.

Blewett, Edward York. "A New Type of Faculty Organization." *Bulletin of the AAUP* 24 (December 1938): 644–51.

Boland, Walter F. "Size, Organization, and Environmental Mediation: A Study of Colleges and Universities." In Baldridge, *Academic Governance.*

Bowen, Howard R. *The Costs of Higher Education: How Much Do Colleges and Universities Spend per Student and How Much Should They Spend?* San Francisco: Jossey-Bass, 1980.

Brauer, Kinley. "The Tenure Crisis at Minnesota." *OAH Newsletter* 24 (November 1996): 3.

Bretz, Julian P. "Selecting a President at Cornell." *Bulletin of the AAUP* 25 (April 1939): 150–57.

Brint, Steven, and Jerome Karabel. *The Diverted Dream: Community Colleges and the Promise of Educational Opportunity in America, 1900–1985.* New York: Oxford University Press, 1989.

Brockliss, L. W. B. "The European University in the Age of Revolution, 1789–1850." In *The History of the University of Oxford,* vol. 6, *Nineteenth-Century Oxford, Part I,* edited by M. G. Brock and M. C. Curthoys. Oxford: Oxford University Press, 1997.

Brubacher, John S., and Willis Rudy. *Higher Education in Transition.* 3rd ed. New York: Harper and Row, 1976.

Burgan, Mary. *What Ever Happened to the Faculty? Drift and Decision in Higher Education.* Baltimore: Johns Hopkins University Press, 2006.

Burke, Colin B. *American Collegiate Populations: A Test of the Traditional View.* New York: New York University Press, 1982.

Burton, Thomas M. "Some Colleges Survived by Lining Up Very Needy 'Students.'" *Wall Street Journal,* December 14, 1990.

Butler, Nicholas Murray. *Across the Busy Years: Recollections and Reflections.* Vol. 1. New York: Scribner's Sons, 1939.

Cain, Timothy Reese, and Steven E. Gump. "John Ervin Kirkpatrick and the Rulers of American Colleges." *Journal of Academic Freedom* 2 (2011). www.academicfreedom journal.org/.

California Public Employment Relations Board. "Higher Education Employer-Employee Relations Act (1979). www.perb.ca.gov/Laws/HERA.aspx.

Campbell, Nancy D., and Jane F. Koretz. "The Demise of Shared Governance at Rensselaer Polytechnic Institute." *AAUP Journal of Academic Freedom* 1 (2010). www.aaup.org /sites/default/files/files/JAF/2010%20JAF/CampbellKoretz.pdf.

Carnegie Commission on Higher Education. *Governance of Higher Education: Six Priority Problems.* New York: McGraw-Hill, 1973.

Carnegie Commission on Higher Education. *Priorities for Action: Final Report of the Carnegie Commission on Higher Education.* New York: McGraw-Hill, 1973.

Carrell, William D. "American College Professors, 1750–1800." *History of Education Quarterly* 8 (Autumn 1968): 289–305.

Carter, Michael J., and Susan Boslego Carter. "Women's Recent Progress in the Professions; or, Women Get a Ticket to Ride after the Gravy Train Has Left the Station." *Feminist Studies* 7 (Autumn 1981): 476–504.

Cattell, James McKeen. *University Control.* New York: Science Press, 1913.

Cheit, Earl F. *The New Depression in Higher Education.* Carnegie Commission on Higher Education series. New York: McGraw-Hill, 1971.

Christensen, Clayton M., and Michael B. Horn. "Colleges in Crisis: Disruptive Change Comes to American Higher Education." *Harvard Magazine* (July–August 2011), 40–43.

Clark, Burton R. *The Distinctive College.* With a new introduction by the author. Chicago: Aldine, 1970; reprint, New Brunswick, NJ: Transaction, 1992.

Clark, Burton R. "Faculty Authority." *AAUP Bulletin* 47 (December 1961): 299–300.

Clark, Burton R. "Faculty Organization and Authority." In *The Emerging University and Industrial America,* edited by Hugh Hawkins. Lexington, MA: D. C. Heath, 1970.

Clark, William. *Academic Charisma and the Origins of the Research University.* Chicago: University of Chicago Press, 2006.

Clarke, Carlene A. "The Yeshiva Case: An Analysis and an Assessment of Its Potential Impact on Public Universities." *Journal of Higher Education* 52 (September–October 1981): 449–69.

Cole, Jonathan R. *The Great American University: Its Rise to Preeminence, Its Indispensable National Role, Why It Must Be Protected.* New York: Public Affairs, 2009.

"The Colleges and the Professors." *Nation,* June 23, 1881.

Collins, Linda. "Shared Governance in the California Community Colleges." *Academe* 88 (July–August 2002): 36–40.

Collis, David J. "The Paradox of Scope: A Challenge to the Governance of Higher Education." In Tierney, *Competing Conceptions of Academic Governance.*

Cooke, Morris Llewellyn. *Academic and Industrial Efficiency: A Report to the Carnegie Foundation for the Advancement of Teaching.* Bulletin no. 5. Boston: Merrymount Press, 1910.

Côté, James E., and Anton L. Allahar. *Lowering Higher Education: The Rise of Corporate Universities and the Fall of Liberal Education.* Toronto: University of Toronto Press, 2011.

Counts, George S. "The Social Status of Occupations: A Problem in Vocational Guidance." *School Review* 33 (1925): 16–27.

Cowley, W. H. *Presidents, Professors, and Trustees.* Edited by Donald T. Williams Jr. San Francisco: Jossey-Bass, 1980.

Creighton, J. E. "The Government of American Universities." In Cattell, *University Control.* Originally published in *Science,* August 12, 1910.

Creutz, Alan. "From College Teacher to University Scholar: The Evolution and Professionalization of Academics at the University of Michigan, 1841–1900." PhD diss., University of Michigan, 1981.

Cross, George Lynn. *The University of Oklahoma and World War II: A Personal Account.* Norman: University of Oklahoma Press, 1980.

Cummings, William K., and Martin J. Finkelstein. *Scholars in the Changing Academy: New Contexts, New Rules and New Roles.* Dordrecht, the Netherlands: Springer, 2012.

CUNY Contingents Unite. "About." Accessed May 25, 2013. cunycontingents.wordpress .com/about/.

Curti, Merle, and Vernon Carstensen. *The University of Wisconsin: A History, 1848–1925.* Vol. 1. Madison: University of Wisconsin Press, 1949.

Danforth, William H. "Management and Accountability in Higher Education." *AAUP Bulletin* 59 (Summer 1973): 135–38.

DePalma, Anthony. "A College Acts in Desperation and Dies Playing the Lender." *New York Times,* April 17, 1991.

Deresiewicz, William. "Faulty Towers: The Crisis in Higher Education." *Nation,* May 4, 2011.

Dill, David D. *Case Studies in University Governance.* Washington, DC: National Association of State Universities and Land-Grant Colleges, 1971.

Dorfman, Joseph. *Thorstein Veblen and His America.* New York: Viking, 1935.

Drucker, Peter F. *Managing in Turbulent Times.* New York: Harper and Row, 1980.

DuBridge, Lee A. Interview by Finn Aaserud. February 14, 1986. Niels Bohr Library and Archives, American Institute of Physics, College Park, MD. www.aip.org/history/ohilist /4582.html.

Duffey, Joseph. "The Board of Regents of the University of Texas System—a Crisis of Confidence." *AAUP Bulletin* 61 (Autumn 1975): 229.

Duryea, Edwin D. *The Academic Corporation: A History of College and University Governing Boards.* Edited by Don Williams. New York: Farmer, 2000.

Dykes, Archie R. *Faculty Participation in Academic Decision Making: Report of a Study.* Washington, DC: American Council on Education, 1968.

Easterby, J. H. *A History of the College of Charleston, Founded 1770.* Charleston, SC: n.p., 1935.

Eckert, Ruth E. "The Share of the Teaching Faculty in University Policy-Making." *AAUP Bulletin* 45 (September 1959): 346–51.

Edel, Abraham. *The Struggle for Academic Democracy: Lessons from the 1938 "Revolution" in New York's City Colleges.* Philadelphia: Temple University Press, 1990.

Ehrenberg, Ronald G. *Tuition Rising: Why College Costs So Much.* Cambridge, MA: Harvard University Press, 2000.

Ehrenberg, Ronald G., Daniel B. Klaff, Adam T. Kexbom, and Matthew P. Nagowski. "Collective Bargaining in American Higher Education." In *Governing Academia,* edited by Ronald G. Ehrenberg. Ithaca, NY: Cornell University Press, 2004.

Eliot, Charles W. "The New Education: Its Organization." *Atlantic Monthly,* February 1869 and March 1869.

Fenlon, Paul E. "State-Wide Coordination and College and University Faculties." *AAUP Bulletin* 53 (Winter 1967): 408–11.

Finkelstein, Martin J. *The American Academic Profession: A Synthesis of Social Scientific Inquiry since World War II.* Columbus: Ohio State University Press, 1984.

Finkelstein, Martin J. "From Tutor to Professor: The Development of the Modern Academic Role at Six Institutions during the Nineteenth Century." *History of Higher Education Annual* 3 (1983): 99–121.

Finkin, Matthew W. "Collective Bargaining and University Government." *AAUP Bulletin* 57 (Summer 1971): 149–62.

Finn, Chester E., Jr., "Context for Governance: Public Dissatisfaction and Campus Accountability." In *Governing Tomorrow's Campus: Perspectives and Agendas,* by Jack H. Schuster, Lynn H. Miller, and associates. New York: American Council on Education / Macmillan, 1989.

Fischer, Karin. "Crisis of Confidence Threatens Colleges." *Chronicle of Higher Education,* May 15, 2011.

Fletcher, Robert Samuel. *A History of Oberlin College: From Its Foundation through the Civil War.* 2 vols. Oberlin, OH: Oberlin College, 1943; reprint, New York: Arno, 1971.

Flexner, Abraham. *Daniel Coit Gilman: Creator of the American Type of University.* New York: Harcourt, Brace, 1946.

Fogel, Daniel Mark, and Elizabeth Malson-Huddle. *Precipice or Crossroads: Where America's Great Public Universities Stand and Where They Are Going Midway through Their Second Century*. Albany: State University of New York Press, 2012.

Freed, John B. *Educating Illinois: Illinois State University, 1857–2007*. Virginia Beach, VA: Donning, 2009.

Freeland, Richard M. *Academia's Golden Age: Universities in Massachusetts, 1945–1970*. New York: Oxford University Press, 1992.

Fuess, Claude Moore. *Amherst: The Story of a New England College*. Boston: Little, Brown, 1935.

Furner, Mary O. *Advocacy and Objectivity: A Crisis in the Professionalization of American Social Science, 1865–1905*. Lexington: University Press of Kentucky, 1975.

Garbarino, Joseph W., in association with Bill Aussieker. *Faculty Bargaining: Change and Conflict*. New York: McGraw-Hill, 1975.

Gates, Charles M. *The First Century at the University of Washington, 1861–1961*. Seattle: University of Washington Press, 1961.

Geiger, Roger L., ed. *The American College in the Nineteenth Century*. Nashville, TN: Vanderbilt University Press, 2000.

Geiger, Roger L. "The Era of Multipurpose Colleges in American Higher Education, 1850–1890." In Geiger, *American College in the Nineteenth Century*.

Geiger, Roger L. *Knowledge and Money: Research Universities and the Paradox of the Marketplace*. Stanford, CA: Stanford University Press, 2004.

Geiger, Roger L. "Introduction: New Themes in the History of Nineteenth-Century Colleges." In Geiger, *American College in the Nineteenth Century*.

Geiger, Roger L. *Research and Relevant Knowledge: American Research Universities since World War II*. New York: Oxford University Press, 1993.

Geiger, Roger L. *To Advance Knowledge: The Growth of American Research Universities, 1900–1940*. New York: Oxford University Press, 1986.

Gerber, Larry G. "'Inextricably Linked': Shared Governance and Academic Freedom." *Academe* 87 (May–June 2001): 22–24.

Gerber, Larry G. "Reaffirming the Value of Shared Governance." *Academe* 83 (September–October 1997): 14–18.

Gilbert, Horace N. "The Executive Council Plan of Administrative Organization at the California Institute of Technology." *Bulletin of the AAUP* 26 (April 1940): 190–96.

Gilman, Daniel Coit. *The Launching of a University, and Other Papers: A Sheaf of Remembrances*. New York: Dodd, Mead, 1906.

Ginsberg, Benjamin. *The Fall of the Faculty: The Rise of the All-Administrative University and Why It Matters*. New York: Oxford University Press, 2011.

Godson, Susan, Ludwell H. Johnson, Richard B. Sherman, Thad W. Tate, and Helen C. Walker. *The College of William & Mary: A History*. Vol. 2, *1888–1993*. Williamsburg: King and Queen Press, Society of the Alumni, College of William and Mary in Virginia, 1993.

Gordon, Larry. "UC Regents Approve Pay Hikes for 12 Staffers." *Los Angeles Times*, December 2, 2011.

Gorman, Robert A. "The AAUP and Collective Bargaining: A Look Backward and Ahead." *Academe* 68 (September–October 1982): 1a–4a.

Gorman, Robert A. "The Yeshiva Decision." *Academe* 66 (May 1980): 188–97.

Graham, Hugh Davis, and Nancy Diamond. *The Rise of American Research Universities: Elites and Challengers in the Postwar Era.* Baltimore: Johns Hopkins University Press, 1997.

Graham, Patricia Albjerg. "Exclusion and Expansion: A History of Women in American Higher Education." *Signs* 3 (Summer 1978): 759–73.

Greenberg, Brian. "Monmouth University." In *Encyclopedia of New Jersey*, edited by Maxine N. Lurie and Marc Mappen. New Brunswick, NJ: Rutgers University Press, 2004.

Griffith, Robert. "Budget Cuts and Shared Governance: An Administrator's Perspective." *Academe* 79 (November–December 1993): 15–17.

Griffith, Sally F. *Liberalizing the Mind: Two Centuries of Liberal Education at Franklin & Marshall College.* University Park: Pennsylvania State University Press, 2010.

Gumport, Patricia J. "The Contested Terrain of Academic Program Reduction." *Journal of Higher Education* 64 (May–June 1993): 283–311.

Haber, Samuel. *Authority and Honor in the American Professions, 1750–1900.* Chicago: University of Chicago Press, 1991.

Hacker, Andrew, and Claudia Deifus. *Higher Education? How Colleges Are Wasting Our Money and Failing Our Kids—and What We Can Do about It.* New York: Times Books, 2010.

Hamilton, Neil. "Comparing AAUP and AGB." *Liberal Education* 85 (Fall 1999): 24–31.

Hawkins, Hugh. *Banding Together: The Rise of National Associations in American Higher Education, 1887–1950.* Baltimore: Johns Hopkins University Press, 1992.

Hawkins, Hugh. *Between Harvard and America: The Educational Leadership of Charles W. Eliot.* New York: Oxford University Press, 1972.

Hawkins, Hugh. *Pioneer: A History of the Johns Hopkins University, 1874–1889.* Ithaca, NY: Cornell University Press, 1960.

Hebel, Sara. "On Campuses: Clashes, Pay Divides, and Thwarted Careers." *Chronicle of Higher Education, Almanac of Higher Education 2013.* Accessed August 20, 2013. chronicle.com/article/On-Campuses-Clashes-Pay/140873/.

Henderson, A. D. "Faculty Participation in the Government of Antioch College." *Bulletin of the AAUP* 27 (April 1941): 178–88.

Herbst, Jurgen. *From Crisis to Crisis: American College Government, 1636–1819.* Cambridge, MA: Harvard University Press, 1982.

Hewett, W. T. "University Administration." *Atlantic Monthly*, October 1882, 505–18.

Hodgkinson, Harold L. *The Campus Senate: Experiment in Democracy.* Berkeley: Center for Research and Development in Higher Education, University of California, 1974.

Hodgkinson, Harold L., and L. Richard Meeth, eds. *Power and Authority: Transformation of Campus Governance.* Jossey-Bass Series in Higher Education. San Francisco: Jossey-Bass, 1971.

Hofstadter, Richard. *Academic Freedom in the Age of the College.* New York: Columbia University Press, 1955.

Hofstadter, Richard, and Wilson Smith, eds. *American Higher Education: A Documentary History.* Vol. 1. Chicago: University of Chicago Press, 1961.

Hutcheson, Philo A. *A Professional Professoriate: Unionization, Bureaucratization, and the AAUP.* Nashville, TN: Vanderbilt University Press, 2000.

Irvine, E. Eastman, ed. *The World Almanac and Book of Facts for 1940.* New York: World-Telegram, 1940.

Jacobson, Jennifer. "Bennington Settles with and Apologizes to Professors It Dismissed." *Chronicle of Higher Education*, January 21, 2001.

James, William. "The Ph.D. Octopus." In *Memories and Studies*. New York: Longmans, Green, 1912. Originally published in *Harvard Monthly*, March 1903.

"James McKeen Cattell." In *Human Intelligence: Historical Influences, Current Controversies, Teaching Resources*, edited by J. A. Plucker. Accessed October 7, 2010. www.intelltheory .com/jcattell.

Jaschik, Scott. "Union Certified at Illinois-Chicago." *Inside Higher Ed*, September 16, 2011. www.insidehighered.com/news/2011/09/16/state_board_backs_adjunct_tenure_track _joint_faculty_union_at_illinois_chicago.

Jaschik, Scott. "Union Democracy for Some?" *Inside Higher Ed*, April 29, 2013. www .insidehighered.com/news/2013/04/29/adjuncts-angry-over-being-excluded-vote-cuny -faculty-union.

"Jasper Adams on the Relation between Trustees and Faculty." In Hofstadter and Smith, *American Higher Education*.

Jencks, Christopher, and David Riesman. *The Academic Revolution*. Garden City, NY: Doubleday, 1968.

Johnson, Eldon L. "Misconceptions about the Early Land-Grant Colleges." *Journal of Higher Education* 52 (July–August 1981): 333–51.

Jones, Gary H. "Universities, the Major Battleground in the Fight for Reason and Capitalism." *Academe* 96 (July–August 2010): 34–37.

Joughin, Louis. "Three Problems of the California State Colleges." *AAUP Bulletin* 53 (Summer 1967): 228–35.

Kaplan, Gabriel E. "How Academic Ships Actually Navigate." In *Governing Academia*, edited by Ronald G. Ehrenberg. Ithaca, NY: Cornell University Press, 2004.

Keller, George. *Academic Strategy: The Management Revolution in American Higher Education*. Baltimore: Johns Hopkins University Press, 1983.

Keller, George. "Does Higher Education Research Need Revisions?" *Review of Higher Education* 21 (Spring 1998): 278.

Kelley, Brooks Mather. *Yale: A History*. New Haven, CT: Yale University Press, 1974.

Kemerer, Frank R., and J. Victor Baldridge. *Unions on Campus*. San Francisco: Jossey-Bass, 1975.

Kennedy, Sister M. St. Mel. "The Changing Academic Characteristics of the Nineteenth-Century American College Teacher." *Paedagogica Historica* 5 (1966): 355–401.

Kilgore, Kathleen. *Transformations: A History of Boston University*. Boston: Boston University, 1991.

Kimball, Bruce A. *The "True Professional Ideal" in America: A History*. Cambridge, MA: Blackwell, 1992.

Kimball, D. S. "Faculty Aspects of University Administration." *Bulletin of the AAUP* 20 (May 1934): 310–11.

Kirkpatrick, John E. *Academic Organization and Control*. Yellow Springs, OH: Antioch Press, 1931.

Kirkpatrick, John E. *The American College and Its Rulers*. New York: New Republic, 1926.

Kirp, David L. *Shakespeare, Einstein, and the Bottom Line: The Marketing of Higher Education*. Cambridge, MA: Harvard University Press, 2003.

Kirshstein, Rita J., and Steven Hulbert. *Revenues: Where Does the Money Come From? A Delta Data Update, 2000–2010.* Washington, DC: American Institutes for Research, 2012. www.deltacostproject.org/pdfs/Revenue_Trends_Production.pdf.

Knoll, Robert E. *Prairie University: A History of the University of Nebraska.* Lincoln: University of Nebraska Press and Alumni Association of the University of Nebraska, 1995.

Koretz, Jane F. "Governance vs. Shared Governance: Rensselaer Polytechnic Institute." *New York Academe* 35 (Winter 2012): 1, 7.

Ladd, Everett Carl, Jr., and Seymour Martin Lipset. *Professors, Unions, and American Higher Education.* Berkeley, CA: Carnegie Commission on Higher Education, 1973.

Larrabee, Harold A. "An Adventure in College Government: The Union Faculty Writes a Constitution." *Bulletin of the AAUP* 28 (October 1942): 494–97.

Larson, Magali Sarfatti. *The Rise of Professionalism: A Sociological Analysis.* Berkeley: University of California Press, 1977.

Lazarsfeld, Paul F., and Wagner Thielens Jr. *The Academic Mind: Social Scientists in a Time of Crisis.* Glencoe, IL: Free Press, 1958.

Le Duc, Thomas. *Piety and Intellect at Amherst College, 1865–1912.* New York: Columbia University Press, 1946; reprint, New York: Arno, 1969.

Lee, Eugene C., and Frank M. Bowen. *The Multicampus University: A Study in Academic Governance.* New York: McGraw-Hill, 1971.

Lehmberg, Stanford, and Ann M. Plaum. *The University of Minnesota, 1945–2001.* Minneapolis: University of Minnesota Press, 2001.

Lender, Jon. "Faculty Gets Recommendations." *Hartford Courant,* February 19, 1980.

Leslie, W. Bruce. *Gentlemen and Scholars: Colleges and Communities in the "Age of the University."* New Brunswick, NJ: Transaction, 2005.

Lieberman, Myron. "Representational Systems in Higher Education." In Baldridge, *Academic Governance.*

Lieberman, Myron. *The Teacher Unions: How the NEA and AFT Sabotage Reform and Hold Students, Parents, Teachers, and Taxpayers Hostage to Bureaucracy.* New York: Free Press, 1997.

Louderback, George D. "Faculty-Administration Cooperation at the University of California." *Bulletin of the AAUP* 24 (April 1938): 349–58.

Lovejoy, A. O. "Annual Message of the President." *Bulletin of the AAUP* 5 (November–December 1919): 10–40.

Lovejoy, A. O. "Organization of the American Association of University Professors." *Science,* new ser., 41 (January 29, 1915): 151–54.

Lucas, Christopher J. *American Higher Education: A History.* New York: St. Martin's Press, 1994.

Lyman, Robert Hunt, ed. *The World Almanac and Book of Facts for 1930.* New York: New York World, 1930.

Magner, Denise K. "Fierce Battle over Tenure at U. of Minnesota Ends Quietly." *Chronicle of Higher Education,* June 20, 1997.

Magner, Denise K. "Minnesota Professors Irate over Plans They Say Threaten Tenure." *Chronicle of Higher Education,* May 17, 1996.

Mallon, William. "Disjointed Governance in University Centers and Institutes." In Tierney, *Competing Conceptions of Academic Governance.*

Mannies, Jo. "Cure for Colleges: 'Just Common Sense.'" *St. Louis Post-Dispatch*, May 7, 1989.

Marmion, Henry A. "Unions in Higher Education." In Baldridge, *Academic Governance*.

Mason, Henry L. *College and University Government: A Handbook of Principle and Practice.* New Orleans, LA: Tulane University, 1972.

McCaughey, Robert A. *Stand, Columbia: A History of Columbia University in the City of New York, 1754–2004.* New York: Columbia University Press, 2003.

McCaughey, Robert A. "The Transformation of American Academic Life: Harvard University, 1821–1892." *Perspectives in American History* 8 (1974): 239–332.

McConaughy, James L. "Report of the Commission on Academic Freedom and Academic Tenure." *Bulletin of the Association of American Colleges* 21 (March 1935): 176–82.

McConnell, T. R., and Kenneth P. Mortimer. *The Faculty in University Governance.* Berkeley: Center for Research and Development in Higher Education, University of California, Berkeley, 1971.

McPherson, Michael S., and Morton Owen Schapiro. "Tenure Issues in Higher Education." *Journal of Economic Perspectives* 13 (Winter 1999): 85–98.

"Measuring Worth." Accessed March 13, 2012, www.measuringworth.com/uscompare /relativevalue.php.

Menand, Louis. "The Trashing of Professionalism." *Academe* 81 (May–June 1995): 16–19.

Metzger, Walter P. "The First Investigation." *Bulletin of the AAUP* 47 (Autumn 1961): 206–10.

Metzger, Walter P. *Academic Freedom in the Age of the University.* New York: Columbia University Press, 1955.

Michael, Richard B. "The American Institute of Instruction." *History of Education Journal* 3 (Autumn 1951): 27–32.

Miller, Gerald Ray. "Budget Cuts and Shared Governance: A Faculty Member's Perspective." *Academe* 79 (November–December 1993): 12–14.

Miller, Kent S., and Ray Bellamy. "Fine Print, Restrictive Grants, and Academic Freedom." *Academe* 98 (May–June 2012): 17–21.

Millett, John D. *The Academic Community: An Essay on Organization.* New York: McGraw-Hill, 1962.

Millett, John D. *New Structures of Campus Power: Success and Failures of Emerging Forms of Institutional Governance.* San Francisco: Jossey-Bass, 1979.

Millikan, Robert A. *The Autobiography of Robert A. Millikan.* New York: Prentice-Hall, 1950.

Morison, Samuel Eliot, ed. *The Development of Harvard University: Since the Inauguration of President Eliot, 1869–1929.* Cambridge, MA: Harvard University Press, 1930.

Morison, Samuel Eliot. *Three Centuries of Harvard, 1636–1936.* Cambridge, MA: Harvard University Press, 1936; reprint, Cambridge, MA: Harvard University Press, 1965.

Morrow, Glenn R. "The University of Pennsylvania: Faculty Participation in the Government of the University." *AAUP Bulletin* 49 (June 1963): 114–22.

Mortimer, Kenneth P., and T. R. McConnell. *Sharing Authority Effectively.* San Francisco: Jossey-Bass, 1978.

"A National Association of University Professors." *Science*, new ser., 39 (March 27, 1914): 458–59.

National Center for Education Statistics. *Digest of Education Statistics: 2005.* Accessed March 22, 2013, nces.ed.gov/programs/digest/d05/.

National Center for Education Statistics. *Digest of Education Statistics: 2011*. Accessed March 12, 2013, nces.ed.gov/programs/digest/d11/.

National Center for Education Statistics. "Fast Facts." Accessed May 22, 2013, nces.ed.gov/fastfacts/display.asp?id=74.

National Center for Education Statistics. *120 Years of American Education: A Statistical Portrait*. Washington, DC: US Department of Education, Institute of Education Sciences, 1993.

Neckers, J. W. "A College Faculty Senate." *Bulletin of the AAUP* 25 (December 1939): 574–77.

Neem, Johann N. "A University without Intellectuals: Western Governors University and the Academy's Future." *Thought and Action* 28 (Fall 2012): 63–74.

Nelson, Cary. *No University Is an Island: Saving Academic Freedom*. New York: New York University Press, 2010.

New York Times, August 7, 1874.

Newfield, Christopher. *The Unmaking of the Public University: The Forty-Year Assault on the Middle Class*. Cambridge, MA: Harvard University Press, 2008.

Nielson, W. A. "MLA Presidential Address." *Bulletin of the AAUP* 11 (March–April 1925): 162–63.

Northwestern University Archives. "The Presidents of Northwestern: Arnold R. Weber." Accessed August 6, 2012. exhibits.library.northwestern.edu/archives/exhibits/presidents/weber.html.

Novick, Peter. *That Noble Dream: The "Objectivity Question" and the American Historical Profession*. New York: Cambridge University Press, 1988.

Oklahoma Historical Society. "Lottinville, Savoie (1906–1997)." In *Encyclopedia of Oklahoma History and Culture*. Accessed March 13, 2012. digital.library.okstate.edu/encyclopedia/entries/L/LO016.html.

Oldfather, W. A. "The Executive Committee System at the University of Illinois." *Bulletin of the AAUP* 27 (April 1941): 188–205.

Padelford, Frederick M. "The Administrative Code of the University of Washington." *Bulletin of the AAUP* 26 (April 1940): 212–16.

Peckham, Howard H. *The Making of the University of Michigan, 1817–1992*. Edited and updated by Margaret L. Steneck and Nicholas H. Steneck. Ann Arbor: University of Michigan Press, 1994.

Perry, Charles M. *Henry Philip Tappan: Philosopher and University President*. Ann Arbor: University of Michigan Press, 1933.

Peterson, George E. *The New England College in the Age of the University*. Amherst, MA: Amherst College Press, 1964.

Peterson, Iver. "State U. Planning a Self-Appraisal." *New York Times*, June 1, 1975.

Polishook Irwin H. "Unions and Governance—the CUNY Experience." *Academe* 68 (January–February 1982): 15–17.

Press, Alexandra. "Student Trustees at Wesleyan Line Up with Plan's Opponents." *Hartford Courant*, December 7, 1979.

Quinterno, John. *The Great Cost Shift: How Higher Education Cuts Undermine the Future Middle Class*. New York: Demos, 2012. www.demos.org/sites/default/files/publications/TheGreatCostShift_Demos_0.pdf.

Rensselaer Faculty Senate. Constitution of the Rensselaer Faculty Senate. Accessed May 24, 2013. facultysenate.rpi.edu/constitution-rensselaer-faculty-senate.

Rhoades, Gary. *Managed Professionals: Unionized Faculty and Restructuring Academic Labor*. Albany: State University of New York Press, 1998.

Ridder-Symoens, Hilde de, ed. *A History of the University in Europe*. Vol. 1, *Universities in the Middle Ages*. Cambridge: Cambridge University Press, 1992.

Ridder-Symoens, Hilde de, ed. *A History of the University in Europe*. Vol. 2, *Universities in Early Modern Europe (1500–1800)*. Cambridge: Cambridge University Press, 1996.

Riesman, David. *On Higher Education: The Academic Enterprise in an Era of Rising Student Consumerism*. San Francisco: Jossey-Bass, 1980.

Ringer, Fritz. "Academic Governance and Collective Bargaining." *Academe* 66 (February 1980): 41–44.

Rivard, Ry. "The Fine Print." *Inside Higher Ed*, May 28, 2013. www.insidehighered.com /news/2013/05/28/documents-shed-light-details-georgia-tech-udacity-deal.

Rodda, Alfred. "Collective Bargaining in California" (1975). *The Back Bench*, "The Rodda Project: The Story of SB 160," August 14, 2007. thebackbench.blogspot.com/2007/08 /collective-bargaining-in-california.html.

Rosenthal, Michael. *Nicholas Miraculous: The Amazing Career of the Redoubtable Dr. Nicholas Murray Butler*. New York: Farrar, Straus and Giroux, 2006.

Ross, Dorothy. *The Origins of American Social Science*. New York: Cambridge University Press, 1991.

Rubiales, David M. "Collective Bargaining at Community Colleges: A Report from California." *Academe* 84 (November–December 1998): 40–42.

Rudy, S. Willis. *The College of the City of New York: A History, 1847–1947*. New York: City College Press, 1949; reprint, New York: Arno, 1977.

Ruml, Beardsley, and Sidney G. Tickton. *Teaching Salaries Then and Now: A 50-Year Comparison with Other Occupations and Industries*. New York: Fund for the Advancement of Education, 1955.

Sabrosky, Curtis W. "The Development of a Divisional Faculty Plan at Michigan State College." *Bulletin of the AAUP* 29 (April 1943): 292–98.

Sagendorph, Kent. *Michigan: The Story of the University*. New York: E. P. Dutton, 1948.

Schmidt, George P. *The Old Time College President*. New York: Columbia University Press, 1930; reprint, New York, 1970.

Schrecker, Ellen W. "The Humanities on Life Support." *Academe* 97 (September–October 2011): 47–53.

Schrecker, Ellen W. *The Lost Soul of Higher Education: Corporatization, the Assault on Academic Freedom, and the End of the American University*. New York: New Press, 2010.

Schrecker, Ellen W. *No Ivory Tower: McCarthyism and the Universities*. New York: Oxford University Press, 1986.

Schurman, Jacob Gould. "Faculty Participation in University Government." In Cattell, *University Control*.

Schuster, Jack H., and Martin J. Finkelstein. *The American Faculty: The Restructuring of Academic Work and Careers*. Baltimore: Johns Hopkins University Press, 2006.

Schuster, Jack H., Daryl G. Smith, Kathleen A. Corak, and Myrtle M. Yamada. *Strategic Governance: How to Make Big Decisions Better*. Phoenix, AZ: American Council on Education/Oryx Press, 1994.

Scimecca, Joseph, and Roland Damiano. *Crisis at St. John's: Strike and Revolution on the Catholic Campus*. New York: Random House, 1967.

Selden, Steven. "Who's Paying for the Culture Wars?" *Academe* 91 (September–October 2005): 35–38.

Slaughter, Sheila. "Retrenchment in the 1980s: The Politics of Prestige and Gender." *Journal of Higher Education* 64 (May–June 1993): 250–82.

Slaughter, Sheila, and Larry L. Leslie. *Academic Capitalism: Politics, Policies, and the Entrepreneurial University.* Baltimore: Johns Hopkins University Press, 1997.

Slaughter, Sheila, and Gary Rhoades. *Academic Capitalism and the New Economy.* Baltimore: Johns Hopkins University Press, 2004.

Slosson, Edwin E. *Great American Universities.* New York: Macmillan, 1910; reprint, New York: Arno, 1977.

Smallwood, Scott. "Union In, Governance Out: The U. of Akron's Board Reacts to a Union by Taking Away Faculty Powers." *Chronicle of Higher Education*, October 10, 2003.

Smith, Wilson. "The Teacher in Puritan Culture." *Harvard Educational Review* 36 (1966): 394–411.

Solomon, Barbara Miller. *In the Company of Educated Women: A History of Women and Higher Education in America.* New Haven, CT: Yale University Press, 1985.

Stadtman, Verne A. *The University of California, 1868–1968: A Centennial Publication of the University of California.* New York: McGraw-Hill, 1970.

Stameshkin, David M. *The Town's College: Middlebury College, 1800–1915.* Middlebury, VT: Middlebury College Press, 1985.

StateUniversity.com. "NASULGC." In *Education Encyclopedia.* Accessed March 20, 2012. http://education.stateuniversity.com/pages/2268/National-Association-State-Universities-Land-Grant-Colleges.html.

Steneck, Nicholas H. "Faculty Governance at the University of Michigan: Principles, History, and Practice." Accessed November 25, 2013. www.sacua.umich.edu/resources/faculty-governance.pdf.

Storr, Richard J. *Harper's University: The Beginnings.* Chicago: University of Chicago Press, 1966.

Story, Ronald. *The Forging of an Aristocracy: Harvard and the Boston Upper Class, 1800–1870.* Middletown, CT: Wesleyan University Press, 1980.

Stratton, George M. "Externalism in American Universities." In Cattell, *University Control.* Originally published in *Atlantic Monthly*, October 1907.

Stripling, Jack. "President's Proposal Renews Debate over How to Measure College Quality." *Chronicle of Higher Education*, September 5, 2013.

Stripling, Jack, and Andrea Fuller. "Presidential Pay Is Still a Potent Political Target." *Chronicle of Higher Education*, May 20, 2012.

Strong, John A. *Running on Empty: The Rise and Fall of Southampton College, 1963–2005.* Albany: State University of New York, 2013.

Sullivan, Teresa A. "Professional Control in the Complex University: Maintaining the Faculty Role." In *The American Academic Profession: Transformation in Contemporary Higher Education*, edited by Joseph C. Hermanowicz. Baltimore: Johns Hopkins University Press, 2011.

Taylor, Angus E. *The Academic Senate of the University of California: Its Role in the Shared Governance and Operation of the University of California.* Berkeley, CA: Institute of Governmental Studies Press, 1998.

Taylor, Mark C. *Crisis on Campus: A Bold Plan for Reforming Our Colleges and Universities.* New York: Knopf, 2010.

Tead, Ordway. "The Place and Function of the Faculty in College Government." *Bulletin of the AAUP* 25 (April 1939): 163–68.

Tewksbury, Donald G. *The Founding of American Colleges and Universities before the Civil War: With Particular Reference to the Religious Influence Bearing upon the College Movement.* New York: Columbia University Press, 1932; reprint, Hamden, CT: Archon Books, 1965.

Thelin, John R. *A History of American Higher Education.* 2nd ed. Baltimore: Johns Hopkins University Press, 2011.

Thorpe, Clarence DeWitt. "The Executive Committee System at the University of Michigan." *Bulletin of the AAUP* 26 (April 1940): 201–11.

Thwing, Charles Franklin. *The German and the American University: One Hundred Years of History.* New York: Macmillan, 1928.

Tierney, William G., ed. *Competing Conceptions of Academic Governance: Negotiating the Perfect Storm.* Baltimore: Johns Hopkins University Press, 2004.

Tierney, William G., and Guilbert C. Hentschke. *New Players, Different Game: Understanding the Rise of For-Profit Colleges and Universities.* Baltimore: Johns Hopkins University Press, 2007.

Tierney, William G., and James T. Minor. *Challenges for Governance: A National Report.* Los Angeles: Center for Higher Education Policy Analysis, Rossier School of Education, University of Southern California, 2003.

Tobias, Marilyn. *Old Dartmouth on Trial: The Transformation of the Academic Community in Nineteenth-Century America.* New York: New York University Press, 1982.

Turner, James, and Paul Bernard. "The German Model and the Graduate School: The University of Michigan and the Origin Myth of the American University." In Geiger, *American College in the Nineteenth Century.*

"2 Faculty Bargaining Units Certified at Illinois-Chicago." *Insider Higher Ed,* June 29, 2012. www.insidehighered.com/quicktakes/2012/06/29/2-faculty-bargaining-units-certified -illinois-chicago.

University of Akron. "History." University of Akron website. Accessed May 16, 2013. www .uakron.edu/about_ua/history/.

University of Michigan. "Financial Statements." Accessed March 13, 2013. www.finance .umich.edu/reports/2010/pdf/FSFY10.pdf.

University of Texas System. "History of the UT System." Accessed June 5, 2012. www .utsystem.edu/about/history-ut-system.

University of Virginia. "Financing the University 101." Accessed March 13, 2013. www.virginia .edu/finance101/answers.html.

US Bureau of the Census. *Historical Statistics of the United States: Colonial Times to 1957.* Washington, DC, 1957.

Van Alstyne, William. "The Specific Theory of Academic Freedom and the General Issue of Civil Liberty." In *The Concept of Academic Freedom,* edited by Edmund L. Pincoffs. Austin: University of Texas Press, 1975.

Veblen, Thorstein. *The Higher Learning in America: A Memorandum.* New York: B. W. Huebsch, 1918; reprint, Whitefish, MT: Kessinger, 2010.

Veysey, Laurence R. *The Emergence of the American University.* Chicago: University of Chicago Press, 1965.

Wagoner, Jennings L., Jr. *Jefferson and Education*. Charlottesville, VA: Thomas Jefferson Foundation, 2004.

Weber, Arnold R., et al. *Faculty Participation in Academic Governance: Report of the AAHE-NEA Task Force on Faculty Representation and Academic Negotiations, Campus Governance Program*. Washington, DC: American Association for Higher Education, 1967.

Weidhorn, Manfred. "The Yeshiva Faculty Union: Tales Told out of School." *Academe* 84 (November–December 1998): 24–26.

Wertenbaker, Thomas Jefferson. *Princeton, 1746–1896*. Princeton, NJ: Princeton University Press, 1946.

Wesleyan University, Office of the President. "Wesleyan's Thirteenth President." Accessed March 27, 2013. www.wesleyan.edu/president/pastpresidents/campbell.html.

Wessel, David. "Wesleyan Faculty Seeking Endowment-Loss Accounting." *Hartford Courant*, May 12, 1978.

White, Andrew Dickson. *Autobiography of Andrew Dickson White*. Vol. 1. New York: Century, 1922.

White, Kenneth B. "Shared Governance in California." *New Directions for Community Colleges* 102 (Summer 1998): 19–29.

Whitehead, John S. *The Separation of College and State: Columbia, Dartmouth, Harvard, and Yale, 1776–1876*. New Haven, CT: Yale University Press, 1973.

Wiebe, Robert H. *The Search for Order, 1877–1920*. New York: Hill and Wang, 1967.

Willey, Malcolm M. *Depression, Recovery and Higher Education: A Report by Committee Y of the American Association of University Professors*. New York: McGraw-Hill, 1937.

Wilson, Logan. *The Academic Man: A Study in the Sociology of a Profession*. New York: Oxford University Press, 1942; reprint, New Brunswick, NJ: Transaction, 1995.

Woodward, William J., Eileen Burchell, Donald R. Wagner, and Jonathan Knight. "Faculty Exigency, Academic Governance, and Related Matters." *Academe* 90 (March–April 2004): 104–12.

Yellowitz, Irwin. "Academic Governance and Collective Bargaining in the City University of New York." *Academe* 73 (November–December 1987): 8–11.

Zabel, Gary. "The Boston University Strike of 1979." In *The Encyclopedia of Strikes in American History*, edited by Aaron Brenner. Armonk, NY: M. E. Sharpe, 2009.

Zweigenhaft, Richie. "Is This Curriculum for Sale?" *Academe* 96 (July–August 2010): 38–39.